CONGRESSIONAL BUDGETING

Congressional Budgeting

POLITICS, PROCESS, AND POWER

Edited by
W. THOMAS WANDER,
F. TED HEBERT,
and GARY W. COPELAND

The Johns Hopkins University Press
BALTIMORE AND LONDON

The Johns Hopkins University Press, Baltimore, Maryland 21218
The Johns Hopkins Press Ltd., London

Library of Congress Cataloging in Publication Data
Main entry under title:

Congressional budgeting.

  Bibliography: p. 239
  Includes index.
  1. Budget—Law and legislation—United States.
2. Budget—United States. I. Wander, W. Thomas.
II. Hebert, F. Ted. III. Copeland, Gary W.
KF6225.C66 1984   343.73′034   84–47943
ISBN 0–8018–2392–7   347.30334
ISBN 0–8018–2396–X (pbk.)

Contents

Preface

On 21 June 1974, the Senate adopted, by a unanimous vote, the conference report of the Congressional Budget and Impoundment Control Act of 1974. In so doing, it ended congressional consideration of the most far-reaching reform of the legislative budget process in more than fifty years. New and potentially powerful budget committees were formed in each house. The fiscal year was altered, and a new legislative schedule that included a timetable affecting the consideration of both authorization and appropriations was devised. Strict limits on new backdoor spending programs were introduced. Congressional controls on presidential impoundments were extended, and an entirely new congressional support agency, the Congressional Budget Office (CBO), was formed to collect, process, and analyze budget-related information.

In short, the changes were extensive. The sight of his colleagues approving all of these major changes in the way that Congress discharges one of its primary responsibilities moved the bill's Senate floor manager, Senator Sam Ervin, to announce: "To my mind, this is the most important piece of legislation that I have worked on during the twenty years that I have served in the Senate. It is the finest example of the legislative process at work that I have ever witnessed."[1] Of course, legislators and their speech writers are not always selective in choosing the objects of this kind of high praise. Any senator or congressman may have two or three "most important bills of my career" in any given session of Congress.

Even discounting for senatorial hyperbole and the exaggerated expectations that generally attend the adoption of major institutional changes, the importance of this particular reform is difficult to gainsay. This new budget process has enabled the president and Congress to place their battle over the budget squarely before the American people in a direct and comprehensive way not previously possible. As a result, the public has been treated to a "news" diet rich with competing budget projections, protean deficits, and incompatible economic assumptions. The process has also provided the forum that has introduced new terms for our political lexicon (e.g., *supply-side economics*), new authoritative voices on budget matters (e.g., Rudolph Penner, Jim Jones, and Pete Domenici), and a search for legislative majorities among various new and exotic congressional "fauna" (e.g, Boll Weevils, Gypsy Moths, and Yellow Jackets).

In sum, the budget process mandated by the 1974 Budget Act appears to have had a significant effect both on the way in which fiscal policy is developed by the federal government and on the institutions that make that policy. To provide an opportunity to assess the degree and nature of that impact, the Carl Albert Congressional Research and Studies Center and the Department of Political Science of the University of Oklahoma convened a conference of leading congressional scholars, present and former members of Congress, congressional staff, and members of the executive branch in February of 1982. This volume grew out of that meeting.

The primary goal of this work is to provide an understanding of how the 1974 reforms have altered the politics and processes of congressional budgeting. This involves discussions of the procedures affecting budget resolutions, reconciliation, impoundments, tax expenditures, and so forth. However, it also involves analyses of the effects of these procedures and the politics surrounding them on institutional arrangements, for example, the intrachamber relations among congressional committees and the relations between Congress and the executive branch. In pursuing this type of understanding, the chapters that follow provide a comprehensive and unified treatment of the current congressional budget process—its origins, evolution, and impact.

It is commonplace to observe that the federal budget is the most political document in Washington. Since 1974, however, it has become increasingly evident that the process that produces the budget in Congress each year is among the most misunderstood, not only by the public but also by members of Congress. Although the chapters in this book are not a curative for this condition, they can certainly ameliorate its worst symptoms as they examine the origins, impact, and possible future directions of the Congressional Budget and Impoundment Control Act of 1974.

The consideration of these issues would not have been possible without the help of many people. The conference from which this volume evolved was funded by the University of Oklahoma Associates and supported by Ron Peters, director of the Carl Albert Center. The organizing of the conference was handled primarily by Jennifer McPhail. She received considerable help from Carl Albert Fellows Ron Grimes, Matt Moen, Mike Sharp, and Frank Smist. All of their efforts are greatly appreciated.

The contributors of this work were, of course, primarily responsible for the success of the conference. However, other conference participants made major intellectual contributions. Those participants were David Bodde, of the Congressional Budget Office; Martin S. Gold, Counsel to the Majority Leader of the U.S. Senate; James McIntyre, Jr., former director of the Office of Management and Budget; Congressmen Mickey Edwards and David Obey; and former Congressman Tom Steed. Henry Bellmon, former Senator and ranking minority member of the Senate Budget Committee was crucial; he helped plan the conference, delivered the keynote address, and made valuable contributions to the conference discussions.

The preparation and repreparation of the manuscript was done by Nita Gaye Dotson. Her tireless efforts merit special commendation.

These people and many more deserve to share the credit for this volume. However, the editors share equally the responsibility for it; the ordering of the names on the title page, therefore, indicates nothing more than the sequence that Tom's daughter, Ashley, selected as she drew our names out of a hat.

1. *Cong. Rec.*, 93rd Cong., 2nd sess., 1974, 120, pt. 15:20464.

I

BUDGET REFORM
AND CONGRESSIONAL
BUDGETING

1 The Politics of Congressional Budget Reform

W. THOMAS WANDER

T his volume is primarily concerned with the consequences of change. How have the processes and the distribution of power within the two houses of Congress been affected by the reforms of the Congressional Budget and Impoundment Control Act of 1974? How have the power relations between the two houses and between Congress and the executive branch been altered by those reforms? What further changes ought to be considered in light of our experience with the new budget process?

The task of this chapter, however, is somewhat different. It considers the prior question, how can one account for the occurrence of such a major change in the first place? It is widely recognized that organizations are generally resistant to major alterations in their basic structures and processes, and the closer one comes to the core of an institution's raison d'être, the more difficult change becomes.

With respect to Congress, nothing is more central to its basic purposes and prerogatives than its power of the purse; it is the very foundation of that body's institutional strength. Taken together, these two points suggest that major changes in the structures and processes through which Congress makes its collective judgments on issues arising under its purse power ought to be relatively rare. In fact, a survey of congressional history indicates that that is the case. Before 1974, only five periods of major reform of the congressional budget process can be identified:

1. the creation of the appropriations committees after the Civil War,
2. the dispersal of the appropriations power in the House between 1877 and 1885,
3. the dispersal of the appropriations power in the Senate in 1899,
4. the consolidation of the appropriations power in the House (1920) and the Senate (1922), and

5. the creation of the legislative budget and the Joint Budget Committee in 1946.[1]

The fact that major reforms occur only rarely suggests that the norm is for the tensions in the budget system to be resolved through minor adjustments worked out both internally and with major environmental actors in an informal manner. Thus, "working relationships" guide much day-to-day activity, and significant changes in those relationships are most often the result of evolutionary processes over a period of years. Only when such adjustments cannot be achieved are major innovations possible (but certainly not inevitable). Therefore, the adoption of significant structural reform of the congressional budget process is not an everyday occurrence. Rather, it is an occasion to the legislator and, to the political scientist, an anomaly requiring explanation.

Such is the task of this chapter with respect to the budget reforms of 1974. That is, the chapter must address two sets of related questions:

1. Given all of the reasons that organizations, including Congress, do not change, why did Congress, in the years 1972–74, decide to change significantly a process that is at the heart of its institutional power and its internal power arrangements?

2. With respect to the adoption of the 1974 Budget Act, how were the various pressures for change (both internal and external) translated into the particular mix of reforms adopted in that year?

Pressures for Change

With respect to the first question (the pressures promoting change), the congressional reform literature indicates that pressure for change comes from both within and without Congress and produces two analytically distinct types of reform. A reform that is a reaction to external pressures and is designed to maintain an organization's viability or autonomy vis-à-vis its environment is an *adaptive innovation*. A reform that responds to the deterioration of internal integration and is designed to relieve those internal tensions might be called *ameliorative change*. Despite the analytical separation of these two modes of organizational behavior, actual reforms generally contain a mixture of both adaptive and ameliorative elements.[2]

This external / internal distinction is an important starting point. Elsewhere, I have used this schema to analyze the five reform periods noted above and have concluded that major institutional changes in the congressional budget process stem, in large part, from some combination of three factors:

1. concern with the congressional capacity to control federal expenditures (as indicated most importantly by federal deficits),
2. shifting relations with the executive branch (particularly the president) over the shaping of the nation's fiscal policy, and
3. internal struggles for control of the purse power (particularly the spending side).[3]

With respect to the adaptive reforms (those stimulated by external pressures), one factor stands out as being extremely conducive to major change—war. In fact, most major congressional budget reforms have occurred near the formal end of significant armed conflict—the Civil War, the Spanish-American War, World War I, World War II, and of course, the 1974 reform instituted as the Vietnam conflict was winding down.

Although armed conflict per se bears little relationship to the internal processes and structures of Congress, the fact that Congress provides the wherewithal to carry on the hostilities establishes a critical link. Simply stated, war puts a tremendous strain on the resources of the federal government. For instance, the two world wars and the Civil War created deficits that were monstrous for their historical eras (see table 1.1).

It seems clear that the economic difficulties engendered by those huge government expenditures place additional burdens on the institution that aspires to control the nation's purse strings. This strain in turn tends to prompt those in Congress to look inward, within their own institution, to see if the legislative process that deals with budgetary matters might be improved and thus made to cope more effectively with such burdens.[4]

A second external factor that appears to facilitate the adoption of congressional budget reform is major change in the relationship between the president and Congress with respect to control of federal budgetary decisions. This factor has been of particular importance in the twentieth century as the institutionalized presidency has come to play an increasingly central role in fiscal policy making.

One prominent context for such change is a wartime condition. Although Congress is generally quite sensitive about executive encroachment on its prerogatives in fiscal matters, in times of armed hostilities the vigilance with which it protects its domain is significantly relaxed. In the immediate postwar period, however, faced with serious economic problems, Congress may well attempt to reestablish its own coequal status by enhancing its capacity for budget control. This was clearly the case in the 1946 reform. As one congressman testified before the reforms of that era, "Decisions will

Table 1.1.   Federal Surplus and Deficit Figures before, during, and after Selected Major Wars (in millions of dollars)

Conflict	Prewar Years		War Years		Postwar Years	
Civil War	1856	+ 4.5	1861	− 25.0	1866	+ 37.2
	1857	+ 1.2	1862	− 422.8	1867	+ 133.1
	1858	− 27.5	1863	− 602.0	1868	+ 28.3
	1859	− 15.6	1864	− 600.7	1869	+ 48.1
	1860	− 7.1	1865	− 963.8	1870	+ 101.6
World War I	1912	+ 2.7	1917	− 853.4	1920	+ 291.2
	1913	− 0.4	1918	− 9,032.1	1921	+ 509.0
	1914	− 0.4	1919	− 13,362.6	1922	+ 736.5
	1915	− 62.7			1923	+ 712.5
	1916	+ 48.5			1924	+ 963.4
World War II	1936	− 4,424.5	1941	− 6,159.3	1947	+ 753.8
	1937	− 2,777.4	1942	− 21,490.2	1948	+ 8,419.5
	1938	− 1.176.6	1943	− 57,420.4	1949	− 1,511.4
	1939	− 3,862.2	1944	− 51,423.4	1950	− 3,112.1
	1940	− 3,918.0	1945	− 53,940.9	1951	+ 3,509.8
			1946	− 20,676.2		

Source: Derived from *Historical Statistics of the United States, 1789–1957*, Department of Commerce, Bureau of the Census, 1960, 711.

have to be made as to when and in what manner the extraordinary and in some respects almost unbelievable powers granted to the executive during this war period are to be taken back into the hands of the people and their Congress where they belong."[5] This type of presidential-congressional conflict played a major role in the adoption of the 1974 reforms.

In addition to these external factors, an examination of major budget reforms must focus on the internal tensions surrounding the congressional budget process. Such tensions are important to the reform process because they seem to produce within the legislature a willingness to examine the ongoing procedures and to make changes in the structures through which they operate.

Not surprisingly, within Congress the primary pressure for change comes from shifts in the power relations of those involved in the struggle for control over spending decisions. The presumption is that those on the losing end of such informal changes will begin to consider reform as a way of regaining some of what they have lost. As Norman Ornstein suggests, "structural reform in Congress is generally a product of those who feel shortchanged of power."[6]

Perhaps the best example of this phenomenon is that provided by the series of changes in the House appropriations process between 1876 and 1885. A change in the House rules in 1876 (the adoption of the Holman

Rule) allowed general legislation in appropriations bills if the effect was to reduce expenditures. This change tremendously increased the jurisdiction of the Appropriations Committee to embrace almost the entire legislative horizon. The domination of the House's most important function could not be tolerated indefinitely by those who did not share meaningfully in its exercise, and the appropriating structure soon collapsed of its own weight. In 1879, the Commerce Committee was granted the authority to report rivers and harbors appropriations. The Appropriations Committee then lost jurisdiction over the agriculture appropriations bill in 1880. Finally, in 1885, five more appropriations bills were dispersed to various House committees.

These changes were precipitated by the passage of the Holman Rule and the growing dissatisfaction of House members with the increasing power of their Appropriations Committee and its chairman, Samuel J. Randall. In an era of government surpluses, this power was often used to frustrate the desire of many members to spend for politically attractive projects such as internal improvements (e.g., rivers and harbors). Looking back on the events of 1885, for instance, Joe Cannon observed that "change is often spoken of as a reform but . . . the purpose, not much disguised at the time, was to cripple the power of Samuel J. Randall."[7]

Such internal tension creates situations in which those who might otherwise oppose reform perceive change not as a threat but as an opportunity to improve their institutional positions. Therefore, in addition to the search for fiscally responsible answers (however defined) to external challenges, the political nature of reform efforts should not be underestimated. Those dissatisfied with the existing conditions, those "short-changed of power," may well be looking for ways to improve their relative power positions in the budget process through such reform. To these efforts, factors such as the massive economic problems left in the aftermath of major wars provide a mantle of legitimacy.

These then are what James March and Herbert Simon have called the "occasions for innovation."[8] They are the internal and external factors that initially direct the attention of Congress (or any organization) to the need for or the possibility of change in its current program of operation. It is to a fuller discussion of those factors crucial to the adoption of the reforms of the Congressional Budget and Impoundment Control Act of 1974 that this chapter now turns.

The Wellsprings of the 1974 Budget Reform

In response to the huge deficits of World War II and the tremendous accretion of power in the executive branch due to that conflict, Congress adopted, as part of the Legislative Reorganization Act of 1946, provisions for a legislative budget formulated by a new Joint Legislative Budget Committee. After two unsuccessful attempts to implement these provisions, however, the legislative budget was abandoned.[9] The external pressures on Congress (preeminently the massive federal deficits created by World War II and the dominance of the president in fiscal matters) that led to the failed postwar reform efforts were ultimately reduced. The huge wartime budget deficits declined and the extreme executive discretion that is typical of such a national emergency was narrowed as the conflict receded and the recovery proceeded. One result was that the sense of crisis that is so often the necessary catalyst for major change simply could not be sustained.

By the end of the 1960s, however, the situation had changed considerably. The external forces challenging the congressional capacity in the budgetary arena had once again intensified and, in so doing, had thrown into sharp relief the increasingly serious tensions and weaknesses present in that process. The conduct of the Vietnam War had heightened congressional sensitivity to presidential dominance, and President Nixon had begun his frontal assault on the fiscal responsibility of Congress. The schisms between the appropriations and authorization committees widened, and the failures of the entire authorization / appropriations process became more pronounced. In addition, there was intense conflict between the keepers of the purse in the House, the Ways and Means and the Appropriations committees. The confluence of these external and internal factors in a time of a troubled economy provided the occasion for another reform of the congressional budget process.

EXTERNAL FACTORS

The Economy.   As suggested earlier, the contest between the executive and Congress for control of fiscal policy decisions is one of long standing. Moreover, that struggle tends to intensify when there are serious problems in the economy, such as the huge deficits brought on by war. Although the figures are not nearly so impressive as those of the Civil War and the two world wars, the budget and the economy became major political issues toward the end of the 1960s as the country began to reap the harvest of Lyndon Johnson's guns-and-butter economics and as the increasing congressional opposition to the Vietnam War "soured" the relations of a Democratic Congress with the president of the same party.

The decline in the economy took several politically significant forms. Inflation was one. It is true that, since World War II, the consumer price index (CPI) had generally moved upward, but from 1952 to 1967 the annual inflation rate had never exceeded 4 percent. From 1966 to 1969, however, the annual rate of increase in the CPI doubled. Wage and price controls in 1971–72 brought inflation under 4 percent again, only to have it jump up to its largest annual rise since 1947, 11 percent, as Congress was considering budget reforms (1973–74).[10]

The recession of 1970 added to the political fallout by increasing unemployment and thereby decreasing the tax revenues necessary to keep the budget in balance. In fact, as table 1.2 indicates, the deficits in the federal funds portion of the federal budget began to increase significantly in Fiscal Year (FY) 1967, rising to $13.1 billion in FY 1970 and ranging between $25 billion and $30 billion in the next three fiscal years. Although such deficits might be the source of considerable nostalgia in times of $200 billion shortfalls, these were considered major indicators of economic illness in the early 1970s.

With respect to the 1974 budget reforms, it is exceedingly difficult to separate the impact of the increasingly troublesome economy from the growing congressional conflict with the president, except to say that the former tended to exacerbate and provide the context for the latter. With the politically damaging deficits rising, along with the concomitant pressures to hold down spending, the struggle to control the increasingly difficult spending decisions was joined. In times of an expanding economy and, more importantly, an expanding federal budget, policy making becomes

Table 1.2. Federal Funds Deficits in the Decade Prior to the Adoption of the 1974 Budget Reform (in billions of dollars)

Fiscal Year	Deficits
1965	3.9
1966	5.1
1967	15.1
1968	28.4
1969	5.5
1970	13.1
1971	29.9
1972	44.7 (estimated)[a]
1973	36.1 (estimated)[a]

Source: Joint Study Committee on Budget Control, *Improving Congressional Budget Control Hearings,* 93rd Cong., 1st sess., 1973, 355.

Note: These figures do not include trust funds.

[a] Estimated figures are displayed here because they were the ones available and employed during the early stages of the reform process. The actual deficits were somewhat lower: $29.2 billion in FY 1972 and $25.0 billion in FY 1973.

primarily a distributive affair in which most programs gain and the only question is, How much? The budget events of 1981, 1982, and 1983 have demonstrated dramatically, however, that when an attempt is made to slow or reverse the growth of nondefense federal spending, when programs face not only reduced increases but also potential cuts, the vested interests of the coalitions that have passed and nurtured these programs are vitally threatened. For this reason, the competition between the president and Congress as well as that within the legislature itself intensifies.

The President. The second major external factor prompting congressional reconsideration of its budget procedures was an increasingly combative relationship with the president in fiscal affairs. For instance, in responding to the nation's economic difficulties outlined above, Congress had approved expenditure ceilings in Fiscal Year 1969, 1970, and 1971. Despite these and other measures, the national deficits, inflation, and unemployment continued to grow.

Finally, in January 1972, President Nixon changed the nature of the dispute over spending levels by suggesting that his budget request of $250 billion become a rigid ceiling for federal spending. Moreover, if program cutbacks were required to meet that limit, he insisted, they should be made at the discretion of the president—a clear violation of the congressional purse power.

Thus, with respect to the FY 1973 ceiling, the president had issued a clear challenge to the legislature. Such a stance, particularly in a time of divided government and in an election year as well, was certain to arouse the institutional and partisan loyalty of Congress and to intensify the conflict with the president.

President Nixon made the budget and federal spending an election-year issue and added significantly to the pressures for some sort of institutional response by Congress with a series of stinging attacks on the "fiscally irresponsible" legislature. On 7 October 1972, just days before Congress considered the spending ceiling that he had requested and less than a month before the congressionl elections, Richard Nixon turned the rhetorical "screws" even tighter. In a nationwide radio address, he warned the public of "the clear and present danger that excessive spending by the Congress might cause a Congressional tax increase in 1973." Moreover, he castigated the congressional capacity for dealing with the budget:

> Let's face it, the Congress suffers from institutional faults when it comes to Federal spending. . . .
>
> Both the President and a family must consider total income and total out-go when they take a look at some new item which would involve

spending additional money. They must take into account their total financial situation as they make each and every spending decision.
    In the Congress, however, it is vastly different. Congress not only
does not consider the total financial picture when it votes on a particular
spending bill, it does not even contain a mechanism to do so if it
wished.[11]

The rhetoric was combative, challenging, tendentious, and, at least with
respect to congressional procedures, pretty much on the mark. In attempting
to place the blame for past and current economic ills on Congress and in
trying to wrest control of spending decisions away from Congress, the
Nixon administration was striking at the fundamental legislative power, the
power of the purse, and finding it soft, weak, and vulnerable.
    As has been indicated, spending ceilings had been set by Congress since
1968, but for Fiscal Year 1973, the president proposed that the $6 billion in
program reductions necessary to reduce a $256 billion budget to $250 billion
should be left to his discretion. Despite the opposition of the Democratic
leadership, that grant of discretionary power was approved by the House. In
the Senate, however, the response to this enlargement of presidential
discretion in spending matters was not as hospitable. That chamber agreed to
the spending limitation of $250 billion but put tight restrictions on the
president's ability to cut those funds. The differences between the two
chambers could not be worked out in conference; therefore, no spending
ceiling was enacted for FY 1973.
    This failed attempt to expand presidential discretion formally was sig-
nificant in a number of ways. It brought home graphically the weakness of
Congress's own budgetary process and its reliance upon the president for the
most important budgeting decisions. The president could shape his budget
priorities directly; as will be seen momentarily, Congress lacked that capacity. The slowing economy had made painful budgeting trade-offs necessary, and the president, through this new spending ceiling proposal and his
scathing rhetoric, had announced that Congress was incapable of making
such choices. Despite its ultimate failure, the experiences with the FY 1973
spending limitation suggested that many members of Congress concurred in
that judgment.
    The combination of an ailing economy and this direct presidential
challenge put the weaknesses of the budget process squarely before Congress in a way that was difficult to avoid. The second form of presidential
challenge in this arena, impoundment, served only to reinforce the image of
congressional impotence in fiscal matters.
    The withholding of duly appropriated funds by the president is not an
entirely new phenomenon. The Nixon administration and others have cited

precedents at least as far back as Thomas Jefferson's withholding of funds congressionally earmarked for naval gunboats. More recently, Franklin Roosevelt impounded Air Force money and canceled a super carrier; Eisenhower, Kennedy, and Johnson all withheld funds in varying amounts.[12]

Nevertheless, Nixon's impoundments were the most explosive politically and helped to create a crisis in congressional-executive relations for at least two reasons: the size and scope of his impoundments were unprecedented, and the number of strictly policy impoundments increased dramatically. In his first term, from 1969 to 1972, Nixon impounded approximately 17 to 20 percent of controllable expenditures, affecting more than 100 programs, most of which were effectively terminated.[13] Naturally, the various coalitions that had been formed to pass and maintain those programs could not be pleased with such a development. As an institution, Congress could not be pleased with its inability to control spending decisions that were seemingly within its purview.

In addition to the economic factors and the issues of impoundment, however, one cannot ignore the partisan dimension of this struggle. It was not an aggressive Democratic president challenging a Congress of his own party for policy leadership (e.g., Lyndon Johnson). It was an aggressively partisan Republican publicly challenging a Congress controlled by the opposition party and blaming it for the economic woes that were causing considerable concern. The inability of the congressional budget process to respond effectively to such challenges, and its patent weaknesses, highlighted by the clashes with the executive, helped to turn congressional awareness briefly to the need to reform that process.

INTERNAL FACTORS

The challenges to the legislature from the outside were effective partly because of weaknesses within. Two of the most pressing problems were severe and longstanding structural flaws in the authorization / appropriations process itself and a growing conflict among committees that dealt with various parts of that process—the authorization, appropriations, and tax writing committees.

The first structural weakness of note was the extremely decentralized nature of the congressional budget process. Since the end of the Civil War, appropriations have been considered separately from expected revenues. Even after the consolidation of the appropriations process in the 1920–22 era, the spending process remained fragmented. Appropriations were generally enacted in thirteen separate bills, formulated independently by the largely autonomous appropriations subcommittees in each house, and passed at different times during the legislative year without being formally related to one another. Thus, it was not possible for Congress to establish program priorities directly; there was no formal mechanism to take money from health programs, for instance, and put it directly into national defense–related appropriations.[14] In a time of tight budgets and necessary funding trade-offs, that situation was increasingly perceived as a serious institutional liability that redounded to the political advantage of the president and his centralizing budget agency, OMB, which could perform prioritizing operations.

Beyond the weakness resulting from the decentralization of the budget process, the authorization / appropriations system appeared to be breaking down. One obvious indicator of this problem was the inability of Congress to pass its appropriations bills in a timely fashion, due at least in part to late authorizations. In FY 1970 (beginning 1 July 1969), for example, $35.8 billion of the budget required authorizing legislation. By 8 October 1969, some three months after the beginning of the fiscal year, only $3 billion worth of the programs had been authorized.[15] With the authorizations coming so late in the year, the appropriations that depended upon them also lagged. It was not unusual during this time to find most of the federal agencies running on continuing resolutions or to find that none of the appropriations bills had been approved prior to 1 July (see table 1.3).

Still another measure of trouble with the system was the growing difference between the amounts authorized by the legislative committees and the amounts approved by the appropriations committees (see table 1.4). For instance, this "full-funding gap" increased from approximately $2.7 billion in FY 1966 to some $8.5 billion in FY 1970 for programs with fixed authorizations. Put another way, of the $24 billion authorized for such

Table 1.3. Appropriations Acts Approved Prior to the Beginning of the Fiscal Years, 1967–72

	1967	1968	1969	1970	1971	1972
Number of Regular Appropriations Acts	12	14	13	13	14	14
Number of Acts Approved Prior to 1 July	2	1	1	0	0	0

Source: Joint Study Committee on Budget Control. *Improving Congressional Budget Control, Hearings.* 93rd Cong., 1st sess., 1973, 362–63.

Table 1.4. Authorizations and Appropriations, Fiscal Years 1966–70 (in millions of dollars)

Fiscal Year	Authorized	Appropriated	Difference	Percentage Difference
1966	14,246	11,561	2,685	18.8
1967	15,192	12,171	3,021	19.9
1968	17,775	12,916	4,859	27.3
1969	21,204	13,337	7,867	37.1
1970	24,381	15,928	8,453	34.7

Source: Joint Study Committee on Budget Control, *Recommendations for Improving Congressional Control over Budgetary Outlay and Receipt Totals*, 93rd Cong., 1st sess., 1973, H. Rept. 93–147, 46; includes only programs with fixed authorizations.

programs in the latter year, less than $16 billion had been appropriated—a loss of almost thirty-five cents out of every authorized dollar.[16] As Allen Schick observes, "One byproduct of this gap has been the transformation of the authorization process from an evaluation of ongoing programs and the determination of new policies into a forum for the advocacy of higher spending by program supporters in Congress."[17]

Given that change and the extent to which the Appropriations Committee (at least in the House) maintained its traditional role as guardian of the federal treasury, the conflict between those two participants in the congressional budget process necessarily intensified.

The frustration, however, was not only on the part of the authorizing committees. In addition to the full-funding gap (and late authorizations), this period of congressional history was characterized by the growing use of so-called backdoor funding mechanisms to bypass the normal appropriations process. The increased use of these backdoor techniques (e.g., contract authority, borrowing authority, mandatory entitlements) meant that, by the early 1970s, fully one-half of all new budget authority was not subject to the effective control of the appropriations committees.[18] As a result, for FY 1969 through FY 1973, congressional action on appropriations bills reduced the requests of the administration for new budget authority by some $30 billion (see table 1.5). During this same five-year period, however, Congress approved, in legislation other than appropriations bills, budget authority that was more than $30 billion above the executive budget estimates.

One special case of intercommittee tension involved the House Appropriations and Ways and Means committees. For much of the 1960s, the Appropriations Committee had been beaten by the revenue committee on the

Table 1.5. Impact of Congressional Action on Administration Requests for Budget Authority, Fiscal Years 1969–73 (in millions of dollars)

Fiscal Year	Appropriations	Other Legislation[a]
1969	− 13,750	+ 737
1970	− 5,436	+ 5,704
1971	− 2,617	+ 8,352
1972	− 2,993	+ 673
1973	− 6,061	+ 15,009
TOTALS	− 30,857	+ 30,475

Source: Joint Study Committee on Budget Control, *Recommendations for Improving Congressional Control over Budgetary Outlay and Receipt Totals,* 93rd Cong., 1st sess., 1973, H. Rept. 93–147, 39.

a Includes "backdoor" and mandatory budget authority.

floor of the House when the interests of the two collided. As one staff member who was with the Appropriations Committee at the time put it: "We were getting our head bloodied during the sixties every time we took Mills on. The tax cuts especially put us in a godawful position in trying to keep the deficits down. But Wilbur won every time."[19]

This confrontation finally spilled over onto the House floor in 1972, during the debate on the $250 billion expenditure ceiling. Congressman Mills had just finished berating Chairman Mahon's substitute for that spending limit, which would have specified whence the $6 billion in spending cuts were to come rather than leaving it to presidential discretion. In a highly unusual public exchange between the two powerful committee chairmen, Mahon vented the frustration of his committee that had built up over the previous decade:

[It] surprises me a bit that my good friend from Arkansas would speak so fervently about the economy and a balanced budget when he has led the fight to bring about the condition with which we are confronted today. Yet he talks about economy and points the finger at the Appropriations Committee, and yet the gentleman from Arkansas has led the fight over the last 10 years that has reduced the revenues of this Government by the equivalent of $50 billion for the forthcoming fiscal year. Except for those reductions, we would be in the black, provided the economy would have behaved as it has.

Yet the gentleman points his finger at the Appropriations Committee. This is not where the problem is. The cutting of revenues and the increasing of spending through the Committee on Ways and Means, through the leadership of the gentleman from Arkansas, have helped bring us to this day of crisis.[20]

Roger Davidson and Walter Oleszek have reminded us that congressional reforms tend to have either external or internal causes and, in most instances, some combination of the two. In the case of the 1974 budget reform, both sources were clearly present, and each was significant. It is impossible to measure the precise degree to which each factor or set of factors contributed to the consciousness of the need for reform among the congressional membership, but each of those factors described above certainly played its part.

However, one distinction can be made. The internal factors were generally problems of long standing, although the severity of some—for example, authorization / appropriations gaps and backdoor funding—had increased around 1970. As indicated earlier, these problems contributed to a condition in which extreme external pressures created an atmosphere of crisis because the established routines simply could not respond effectively; the central congressional power, the power of the purse, was challenged at a time when it was in relative disarray.

However, it seems clear that it was the nature of the external pressure, the unparalleled efforts of the Nixon administration to control fiscal policy decisions, that precipitated the crisis. It was partly the public attacks and the harsh political rhetoric, but verbal assaults on Congress by the Chief Executive are not particularly rare on the American political stage. That combative rhetoric, reinforced by sweeping impoundments that seriously undermined the efficacy of congressional spending decisions, however, was a combination that raised deep concern in Congress. As Louis Fisher concluded: "The Nixon impoundments were unprecedented in their scope and severity. Never before had congressional priorities and prerogatives been so altered and jeopardized."[21]. The congressional response is nicely summarized in a staff memorandum to then Speaker Carl Albert:

> Impoundment question is really a "political" controversy rather than a Constitutional or legal one. Is a struggle for power between the President and Congress. Even if Congressional Democratic leadership is not positive as to Constitutional line of demarcation on matters between President and Congress, and is not absolutely certain any legislative proposal provides the answer, the practical political situation of the power struggle requires Congress to act and act promptly.[22]

In other words, the impoundment controversy had finally created an atmosphere in which serious scrutiny of the congressional budget process could be undertaken, and, in fact, could hardly be avoided. Thus, in the same bill that ultimately rejected the $250 billion spending ceiling, Title III established an ad hoc Joint Study Committee on Budget Control to examine congressional budget procedures and recommend changes therein.

The Joint Study Committee on Budget Control

The Joint Study Committee on Budget Control (JSC) was established on 27 October 1972. Significantly, its membership was composed almost entirely of members of four congressional committees—the House Ways and Means and Appropriations committees and the Senate Finance and Appropriations committees. Only two members of the sixteen-person delegation from each chamber were selected at-large, with primary institutional loyalty to the other standing committees. Consequently, from its very inception, the deliberations of the JSC were dominated by the interests of the fiscal committees of Congress.

However, it must be added that the interests of those fiscal committees were not always identical. For the Ways and Means Committee, the overriding weakness of the congressional budget process was the inability of that process to control spending. This deficiency and the budget deficits that resulted from it limited the ability of the revenue-raising committees to provide the tax cuts and tax incentives that reduced the flow of revenue into the federal treasury but made the Ways and Means Committee a politically powerful place to be. Therefore, in order to insure its continued flexibility in pursuing tax policy, the major substantive goal of the Ways and Means Committee was to place an early ceiling on spending. This it hoped to do by routing more spending decisions through the appropriations process and by putting a cap on appropriations early in the legislative year.

In many ways, the House Appropriations Committee had quite a different agenda. As was suggested earlier, it had been "bloodied" in legislative battles with the Ways and Means Committee during the previous decade. In addition, it had borne much of the burden and taken much of the political heat for the large budget deficits that had developed over that same time period.

At a minimum, then, the appropriations committees wanted these inequities rectified in the proposed budget reform. One staff member involved in the negotiations over the terms of the budget reform for the House Appropriations Committee put it this way:

> What Appropriations wanted was very simple. We wanted the backdoor closed. We wanted spending bills identified as such and routed through the appropriations process. We wanted the budget process, whatever it turned out to be to focus on revenue and outlays. So many of the people around here including those from Ways and Means focus entirely on the spending side. For them, spending is the budget and nothing else exists. We wanted to change that institutionally. Finally, we wanted the authorization process to conform to the House rules. Appropriations shouldn't proceed until the authorization had been enacted and to do that we wanted authorizations to be passed early in the legislative year.

Unlike the well-articulated reform objectives of the fiscal committees, the agenda of the authorizing committees in both chambers was notably ill-defined early in the reform process. They had only minor complaints about the existing system and probably underestimated the probability that some form of budget reform would be adopted. Once it became clear that some alterations in the budget process were all but inevitable, those concerned about the prerogatives of the authorizing committees attempted simply to minimize their losses.

Not surprisingly, the final report issued by the JSC reflected the institutional interests of its members and put forward the claims of the fiscal committees (particularly, the tax writing committees) in the strongest possible way. For instance, it recommended the creation of new budget committees in each house, two-thirds of whose members would be from the fiscal committees in that chamber (one third each from the taxing and spending committees). Only the remaining one-third would come from the authorizing committees.

In addition, the taxing committees won a provision for an early and detailed spending ceiling. The first budget resolution would, by 1 May, establish ceilings and subceilings (by appropriations subcommittee and / or program levels) on budget outlays and new budget authority, levels of revenue and debt, and the appropriate level of surplus or deficit. Moreover, according to the so-called rule of consistency, members desiring to amend the resolution would not only have to secure majorities for a proposed increase in funds for their favorite program but would also have to build a majority coalition behind the specific cuts in other parts of the budget to compensate for it. Building one majority for a floor amendment in Congress is no simple matter; the necessity of forging two separate majorities for the same amendment would make the resolutions virtually amendment free. Thus, for those on legislative committees, particularly liberals who would presumably be underrepresented on the new budget panels, it would be very difficult, under these procedures, to have a decisive impact on the emerging budget, either in committee or on the floor.

Only after the first resolution's ceilings were in place could Congress move on to consider the appropriations bills, and any measure that exceeded those ceilings would be subject to a point of order that could be waived only by a two-thirds vote. Such an early limit on spending down to the program or subcommittee level would seriously curtail the flexibility of the appropriations committees, and therefore, its presence in the final report represented a clear victory for the taxing committees.

For their part, the appropriations committees did succeed in closing the back door to new spending programs immediately and to some existing programs eventually but not to those financed through their own trust funds (e.g., Social Security). The appropriations committees wanted to eliminate the backdoor programs entirely, to have all spending counted as such, and to have it pass through the appropriations process. The Ways and Means and Finance committees, on the other hand, had increased their budgetary clout over the years by creating and maintaining within their jurisdictions some of the largest backdoor programs, including all Social Security legislation. As a result, the full implementation of the appropriation committees' goal would have seriously undermined the power base of their taxing colleagues on the Joint Study Committee. In the compromise reached within the JSC, the spending committees settled for significantly less than they had sought, so that power was left intact. As Allen Schick concludes, with respect to this report, "the preferences of the tax committees prevailed. The treaty forged in the JSC had a pronounced tilt toward tough spending controls."[23]

Thus, the JSC in fashioning its response to the external challenge posed by the executive, weighted its recommendations heavily in favor of the internal interests of its own membership. The taxing committees secured both of their major objectives—significant representation on the new budget panels and early and detailed spending ceilings that were extremely difficult to amend. The appropriations committees did not get all of the items on their agenda, but they did get the restrictions on new backdoor programs, which would stem the tide of funding decisions made outside of the appropriations process. They, too, were well represented on the new budget committees under the provisions of the JSC report. Finally, they hoped to eliminate the problem of late authorizations with the provision that authorizations would take effect no earlier than the fiscal year after they had been enacted.

The legislative committees, however, did not fare well. They lost the backdoor for new programs, although existing backdoor funding was not threatened. They had minimal representation on the new budget committees, and the floor procedures made it extremely difficult for them to amend the resolutions produced by those committees or to wage full-funding fights during floor consideration of appropriations bills.

This was not the end of the reform process, however, and the strategic position of the relevant institutional players changed substantially, as did the content of the reform package as a result of a new round of deliberations in each house.

Budget Reform in the House

In the House, the reform process moved from the Joint Study Committee to the House Rules Committee. Much more was involved with that move, however, than a simple change of venue. As was indicated, the JSC was thoroughly dominated by the fiscal committees of Congress. The House Rules Committee, however, since its expansion in 1961, had become an ally of the Democratic leadership in the House. As such, its responsibility in considering H.R. 7130 was to respond to the concerns and interests of various factions within the Democratic party, interests that were largely ignored by the JSC. The support of the Ways and Means and Appropriations committees could not now be written off, but that of the legislative committee members was critical to the survival of the budget reform process.

As a result, new political alliances were formed as the Rules Committee began its deliberations. One major consequence was that the Ways and Means Committee found itself politically isolated. Under the leadership of Richard Bolling (D, Mo.), the Democratic party leaders were joined by the party liberals and the Appropriations Committee (whose interests were not completely well served by the JSC report). One of those intimately involved in the negotiations that produced this alliance "sized up" the political situation:

> After the Joint Committee's report, Ways and Means found itself pretty much alone defending it . . . . Appropriations all it wanted was . . . well two things really. First, it wanted to end backdoor spending—you take away the rest of the bill and they would support it if it eliminated the backdoor spending and without it they wouldn't support the bill at all. They also wanted to maintain their slots on the committee . . . .
>
> The liberals (the DSG and Labor) they didn't want a bill at all but if a bill was coming out of Rules they wanted as weak a process as they could get. What the conservatives were calling fiscal responsibility, putting our house in order, etc., the liberals saw as an outright threat to their social programs. They, especially the unions, were going along with Bolling on this one, the Republicans were following Rhodes and southerners were going with Mahon, all supporting the Appropriations route. So, as I said, Ways and Means was left out there by themselves with no firepower.

As this quote suggests, the liberals really preferred no bill at all, primarily because the programs they supported would probably fare much worse at the hands of a centralized, coordinated budget system dominated by conservatives than they had under the existing decentralized, uncoordinated system of appropriations and backdoor financing. Nevertheless, blocking budget reform entirely appeared to be impossible, even to those who would benefit most from such a strategy; thus, they had to choose between strengthening the Appropriations or the Ways and Means committees.

With Ways and Means isolated and the House liberals in an uneasy alliance with the Appropriations Committee and the Democratic leadership, the Rules Committee began fashioning a compromise that would attract majority support in the House. In the Rules Committee version of H.R. 7130, the basic skeleton of the JSC report was retained, but much of the flesh was derived from a proposal by the Appropriations Committee's leading representative on the JSC, Jamie Whitten (D, Miss.), and modified somewhat to appeal more directly to House liberals and members of that chamber's legislative committees.

The major goals of the Appropriations Committee were achieved in the bill reported out by the Rules Committee. The overriding concern of the Appropriations Committee to reestablish and maintain its control over spending decisions was upheld for most legislation having provisions for new spending authority. As the committee report suggests, ''This means that backdoor spending would have the status of any ordinary authorizing legislation which must go through the regular appropriations process for funding.''[24]

The Appropriations Committee's interest in arresting the flood of late authorizations was accommodated by a requirement that authorizing legislation be passed before 1 April, unless an emergency waiver was granted by the Rules Committee. In addition, the fiscal year was changed from 1 July through 30 June to 1 October through 30 September to give Congress an additional three months to consider the spending bills and other items in the congressional budget.

Finally, the Appropriations Committee was granted five seats on the twenty-three person committee. This, combined with the five slots reserved for Ways and Means, gave the fiscal committees far less than the two-thirds majority they had originally proposed, but it still retained the principle of representation on the new budget panel and gave them almost 50 percent of the membership.

The Ways and Means Committee clearly suffered major setbacks in the Rules Committee's phase of these deliberations. This was an era of major changes in the power position of that committee,[25] and although it did not lose everything it had gained in the JSC report, it did lose its single most important objective—the imposition of an early ceiling on the spending process. Under the Rules Committee bill, the first budget resolution would establish only guidelines, not firm ceilings and, therefore, would not restrict the flexibility of the Appropriations Committee's deliberations and spending decisions. After a decade of supremacy, the Ways and Means Committee appeared to have lost an important contest with its major rival in the congressional budget process.

The House liberals and legislative committees did not fare particularly well, but, given the strong pressure for reform, they probably minimized the damage to their own interests. The greatest damage was incurred when they lost the "backdoor" as an alternative funding source for the programs under their jurisdictions. The closing of the backdoor certainly limited the options and the leverage available to the authorizing committees in the struggle to fund their programs. Despite this weakness, however, House liberals did succeed in preventing the emergence of a "super" Budget Committee, heavily conservative and strongly inclined to cut back on the social programs they favored.

Of greatest importance, however, the Rules Committee suggested a unique, rotating membership for the new budget panel. Under this provision, no member could serve more than four years out of any ten.[26] The rotating membership, it was hoped, would preclude the development of entrenched power within the committee. No one was going to make a legislative career out of service on the Budget Committee, and consequently, there would be no burning interest among members to increase greatly the committee's power, prestige, and influence within the House. The fear of House liberals that the new Budget Committee would be yet another conservative power center was eased considerably.

IMPOUNDMENT

One of the major factors precipitating the full-scale movement toward budget reform was the presidential challenge to the congressional power of the purse in the form of impoundment. In fact, from a political and institutional point of view, this was the preeminent issue, because this latest incarnation of a longstanding presidential practice was striking at the "taproot" of congressional power. Thus, anti-impoundment legislation headed the House Democratic leadership's list of necessary budget reforms and was perhaps the only part of budget reform that attracted the support of most liberals in Congress.

The anti-impoundment bill reported out by the Rules Committee, H.R. 8480, provided for a one-house veto, under which any impoundment must cease if, within sixty days, *either* house of Congress passed a resolution of disapproval. Obviously, it is much easier to gain agreement to such an action in one house than in both; still, if both houses did nothing, the impoundment would remain in effect.

H.R. 8480 was reported from the Rules Committee and passed by the House on 25 July 1973. Before passage, the bill was amended on the floor to make the anti-impoundment procedures effective for only one year. The amendment was approved with the understanding that, when budget control legislation was finally developed, it would contain permanent impoundment controls. The anti-impoundment provisions of H.R. 8480 were attached to H.R. 7130 by the Rules Committee, and the entire package was reported out of that committee on 20 November 1973.

This series of reforms, formulated largely during the Rules Committee deliberations, was maintained with almost no exceptions on the floor of the House. No major amendments were adopted in the two days of debate, and the measure passed, 386 to 23.

Budget Reform in the Senate

In the Senate, the work of the Joint Study Committee passed through two committees on its way to the floor. Its first stop was in the Government Operations Committee. Initially, that committee received from its Subcommittee on Budgeting, Management, and Expenditures a bill at least as restrictive and unfavorable to the interests of liberals and the appropriations committees as the JSC recommendations. Among its main provisions, the bill provided for a budget resolution to be adopted by 15 April which, in addition to overall spending, would set ceilings for appropriations committees and subceilings for appropriations subcommittees and "major program groupings." A form of the "rule of consistency," to restrict amendments to the budget resolution, was also included.

That bill represented a narrow conservative triumph (the vote for approval was 5–4), but because it ignored or actively undercut significant interests of major congressional actors, it was a victory that could not be sustained for long. The first imperative of the full committee, therefore, was to fashion a compromise measure that would obscure the conservative-liberal divisions within its membership and thereby present the Senate with a united front. The result was an amalgam, a "Rube Goldberg" combination of targets, ceilings, triggering, and enforcement legislation that would retain the early ceiling on total spending, but only in the context of other provisions that were so complex and cumbersome that there was almost no support for them beyond the committee.[27]

S. 1541 AND THE SENATE RULES AND ADMINISTRATION COMMITTEE

Since the bill reported by the Government Operations Committee affected the Senate rules in several ways, the second step in the Senate process was the consideration of S. 1541 by the Senate Rules and Administration Committee. Although the version reported out by Government Operations had apparently been successful in reconciling the different points of view on that committee, the committee had not ventured far beyond its own members to consider which institutional interests were being affected by the proposed legislation. For instance, a letter sent to all the Senate committee chairmen by the Rules Committee Chairman, Howard Cannon, noted, with respect to the subcommittee deliberations: "It does not appear that any committee chairman was specifically asked for his views . . . [and] since this bill directly affects the work of the Senate and many of its committees, it is important that each committee carefully consider the impact of all of its provisions on their operations."[28]

In order to address this concern, obtain the broadest input into the development of this bill, and most importantly, produce a consensus measure that would evoke little or no opposition in the chamber, Senator Byrd (D, W. Va.) created an ad hoc staff group to consider the various options available for budget reform. All standing committees were permitted to designate representatives to the group, and ten did so. In addition, the group included representatives from four joint committees, the House Appropriations Committee, the Congressional Research Service, and the Office of Senate Legislative Counsel.[29]

The measure produced by this group of approximately forty-five staff members was, in turn, revised by Senator Byrd himself. As one who participated in the staff group put it: "I had never seen anything like it. Byrd almost literally locked himself in a room for two or three days and went over every sentence in that bill and reworked much of it. He wanted to make sure there were no screw-ups . . . nothing that was going to tie the Senate up for weeks on end."

What Byrd and the staff group produced was, in the words of the committee report, "a bill which is (a) enactable, (b) workable, and (c) useful"; that is, its product possessed those qualities lacked by the earlier Government Operations bill. It had taken into account the broader range of institutional interests that existed in the Senate; it had simplified the proposed budget procedure and made it more flexible; therefore, it was a bill that would be much more acceptable to the Senate membership as a vehicle for change than the earlier versions had been.

For instance, the first budget resolution provided for in the earlier legislation was altered substantially in the substitute bill. Rather than set early ceilings, the substitute measure conceived of the first resolution in terms similar to those developed by the Rules Committee in the House. It was to set guidelines or targets for the appropriate levels of budget authority, outlays, revenues, surplus or deficit, and debt levels. These figures would, in turn, guide congressional considerations of appropriations and other spending measures later in the legislative year. Rather than the cumbersome ceiling enforcement mechanism of the Government Operations bill, the Rules Committee provided for a second resolution and a reconciliation procedure. Under these provisions, the mandatory second resolution would be reported in August, shortly after action had been completed on the appropriations measures. Among other things, it would set a firm ceiling on spending and a floor for revenues. Finally, under the reconciliation provisions, if these totals were out of line with the revenue and / or spending totals already approved, the relevant committees could be directed to make adjustments in the taxing or spending measures under their jurisdictions in order to bring the two into conformity.

With these and other provisions in place, the Senate Rules Committee agreed unanimously to the revised version of S. 1541, and the bill was reported to the Senate.

IMPOUNDMENT

In the Senate, as in the House, the impoundment control provisions were passed separately from the budget control act. The most important provision of S. 373 was the requirement that impoundments be reported to Congress by the president and that the appropriated money be spent unless both houses passed a concurrent resolution approving the impoundment. If Congress did nothing, the impoundment would, in effect, be disapproved. This was a much tougher impoundment provision than that passed by the House, which required at least one house to take action in order to disapprove an impoundment.

Finally, the passage on the Senate floor was similar to that in the House. The major divisions in the Senate membership that were to be affected by budget reform had been taken into consideration in the process of creating the reform package, and the series of compromises held together very well on the floor. In fact, the only major amendments adopted represented small victories for the conservative camp as they tightened, to some extent, the control of appropriations and entitlement programs. With that exception, the structure finally devised in the Senate Rules Committee remained unchanged, and the upper house passed its version of congressional budget and impoundment control unanimously, 80 to 0.

The reform process in the Senate occurred in a manner similar to that of the House, and the reform measure it produced was not radically different. It provided for new budget committees that would report two budget resolutions each year, setting first targets and then ceilings on federal budget authority and outlays and a floor for revenue. The Senate package also provided for a reconciliation process that would allow the second resolution to direct committees of Congress to raise more revenue or to cut back in programs and funding they had already approved in order to bring total government expenditures under the spending limit.

As in the lower chamber, different institutional interests within the Senate met with varying degrees of success in improving or maintaining their positions within the budgetary process. Again, once the reform measure had been put before the Rules Committee, the appropriations committees successfully resisted attempts to establish early ceilings on expenditures in favor of targets established by the first resolution, which were intended to guide rather than restrict the appropriations process. Given these provisions and others to restrict new entitlement legislation, the spending committees emerged from the reform process with a much improved institutional position. The authorizing committees and Senate liberals, on the other hand, could only hope to minimize their losses in the face of the overwhelming sentiment for budget reform of some kind. They did that by securing the adoption of a strong anti-impoundment measure. Moreover, they altered the requirement that authorizing legislation be passed early in the year to one that required only that such legislation be reported by 15 May.

The issue of Budget Committee membership, which was of such great import in the House, did not become a test of strength, since it was decided quite early in the process to select the members of that body by routine methods and to grant guaranteed representation to no committee.

Conference

Unlike the relative ease with which the separate versions of the budget reform passed in their respective houses, the conference committee compromise was not concluded easily. It is true that the budget control features of the legislation were handled expeditiously. As expected, the conferees agreed to the creation of two new budget committees, with the sole responsibility of reporting two resolutions each year—the first to set targets, and the second to set ceilings and include reconciliation, if necessary. Each house was permitted to set the conditions for the membership of its own budget committee. The conferees selected the more lenient Senate requirement with respect to authorizations, that is, in order to be considered on the floor, authorizations must be reported (but not necessarily passed) by 15 May.

After all these matters had been settled, however, the conference committee was left with perhaps the most important presidential challenge to congressional prerogatives in the budgeting field—impoundment. The Senate had passed an impoundment control measure such that an impoundment would be terminated automatically unless both houses passed a concurrent resolution approving of the impoundment within sixty days. The House, on the other hand, had passed a weaker version of impoundment control that would end any impoundment only if one house of Congress disapproved of it within sixty days.

After a lengthy deadlock over these provisions, the conferees followed that time-honored conference committee tradition of "splitting the difference." They divided impoundment into two categories—rescissions and deferrals. The former, withholding funds on a permanent basis, requires the approval of both houses of Congress, which was the Senate impoundment control provision. The latter, the temporary withholding of funds, is permitted unless one house passes a resolution of disapproval; this was the House impoundment control provision.

With that thorny issue resolved, the final budget reform package was reported out of the conference committee and approved overwhelmingly by the House on 18 June 1974, by a vote of 401 to 6, and by the Senate on 21 June 1974, by a vote of 75 to 0.

Conclusion

The reform of the congressional budget process in 1974 was a major event in the history of Congress. As such, it commands one's attention not only for its consequences, which are examined in later chapters, but also for what it illustrates about the process of change in Congress. In view of the latter concern, I have approached this latest and most extensive reform, asking two related questions: Whence comes the impetus for this type of major change? And secondly, How are the various internal and external pressures for change translated into a reform package that wins the approval of both houses of Congress?

With respect to the first question, I have employed a schema that distinguishes between external and internal sources of reform pressure. Adaptive reforms are those that are stimulated by external factors, such as the economic consequences of war or presidential challenges for control of fiscal policy. Ameliorative changes are attempts to ease internal tensions (e.g., disputes over spending "turf").

As the 1974 reforms illustrate, major reforms are often spawned by a mixture of internal and external pressures. The dominant and decisive stimulus to change in this case was the external challenge of the executive branch, primarily through policy impoundments, but there were also significant strains caused by internal weaknesses in the congressional budget process. Thus, some elements of the reform package, such as the impoundment provisions, responded directly and completely to the external pressures, but many responses were tempered by internal considerations. For instance, in designing the "shape" of the House Budget Committee, an important consideration was to avoid intensifying the internal conflicts while creating a unit that would be able to respond effectively to the challenges of the president and the economy. In both the House and Senate, proposals for establishing spending ceilings early in the legislative year were amended partly in response to the institutional memory of the ill-fated ceilings associated with the 1946 reforms but also in deference to the institutional interests of the appropriations committees. These committees did not want to be restricted in their deliberations.

The process of balancing the opposing forces generated by internal stresses and external pressures generally occurs prior to the formal adoption stage of deliberations. The *search process* is the key to fashioning a reform package that will be adopted by the members of Congress and is, therefore, also the key for political scientists who wish to explain the outcomes of reform movements in Congress.

Consistent with this account of the recent budget reforms, one of the first imperatives of the successful search process appears to be a willingness to seek out the views of those members of Congress who will be affected in a significant way by the proposed changes. Thus, with respect to the 1974 changes, one important factor that lengthened the search process was the inability or unwillingness of two of the search units to satisfy this elementary condition. The Joint Study Committee, for example, was weighted too heavily in favor of the fiscal committees to provide a proper forum for the serious consideration of other political interests affected by the reform proposals. When it became clear that even the interests of one of the main fiscal units, the appropriations committees, were not being well served, the success of the JSC recommendations became problematic at best.

In the same way, the network consulted by the Government Operations Committee before making its recommendations to the Senate was too restricted to allow the fashioning of a proposal that could attract majority support within its own body. This situation prompted Senator Cannon's letter to the other committee chairmen bemoaning the fact that they had not been asked to testify before the relevant subcommittee and suggesting that "since this bill directly affects the work of the Senate and many of its committees, it is important that each committee carefully consider the impact of all of its provisions on their operations."[30]

That type of reaching out to the various factions within its chamber was one function performed by the rules committees in the House and the Senate. Having little or no voice in the deliberations of the JSC, House liberals and the authorizing committees found in the Rules Committee a forum where they could present their cases. Sentor Byrd's ad hoc staff committee provided a similar forum for such interests in the Senate.

The foregoing is not meant to suggest that all views or interests are weighted equally and that all are therefore accommodated to the same degree in some magical way. In the reform process, there are winners and losers. Once the scope of conflict had expanded in the House, for example, the Appropriations Committee secured almost every item on its agenda. After more than a decade of lessening power and of defeat by the Ways and Means Committee, members of Congress perhaps felt the need to "shore up" that wing of their fiscal house. Thus, the taxing committee lost most of what it had gained in the JSC recommendations.

Those on the losing end of the arrangements made at the search stage may, of course, carry their fight to the floor. If the search committee is relatively representative of or sensitive to the divisions of power within its chamber, such a strategy will meet with limited success; this was the experience of the various factions in both houses during the 1974 reform process.

Finally, it must be emphasized that in Congress, as in other organizations, the search process is a political one and not simply a mechanistic matching of problems and solutions. The pressures from the executive in the early 1970s, coupled with the long-standing weaknesses within the congressional budget process, offered the opportunity for reform; it did not preordain the outcome. Some units, such as the House Appropriations Committee, came to the process with a fairly elaborate agenda of provisions and preferred outcomes. Others, such as the authorization committees, pursued very little in the way of specific changes initially, in part because they were fighting a rear-guard action—trying simply to defuse attempts to undermine their current advantages. For instance, the creation of the House Budget Committee was not simply a question of forming the most powerful, centralizing committee in the House to take care of budgeting issues for that body. Rather, the design of that committee was the outcome of a much more complex political process. In order to assure broad and deep support once their proposals got to the House floor, the Rules Committee needed to reduce the potential opposition of the disaffected liberals who feared the creation of a new, fiscally conservative power center and to retain the support of those conservatives who had served on the JSC. The outcome was a somewhat bizarre committee design with slots reserved for the fiscal committees, the authorizing committees, and the party leadership and with a rotating membership to still the fears of the House liberals.

It is true that not all the provisions of this reform required this type of intricate political balancing. The impoundment provisions, although they created some interchamber conflict, were a relatively straightforward response to the external challenge posed by the president; the only question was how strong they should be. Nevertheless, even those provisions are a part of the overall package (i.e., impoundment control provisions accepted as the price for spending controls, and vice versa), and it is a package of reforms, a compilation of carefully balanced compromises acceptable to a majority of both houses of Congrerss, that the search process is supposed to produce.

This chapter has examined the "choice" made by Congress to reform its budget process in 1974. As Cohen et al. have noted, in such a context, "choices are made by forming a group with sufficient power to enforce a joint solution to a problem."[31] This type of coalition formation results from the balancing, negotiating, and compromising that are at the heart of the successful search process. As such, this stage of reform holds the key to an understanding of how the various pressures for reform, both internal and external, are translated into a successful reform package, such as the Congressional Budget and Impoundment Control Act of 1974.

2

Congressional Budgeting, 1977–1983: Continuity and Change

F. TED HEBERT

The congressional budget process was challenged during the early Reagan administration by events unlike any since its implementation—by the actions of a president determined to restructure spending and revenue policies and a Congress divided along party lines for the first time in twenty-six years. President Reagan used the budget procedures to achieve his much acclaimed initial victories over congressional Democrats, but in doing so he may have both strengthened those procedures and stimulated efforts to change them. Indeed, some members of Congress are calling for such changes.[1]

Chapters that follow examine in detail the effects of the congressional budget process on the politics of Congress and on congressional relationships with other institutions. To provide a background for such examination, this chapter explores developments in the budgetary process since the FY 1977 implementation of the Congressional Budget Act. Some of these developments are mere extensions and elaborations of practices in place before passage of the act (e.g., the use of tax expenditures and entitlements), whereas others flow directly from procedures required by the act (e.g., budget resolutions).

The Budget Schedule: Can Congress Maintain It?

A notable feature of the Budget Act was the establishment of a schedule for Congress to follow in acting upon the budget and related legislation. Adoption of this schedule arose, at least in part, from the frustration that members of Congress felt at their own inability to enact appropriation legislation in a timely manner. In every year of the decade preceding enactment of the Budget Act, Congress had failed to pass important

31

appropriations bills before the start of the fiscal year. In fact, in not one of those years did as many as one-half of the major bills pass on a timely basis.

To give itself greater opportunity to consider appropriations legislation, Congress shifted the starting date of the fiscal year, effective for FY 1977. The Budget Act provided that FY 1976 would end as scheduled on 30 June, 1976 but that it would be followed by a "transitional quarter," extending through 30 September. FY 1977 would being on 1 October, as would all succeeding fiscal years. Since the act did not alter the existing requirement that the president's budget be received early in the calendar year (within fifteen days after Congress convenes), Congress provided itself three additional months to consider the president's requests.

Perhaps even more important, Congress imposed upon itself a number of deadlines to stimulate timely consideration of the budget. Figure 2.1 schematically presents the procedure Congress adopted, a procedure that incorporated actions by the appropriations committees (most of which were longstanding practices) and those of the budget committees and the Congressional Budget Office, the new institutions established by the act.

In the following chapters, many references will be made to specific steps required by the Budget Act. It is appropriate to mention some of these here and to note the difficulty that Congress has had in meeting the established deadlines.

The budget committees face the earliest major deadline, a requirement that they report a "first concurrent budget resolution" to their chambers by 15 April. The committees are to have reviewed the president's request and received comments from other committees and reports from the Congressional Budget Office. The first resolution is required to contain a statement of the appropriate level of total budget outlays and budget authority for the coming fiscal year, a recommended level of federal revenue, and an appropriate deficit or surplus level, if any. Further, it is to contain appropriate levels of outlays and budget authority for each major functional category of federal activity.

Congress has one month in which to consider the resolutions proposed by its budget committees. Final action—including resolution of any differences between the two chambers—is to be completed by 15 May. This resolution then serves as a guide to the appropriations committees and to the two chambers as they act upon appropriations bills.

In an effort to correct its own previous failings, Congress set for itself the deadline of seven days after Labor Day for completion of actions on all major appropriations bills for the new fiscal year. The Budget Act did not require that these bills conform to the first concurrent resolution. In fact, in anticipation of nonconformance, it provided for congressional adoption (by

15 September) of a second concurrent budget resolution, one that would reaffirm or revise the first one. Should Congress determine that some or all of the appropriations or revenue bills did not conform with the second resolution, it could bring into use a reconciliation procedure. Under this procedure (to be completed by 25 September) Congress would adopt necessary changes in previously passed bills or resolutions.

THE RECORD

Just how well has Congress performed in meeting the deadlines it established for itself? Before addressing that question, it is important to examine the phrase, "for itself." Congress attempted to provide deadlines, but there is little that can be done to assure adherence to them. Although the Congressional Budget Act was made law in 1974, later Congresses might choose to ignore it or to follow only parts of it. Much depends upon the willingness of the members, themselves, to meet the deadlines established.

In the first years after implementation, Congress adhered to the new requirements rather well, even passing all thirteen appropriations bills prior to the start of FY 1977 (see table 2.1). In calendar year 1978, performance began to deteriorate, approaching failure to conform to the provisions of the act in 1981. As will be noted below, adoption of the second budget resolution, on 10 December, 1981, was a desperate effort to conform procedurally with the act's requirements (if not its deadlines) while ignoring its substantive intent.

Regarding passage of appropriations bills, Congress is performing no better today than in the years immediately preceding adoption of the Budget Act. Not only is passage of many bills late, but in several instances continuing resolutions have been used to fund agencies for an entire fiscal year.

The obvious deterioration of adherence to Budget Act deadlines may be due, in part, to a decrease in the novelty introduced by the act. More important, however, is the difficulty of budget issues with which Congress has been forced to deal in recent years. Pressure for a balanced budget at a time of worsening economic conditions has compelled Congress to address issues that, in earlier years, could be pushed aside by appropriating growth revenues. Most likely, the difficulty of reaching compromise solutions— and thereby passing appropriations bills on time—has been aggravated by the divided party control in Congress and by differences between the Democratic-controlled House and the Republican administration. This is not to contend that return to united party control will automatically restore

Approximate timing

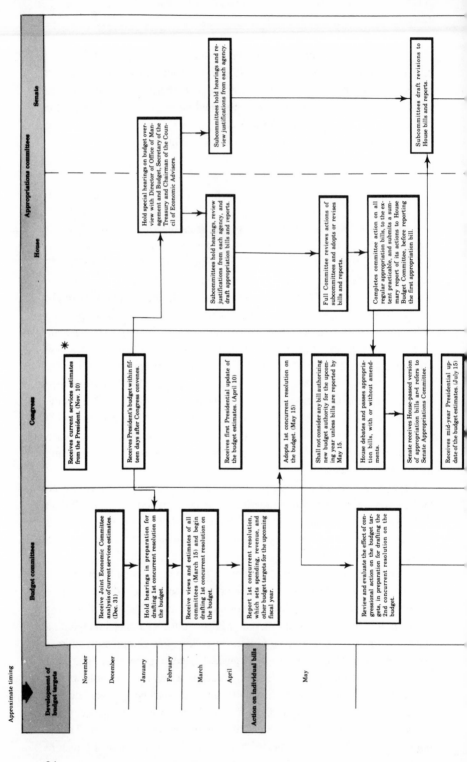

34

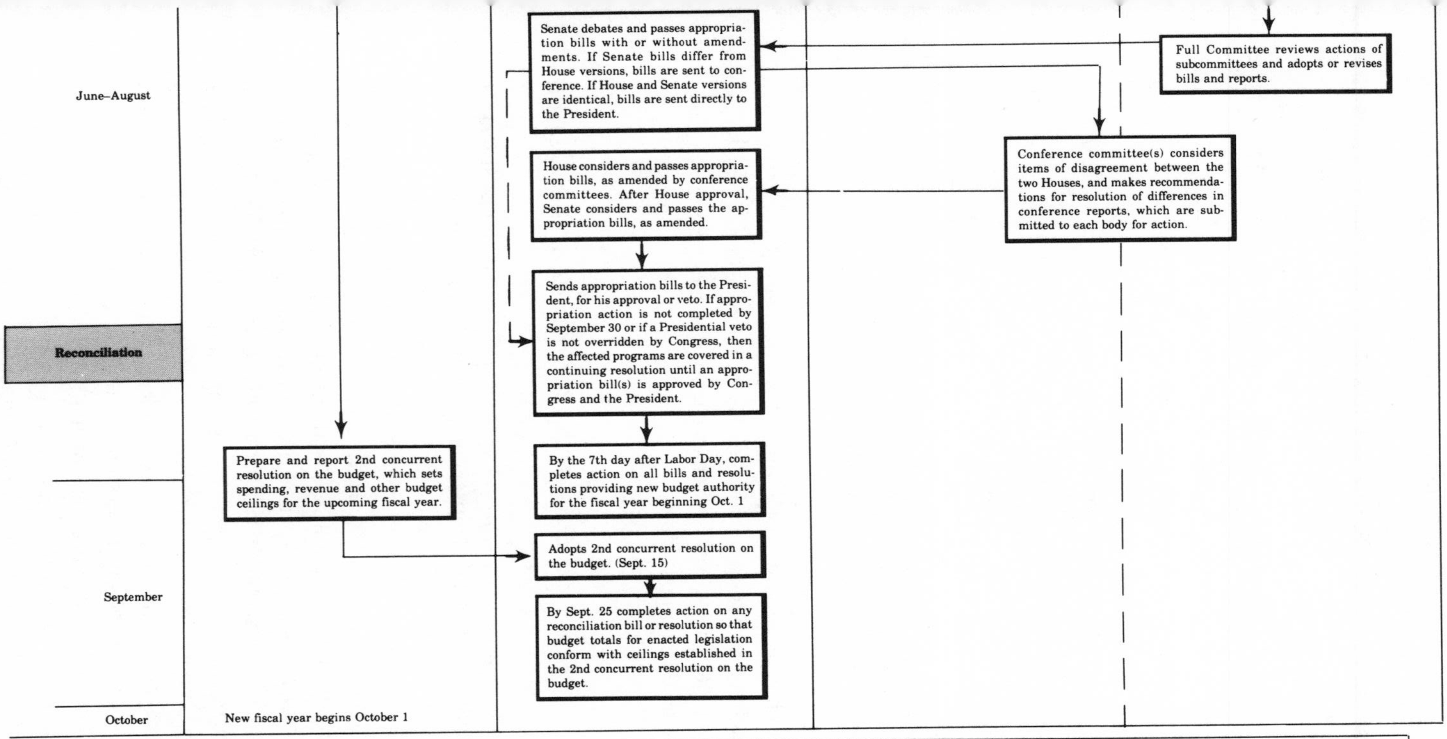
June–August
Reconciliation
September
October
New fiscal year begins October 1
Prepare and report 2nd concurrent resolution on the budget, which sets spending, revenue and other budget ceilings for the upcoming fiscal year.
Senate debates and passes appropriation bills with or without amendments. If Senate bills differ from House versions, bills are sent to conference. If House and Senate versions are identical, bills are sent directly to the President.
House considers and passes appropriation bills, as amended by conference committees. After House approval, Senate considers and passes the appropriation bills, as amended.
Sends appropriation bills to the President, for his approval or veto. If appropriation action is not completed by September 30 or if a Presidential veto is not overridden by Congress, then the affected programs are covered in a continuing resolution until an appropriation bill(s) is approved by Congress and the President.
By the 7th day after Labor Day, completes action on all bills and resolutions providing new budget authority for the fiscal year beginning Oct. 1
Adopts 2nd concurrent resolution on the budget. (Sept. 15)
By Sept. 25 completes action on any reconciliation bill or resolution so that budget totals for enacted legislation conform with ceilings established in the 2nd concurrent resolution on the budget.
Full Committee reviews actions of subcommittees and adopts or revises bills and reports.
Conference committee(s) considers items of disagreement between the two Houses, and makes recommendations for resolution of differences in conference reports, which are submitted to each body for action.

General Notes

Action represented in the column labeled "Congress" reflects action of one or both bodies of Congress (House and Senate), as specified. Information is also included on reports sent to Congress as a whole.

Action on revenue measures follows the same general procedure as action on appropriation bills, except that revenue measures are reported by the Ways and Means Committee in the House, and by the Finance Committee in the Senate.

Figure 2.1. Congressional budget process. (*Souce:* Executive Office of the President, Office of Management and Budget.)

*Although the current services budget is required in November by the Budget Act, it is now submitted in January with the president's budget.

Table 2.1.   Congressional Adherence to Deadlines of the Congressional Budget Act

Calendar Year	1st Resolution Adoption Date	2nd Resolution Adoption Date	Number of Appropriations Bills Passed on Time[a]	Number of Appropriations Bills Passed by Oct. 1[a]
1976 (FY 77)	May 13	Sept. 16	9	13
1977 (FY 78)	May 17	Sept. 15	9	10
1978 (FY 79)	May 17	Sept. 23	3	7
1979 (FY 80)	May 24	Nov. 28	2	3
1980 (FY 81)	June 12	Nov. 20	0	3
1981 (FY 82)	May 21	Dec. 10	0	0
1982 (FY 83)	June 23	Oct. 1[b]	0	1
1983 (FY 84)	June 23	Oct. 1[b]	4	6

Sources: Congressional Quarterly Almanac, various volumes, and *Congressional Quarterly Weekly Reports,* various issues.

[a] In each of these years there were thirteen major appropriations bills.

[b] No second resolution was adopted in 1982 or 1983, but the first resolutions became binding on Oct. 1.

adherence to budget deadlines. Unfortunately, the willingness of members of Congress to compromise on complex issues in order to meet the budget schedule may have been lost. Whether such willingness can be regained cannot now be determined.

Federal Spending and the Deficit

Passage of congressional budget reform in 1974 came about, at least in part, as a result of the hope that closer congressional scrutiny of budget totals would result in Congress sharing with the president efforts to restrict both spending and the deficit. Figure 2.2 shows the upward trend of spending and the annual deficit prior to 1974. Having passed the $100-billion mark in 1962, federal spending topped $200-billion in 1971. Deficits, although common during the post-1950 period, had remained under $10 billion in all years prior to 1971, except for 1959 and 1968. Efforts in Congress and by President Nixon to curtail spending through establishment of ceilings enforced by impoundments were generally unsuccessful, although the impoundments raised the ire of many members of Congress.[2] Could congressional procedures be changed so that Congress could succeed in preventing deficits and in slowing (or stopping) spending growth when both Congress and the president had previously failed? Could Congress simultaneously restrict the president's impoundment authority and take upon itself responsibility for managing federal spending and deficit totals? These

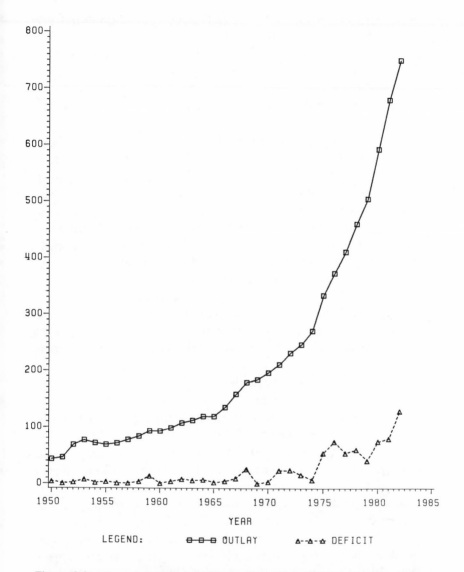

Figure 2.2. Annual outlays and deficits, 1950–82 in billions of dollars. This includes off-budget outlays since 1973. Surpluses were recorded in the following years in the amounts indicated but are plotted here as zero deficits: 1951, $6.1 billion; 1956, $4.1 billion; 1957, $3.2 billion; 1960, $0.3 billion; 1969, $3.2 billion. *Source: The United States Budget in Brief FY 1984* (Washington, D.C.: Executive Office of the President Office of Management and Budget, 1983).

were among the questions raised by adoption of the Congressional Budget and Impoundment Control Act of 1974.

What does the record show? What has happened to spending and deficit levels since 1977, the first year of the act's implementation? Spending has continued to grow and deficit levels have been more than $40 billion annually, considerably higher than any during the 1950–74 period (see figure 2.2).

One important qualifier needs to be interjected here. The 1970s was a period of high inflation. Costs to government were pushed upward during this period, much as were costs to individuals. In addition to attempting to meet increased prices of goods and services, governments were under great pressure to ensure that payments to individuals (e.g., Social Security and retirement benefits) kept pace with the rising cost of living. To help assess the impact of such inflation, Figure 2.3 presents data on outlays and deficits expressed in constant (1967) dollars. The differences between figures 2.2 and 2.3 are rather sharp. Most notable is the reduction of spending growth (see figure 2.3). Whereas figure 2.2 shows current dollar growth of 101 percent since 1976, the growth in constant dollars is only 22 percent. Similarly, the size of deficits in recent years is not as large as figure 2.2 suggests; in fact, the 1981 deficit was smaller than those of 1975 and 1976, the years just before implementation of the Congressional Budget Act, and the 1982 deficit was only slightly larger.

These data do not permit any firm conclusion that the Budget Act has succeeded in reducing spending or deficits below the levels they would otherwise have attained. Of course, it is impossible to know with certainty the levels they would have reached. One thing the act clearly did not produce, however, was a reduction in the level of demands for restraint on spending and deficits. The movement for adoption of some form of constitutional amendment—to balance the budget, to restrict spending growth, or both—has gained momentum since 1977, a development considered in greater detail below. Finally, those closest to the process, members of the House and Senate budget committees, cannot agree on the act's impact; some claim it has produced large savings, although others see no such results.[3]

Spending Growth and Entitlements

There are many ways to analyze federal spending, but one that has received increased attention in recent years addresses controllable versus uncontrollable expenditures. Particularly important in the latter category are

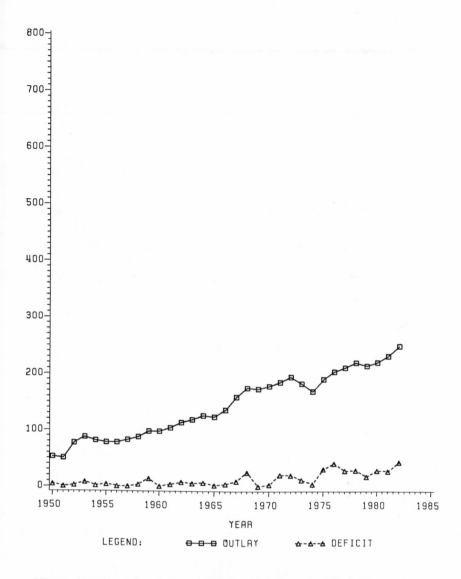

Figure 2.3. Annual outlays and deficits, 1950–82, in constant dollars (1967 dollars, in billions). This includes off-budget outlays since 1973. Surpluses were recorded in the following years in the amounts indicated but are plotted here as zero deficits: 1951, $6.7 billion; 1956, $4.5 billion; 1957, $3.5 billion; 1960, $0.3 billion; 1969, $3.0 billion. Source: Author's calculations deflating data shown in Figure 2.2, using producers price index, all commodities, obtained from Department of Commerce, *Business Conditions Digest,* various issues.

entitlement programs. As defined by the General Accounting Office, these are programs established by "legislation that requires the payment of benefits (or entitlements) to any person or unit of government that meets the eligibility requirements established by such law."[4] These laws constitute a binding obligation on the federal government, giving eligible recipients legal recourse in the event the obligation is not met.[5] The Office of Management and Budget reports that entitlements have expanded dramatically in recent years, growing at a rate faster than total outlays. An expanding portion of the budget is accounted for by entitlements and other "uncontrollable" spending (see table 2.2). The principal type of entitlement—and the one that grew quite rapidly—is payments to individuals, including such programs as Social Security, federal employee retirement benefits, unemployment compensation, student loan insurance, and so forth. The wave of social reform in the 1960s contributed to this growth, as did the congressionally adopted policy of indexing many benefits for inflation. In the early 1970s, general revenue sharing, a form of entitlement designated for state and local governments rather than individuals, was added to these and resulted in $4.6 billion in outlays in 1982.

Table 2.2.   Relative Controllability of Federal Budget

Fiscal Year	Relatively Uncontrollable[a]	Relatively Controllable
1970	63.2	36.8
1971	65.6	34.4
1972	65.4	34.6
1973	69.2	30.8
1974	71.3	28.7
1975	72.0	28.0
1976	72.3	27.7
1977	72.3	27.7
1978	73.4	26.6
1979	73.5	26.5
1980	75.1	24.9
1981[b]	73.1	26.9
1982	74.6	25.4
1983	75.5	24.5

Source: Office of Management and Budget, *Budget of the United States Government, Fiscal Year 1984* (Washington, D.C.: Government Printing Office, 1983). The issues for FY 1980 and FY 1982 were also used.

[a]Percentages shown are slightly different from those reported in the budget documents. Amounts of undistributed employer share of employee retirement were omitted in these calculations.

[b]Basis of figures for 1981, 1982, and 1983 is different from that used in prior years, due to reassignment of some items by the Office of Management and Budget.

Entitlements and some other spending categories (e.g., interest on the debt and liquidation of obligations created by contracts executed in prior years) are frequently identified as spending that is "relatively uncontrollable under present law." According to the 1984 budget, such spending accounted for more than 75 percent of total outlays in 1983. It is projected to increase to more than 76 percent in 1984, despite attempts by the Reagan administration to reduce growth in numerous entitlement programs.[6]

If one accepts the label *uncontrollable* as truly reflecting the nature of these outlays, the amount of discretion available to the president and Congress is small indeed—and growing smaller. However, this label may overstate the degree to which these items are untouchable. Some observers contend that the label provides a convenient means of obscuring a lack of fiscal discipline:

> The notion of spending being 'uncontrollable' is both inaccurate and harmful. It is harmful because it narrows our range of perceived alternatives and thwarts useful debate concerning the realignment of federal budget priorities. It is inaccurate because it implies that a budget item is preordained and beyond the discretion of politicians to reduce or eliminate. With only one exception—payment of interest on the national debt—the term 'uncontrollable' is applied to spending that politicians can change but will not, often because of simple lack of fortitude.[7]

From the congressional perspective, however, there is an important distinction between much of this so-called uncontrollable spending and that which is more easily controlled. Specifically, some entitlements do not require annual appropriations but are, rather, funded on the basis of actions taken on legislation reaching the floor of the House and Senate through the authorizing committees. Although some other entitlements require action by the appropriations committees, that action is virtually mandatory.

Despite inclusion in the Budget Act of provisions designed to give appropriations committees and budget committees a degree of control over new entitlement programs, the extent of control exercised over total entitlement spending remained quite limited until extraordinary procedures were followed in 1980 and succeeding years. However, the act may have reduced expansion of entitlement programs. Allen Schick notes that "virtually all of the 1977–79 increase [in entitlements, other than interest on the debt] was due to the mandatory rise in existing entitlements rather than to congressional action. It is hard to ascertain whether the pronounced slowdown in new entitlements has been due primarily to the operations of the Budget Act or to the fiscal temper of Congress, but it seems reasonable to conclude that both factors have been relevant."[8]

Tax Expenditures

Of the widely used expressions employed in today's federal budgetary process, *tax expenditures* may be the most difficult to define precisely. The Congressional Budget Act includes an effort to do so, an effort Schick refers to as a "groundbreaking" definition. It defines tax expenditures as "revenue losses attributable to provisions of the Federal tax laws which allow a special exclusion, exemption, or deduction from gross income or which provide a special credit, a preferential rate of tax, or a deferral of tax liability."[9] Inclusion of this definition in the act indicated that the expression was coming into common use. The Treasury Department had been reporting tax expenditures since 1967.

Despite this formal acceptance of the expression, some people continue to object to its use. To apply the concept with precision, a standard or normal tax structure must be agreed upon; deviations from this structure that result in lower tax revenues would then be considered tax expenditures. Of course, many exemptions and preferential rates are of long standing, prime examples being the "preferential" rate accorded lower income individuals by the progressive income tax and the preferential rate applied to capital gains. Other examples—those often referred to as "loopholes"—are more readily agreed upon as being tax expenditures.

Some critics take an extreme position in considering the tax expenditure concept. William Bonner, treasurer of the National Taxpayers Union, rejects its usefulness, noting that "to equate spending with not taking suggests that government owns everything."[10] In other words, under the tax expenditure notion, it is possible for almost anything left in private hands to be considered a tax expenditure.

Clearly, most of those who use the expression *tax expenditure* mean something much narrower. It is impossible to look at the tax actions of recent sessions of Congress and not conclude that decisions have been made to forgo collection of large amounts of money. In many cases, these were specific decisions to amend tax provisions in order to create new deductions or exemptions. The Economic Recovery Tax Act of 1981 created new tax expenditures of $82 billion in FY 1982 through FY 1984, according to Congressional Budget Office calculations. (However, according to the administration's definition, the increase was only $14.5 billion.)

Taking a longer perspective, table 2.3 presents data from testimony of then CBO Director, Alice Rivlin, before the House Rules Committee, which considered legislation to include tax expenditure ceilings in congressional budget resolutions. The $36 billion in tax expenditures shown for 1967 resulted from fifty tax expenditure items. In her prepared statement, Rivlin noted that in 1982 there were 104 items totaling $266.3 billion.[11]

Table 2.3.   Tax Expenditures, 1967–81

Year	Tax Expenditures (in millions)	Percentage of Federal Outlays
1967	36,550	20.5
1969	46,635	23.7
1971	51,710	22.3
1973	65,370	24.3
1975	92,855	28.5
1977	113,455	28.2
1979	149,815	30.3
1981	228,620	34.6

Source: House Committee on Rules, *Hearings on H.R. 4882 to Amend Congressional Budget Act of 1974,* 97th Cong., 1st sess., 142.

Note: Tax expenditure estimates for calendar years 1967 through 1973 are compared with outlays for Fiscal Years 1968 through 1974.

The increases in recent years have occurred with the congressional budget process in place. Under the present process, no effort is made specifically to limit tax expenditures. The Congressional Budget Office is required by section 308(c) of the Budget Act to report on tax expenditures each year, and the president is subject to a similar requirement. The budget committees have reported on tax expenditures in their reports accompanying the budget resolution and have even made specific recommendations for cuts. Yet, at no point are limits or target figures adopted by the Congress. Of course, acceptance of the total revenue floor in the second budget resolution does preclude enactment of tax expenditures that would result in total revenue falling below that floor.

In 1981 the House Rules Committee held hearings on H.R. 4882, a bill that would have required that budget resolutions fix the level of tax expenditures each year. Further, under it, tax expenditures would have been treated just like revenue reductions. Senate hearings were held on legislation that would have prohibited adoption of a first budget resolution if tax expenditures exceeded an amount equal to 30 percent of the level of net revenue reported in the resolution. This Senate bill also would have required that all tax expenditure legislation be referred both to the authorizing committee with jurisdiction over the affected activity and to the budget committees. Finally, it would have required that tax expenditures be reported in the House and Senate by 15 May, before the beginning of the affected fiscal year. Neither the House nor the Senate bill was reported from committee.

Much of the testimony on these proposed pieces of legislation indicated grave concern for the difficulty of defining tax expenditures. However, there were some—including members of Congress—who contended that, after enactment of a limit, agreement on a workable definition would be reached. Congress would, at the very least, examine the changes being proposed in tax expenditures each year, under whatever definition was employed. The only necessity would be that the definition be kept constant from year to year.

The Budget Resolutions

Actions to adopt the first and second concurrent resolutions on the budget are the most important steps required by the Congressional Budget Act. Use of a resolution to set a budget target had been attempted in the late 1940s, under requirements of the Legislative Reorganization Act of 1946. It required that Congress adopt by 15 February a revenue total and spending ceiling for the coming fiscal year. That effort was almost a complete failure. Only in 1948 could agreement on such a resolution be reached, and in that year the spending limit set was surpassed by the appropriations adopted.

Procedures established in 1974 differed in important ways from this earlier effort, although they have confronted many of the same difficulties. The present system recognizes that circumstances might change following adoption of the resolution and, therefore, that a resolution might be more useful as a guide than as a rigid ceiling to which later actions must conform. Further, unlike the reform of the 1940s, which required a joint committee to develop the resolution, the 1974 act permits each chamber's Budget Committee to do so independently and uses the conference committee process to deal with differences.

In the eight years for which resolutions have been adopted, the political enormity of the task has become evident. Even though many decisions can be side-stepped—left to the appropriations committees and others—the totals that the budget committees must attempt to set have the potential for affecting virtually every government agency and interest group. Although a major purpose of the Budget Act was to provide Congress with a mechanism for setting economic policy at the highest and most general level, the committees are forced to make innumerable decisions on lesser issues as they approach that task. This is the case even though the first resolution figures are not binding on Congress.

The opportunity to set binding limits arises just before the start of the fiscal year, when Congress is required to enact the second budget resolution. Under the act, it is expected that this affords the budget committees the opportunity to see how well appropriations and authorizing committees have followed the guidance of the first resolution. Failure to pass appropriations bills on a timely basis alters the process; the second resolution must contain allowances for those bills not yet passed. In all of the years since implementation of the act, it has been necessary for Congress to pass third or even fourth resolutions. In 1982, Congress waived provisions of the Budget Act that make the second resolution binding.

In none of these years has Congress successfully used the second resolution reconciliation procedure, which the Budget Act permits. This failure partially explains the need for resolutions beyond the second. In 1979 the Senate included in its version of the second resolution a requirement that various committees report legislation to reduce spending by $3.6 billion. The House refused to accept a conference committee report including a reconciliation requirement. With federal outlays clearly set to exceed the second resolution, Congress was only able to modify the second resolution and thereby allow for the higher expenditures.

In the following year, there was a change. Not only did Congress include a reconciliation requirement, but it did so in the first resolution. Intent on adopting a resolution that would accord with President Carter's effort to achieve a balanced budget—and mindful of the fast approaching election—Congress passed the first resolution in June and with it instructed the appropriations committees, eight House and ten Senate authorizing committees, and the Finance and Ways and Means committees to report legislation adjusting spending and revenue amounts. The budget committees combined these reports into a reconciliation bill passed by Congress in November, following the election. Provisions were included to reduce 1981 outlays by $4.6 billion and to increase revenues by $3.6 billion.[12] Thus, the first use Congress made of the reconciliation process was at variance with the procedures anticipated by the Congressional Budget Act.

Upon initial examination, one might think it inappropriate to apply the label *reconciliation* to a requirement placed in the first resolution. The term, as employed in the Budget Act, applied particularly to reconciliation of the appropriations bills just passed with the second resolution. Since the actual use made of the procedure occurred before appropriations bills were passed, it might seem that there was nothing to be reconciled. In fact, this is not true. Much federal spending (outlays) depends upon authority granted in prior years, through multiyear appropriations or entitlements. The reconciliation requirement in the first resolution was directed toward reduction of this previously enacted authority and toward changes in previously enacted revenue measures.

In 1981, President Reagan's first year in office, reconciliation was used even more extensively. It was again made a requirement of the first resolution. Fourteen Senate and fifteen House committees were required to cut 1982 outlays by $36 billion. Unlike 1980, when legislation to effect reductions was not passed until almost the end of the year, this time legislation was passed in July to cut outlays by $35.2 billion.

If one is to judge the effectiveness of the Budget Act according to the strength of actions taken under its provisions, use of the reconciliation practice in 1981 to provide President Reagan with his budget victory would have to assure it high marks. Unfortunately, an opposite extreme was reached when Congress attempted to pass the second budget resolution that year. Neither chamber passed a realistic resolution. In an effort to meet the letter of Budget Act requirements, they adopted the amounts accepted in the first resolution, despite widespread knowledge that federal spending would substantially exceed this outlay level and that the deficit would most certainly be in excess of the $37.65 billion permitted.

In 1982 and 1983, Congress again included reconciliation instructions in the first resolution. Additionally, language was included that made the first resolution binding upon failure of Congress to adopt a second resolution. In both years, no second resolution was adopted by 1 October, so the amounts set in the first resolution became binding.

Impoundment

In combining impoundment control with establishment of congressional budget procedures, Congress responded to the outrage of its own members and others (especially officials of cities being denied federal grants) at impoundments imposed by President Nixon. To many members of Congress, this extensive use of impoundments represented a frontal attack by the president on the fundamental right of Congress to control federal spending and, more importantly, to establish program priorities. The priorities that Congress set by passing appropriations bills were being altered by the president as he selectively refused to allow obligations of funds.

Impoundment did not begin with President Nixon. Its history dates back at least to the presidency of Thomas Jefferson. But Nixon increased the extent of impoundment beyond levels set by previous presidents and undertook what many members of Congress saw as an attempt to keep impoundment actions secret by failing to report on them when Congress so requested.[13] The result was action by Congress to restrict presidential impoundment power through the prohibition of policy impoundments and the establishment of procedures for congressional review of rescissions and deferrals.

Joel Havemann has reported on the first several years' experience under these new procedures.[14] In general, it can be said that Congress has rarely overturned a deferral but has often refused to rescind funds at presidential request. Of the three years Havemann examined, the largest rejection rate of deferrals came in the first, 1975, when 38 percent of the dollar amount proposed was rejected. The difference in treatment of rescissions is made clear by noting the rejection of 91 percent of the dollar amount of rescissions that year.

The pattern over four recent years is shown in table 2.4. Even noting the extraordinarily large amount of deferred funds overturned in 1980, the pattern that Havemann identified seems to hold. Presidents are relatively free to use their deferral authority without much chance of congressional action to require obligation, but it is not as easy for them to secure rescissions. Even with rescissions, however, presidents have had considerable success. Only in 1980 was more than 50 percent of the rescinded amount rejected by Congress.

Incorporation of these new impoundment features in the Congressional Budget and Impoundment Control Act did not end the controversy over impoundment. Neither it nor various federal court decisions settled the question regarding a possible constitutional impoundment authority available to the president. Further, there have been disagreements between the

Table 2.4. Deferrals and Rescissions in 1979–81 (in billions of dollars)

	1979	1980	1981	1982
Deferrals				
Proposed	4.6	10.5	9.5	8.2
Released	1.7	2.4	5.5	5.4
Overturned	0[a]	5.5	0.4	0.4
Before Congress	2.9	2.7	3.7	2.4
Percentage overturned	0%	52.4%	4.2%	4.9%
Rescissions				
Proposed	0.9	1.6	15.4	7.7
Accepted	0.7	0.5	11.7	4.1
Rejected	0.2	1.1	3.0	3.2
Pending[b]	0	0	0.6	0.4
Percentage rejected	22.2%	68.8%	19.5%	41.6%

Source: House Documents, *Cumulative Report on Rescissions and Deferrals, September 1982: Communication from the Director of the Office of Management and Budget* (Washington D.C.: Government Printing Office, 1982), and documents in the same series for 1979 through 1981.

[a] Congress overturned $8 million in deferrals.

[b] Pending status, as of the September report for each year.

Office of Management and Budget and the General Accounting Office as to whether certain actions should be classified as rescissions or deferrals. The executive branch still has a degree of latitude in the reprogramming and transfer of funds; some members of Congress find this objectionable.[15]

Conclusion

Developments described in this chapter can be characterized, to a large extent, as continuations of those under way prior to adoption of the Congressional Budget Act. Procedures implemented under the act did not bring a swift halt to rising federal spending, nor did they assure a balanced budget. Congress, in any given year, remains confronted by the decisions taken in prior years, in the form of "largely uncontrollable expenditures." Tax decisions continue to be made piecemeal, through adoption of an ever-growing number of tax expenditures, by almost anyone's definition.

Should the process be declared a failure because it did not interrupt these trends? Perhaps not. There are other bases on which it must be judged. The process was clearly intended to alter the responsibility of members of Congress, collectively and individually, as they deal with one another and with the executive branch. It has survived two changes in presidents, changes in budget committee leadership, and a change of party control in the Senate. In addition, it has been adapted to changing needs, as reflected by the use made of the reconciliation procedures. Perhaps the continuity of the process itself gives some indication of success. The following chapters will address its impact upon relationships within Congress and between Congress and the executive branch.

II

THE INSTITUTIONAL
IMPACT OF
CONGRESSIONAL
BUDGET REFORM

3 Changes in the House of Representatives after the Passage of the Budget Act of 1974

GARY W. COPELAND

T he focus of this chapter is the ways in which the Congressional Budget and Impoundment Control Act of 1974 has changed the House of Representatives. In the normal legislative process, there are patterns of behavior and positions of influence that persist over time. When the normal legislative process is changed, those behavioral patterns are altered and influence may be redistributed among the various actors in the system. A change in the rules and procedures of a legislative institution changes that institution. This chapter concentrates on the ways in which the changes enacted in the 1974 Budget Act have influenced the House's conduct of its business and on the alteration of distribution of power within that body.

The primary purpose of the Congressional Budget Act was very simple—to restore to Congress control over governmental spending.[1] That control, according to the act's advocates, was lacking because Congress failed to consider either fiscal policy or spending priorities on a systematic basis, lacked the expertise to do so even if its members so desired, and had lost much of its control over expenditures to the president.

To compensate for the first problem, the act's centerpiece required that Congress adopt two budget resolutions each year. The resolutions would coordinate taxing and spending policies by including recommended levels of revenues and expenditures (both outlays and budget authority) and, therefore, an implied fiscal policy. They would also establish priorities for spending among nineteen functional areas. The figures in the first resolution would be allocated to appropriations subcommittees to be used in consideration of appropriations measures. The figures in the second resolution would be loosely binding, and Congress could order its committees to reconcile differences between the second resolution and actual revenue and spending decisions previously made.

The Act also recognized the problem of expertise and established the Congressional Budget Office (CBO). The CBO was empowered to collect information regarding the economy and the activities of government so that Congress would not have to rely solely on information delivered to it by the executive branch or the private sector. Each house also created its own budget committee, which would recommend the budget resolution to the whole body and would employ a sizable professional staff.

Finally, to overcome the third problem, the act clarified the legal status of impoundments and ensured that Congress would have the final say over whether money it had appropriated could remain unspent.

The fundamental changes enacted in 1974 necessarily modified the House and its intrainstitutional relations. The act altered the interactions among the various actors within the House and established a new set of contenders for power, thus changing the balance that had existed within that chamber. The specific institutional alterations on which this chapter concentrates are the changes in (1) the provision of staff to provide expertise on budgetary matters, (2) the allocation of time within the House, (3) the committee structure of the House, (4) the activities on the floor of the House, (5) the interactions between the parties, (6) the influence of the ideological wings within Congress, and (7) the resources given to the House leadership to establish and pursue a budgetary program.

Structural Changes in the House

The specific requirement that Congress pass two budget resolutions a year led directly to a number of important modifications in the institutions and processes of the House. The creation of the budget committees and the Congressional Budget Office provided a locus for budgetary and fiscal debates and supplied new and valued expertise. This section will first consider the impact of the requirement for a budget, then of the expertise it brought with it. Finally, the increasing time pressures on the House will be considered.

NEW BUDGET RESPONSIBILITIES

Prior to the changes in congressional budget making that were enacted in 1974, Congress did a very poor job of considering budgetary issues. James Sundquist described the prereform budget as

> whatever emerged from a piecemeal and haphazard legislative process.
> The President was directed, by the Budget and Accounting Act of 1921,
> to present each year a comprehensive and coherent program. But there
> was no compulsion on the Congress to act on that program in a similarly

consistent and orderly way. The President's program was pulled apart. Its taxing and spending halves were assigned to different committees and acted on quite separately. The spending half was handled in a host of different measures: more than a dozen bills were produced by the appropriations committees but handled by separate subcommittees and considered independently of one another throughout the legislative process.[2]

Certainly various members and committees considered what fiscal policy might be appropriate in any given year or what policy areas should have higher or lower priority than other areas, but no one had the formal responsibility, nor was there a forum to lead that debate and to make recommendations to the body as a whole. The creation of the budget committees and their responsibility for budget resolutions corrected those deficiencies.

The House Budget Committee was made responsible for hearing testimony, collecting and evaluating economic data, considering fiscal policy, and weighing alternative allocations of the limited governmental resources. After gathering the information and about six months prior to the start of a new fiscal year, it makes recommendations to the House as a whole on the general outlines of the federal budget. This first budget resolution is intended to serve as a guide for the House as it works through the summer, preparing appropriations and taxing measures for the coming year. Just prior to the start of the new fiscal year, the Budget Committee considers interim legislative action and reworks its original estimates and recommendations before proposing a second resolution. According to the plan envisioned in the law, if the second resolution and the previous actions of Congress are at variance, the resolution can require other committees to reconcile the differences.

New requirements, then, were made of the Budget Committee and more generally of Congress. Members are now required to consider systematically issues that had been considered only superficially in the past and to decide explicitly on fiscal policy and the appropriate level of federal deficit (or, conceivably, surplus). They are forced to weigh directly competing claims on the federal treasury and to decide how to allocate its resources among those claims. The debate and adoption of a specific budget statement by the Budget Committee and, ultimately, by Congress are the major innovations in the Budget Act.

NEW BUDGET EXPERTS

Beyond the budgetary and fiscal debate, concomitant changes supplied the requisite expertise to make the deliberations meaningful. The allocation of staff to deal with budgetary and economic issues has increased dramatically. The House Budget Committee has a staff of over one hundred professionals, including a small number specifically assigned to the minority. About thirty others, called associate staff, provide expertise directly to the offices of various members by being answerable to the member but being paid by the Budget Committee. The Congressional Budget Office, which is the prime source of economic information and which makes its own economic, spending, and revenue estimates, has over two hundred professional staff positions. Between the two organizations, the members of the House of Representatives now have considerable talent upon which they can draw to aid their decision making on fiscal and spending policies. To help them deal with the more routine budgetary matters, most members assign one of their personal legislative assistants to work at least part-time on this topic. Thus, Congress has, for the first time, an adequate supply of expertise to deal with a wide range of budgetary concerns.

A more impressive change has taken place within the membership of the House. Largely because of the new budget procedures, members of Congress are much more conversant in fiscal policy and budgetary matters than they have ever been in the past. The new processes (coupled, undoubtedly, with the troubled state of the economy) have forced members to pay more attention and to learn about the matters on which they are voting. In the past, individual members could ignore this whole range of issues because they were not forced to make any general decisions regarding them. Now they must make a summary judgment concerning the preferred levels of revenue and spending and the allocation of federal dollars across a range of functional categories. This need, along with the educational efforts of the CBO and the staff and members of the Budget Committee, has created considerable economic and budgetary literacy on the Hill. Our representatives spend so much time poring over budget figures that many of them must feel like the member who pointed to a stack of papers that he had been working through and said, half in exasperation and half in pride, "You know, most of the time any more I feel more like a CPA than a Congressman."[3]

THE ALLOCATION OF TIME WITHIN THE HOUSE

The addition of new responsibilities and the presence of budgeting experts have led the House to spend more time on the budget than ever before. In fact, the time factor has been an important focus of dissatisfaction with the process. Since the implementation of the Congressional Budget Act, the House has been working longer, devoting less time to other matters, and still not achieving the timetable found in the budget law.

Prior to the first use of the budget procedures in 1975, the time the House spent in session had generally been declining (see table 3.1). The House spent about 1,600 hours in session in both the 90th and 91st Congresses. During the next session, it dropped to 1,429 hours, before showing a minor rise to 1,487 hours in the 93rd Congress. Along with this trend was an obvious and consistent decline in the number of bills introduced during each session. In the 94th Congress, the first time the budget process was used, the number of hours in session jumped to 1,788—an increase of over 20 percent—and the number of hours has grown each session since then. Conversely, the number of bills introduced has continued to decline, indicating that the increasing length of the session cannot be attributed to an increase in the amount of legislation. The number of laws enacted shows the same general pattern of decline since the establishment of the budget procedures. The first three Congresses after the implementation of the budget process enacted an average of 612 bills; in the previous three sessions, Congress had enacted an average of 650. The 97th Congress reached a post–World War II low for the amount of legislation enacted. Thus, under the Budget Act, Congress has worked longer, but other standard measures of work load have declined; something has been consuming that time.

For the first time, Congress was allocating part of its floor time to debate over budget resolutions. To account for the increase in the length of the sessions solely by the changes due to Public Law 93–344 requires sub-

Table 3.1. House Business, 89th to 96th Congresses

Congress	Calendar Years	Bills Introduced	Public Bills Passed	Hours in Session	Budget Debate[a]
89th	1965–66	19,874	810	1,547	—
90th	1967–68	22,060	640	1,595	—
91st	1969–70	21,436	695	1,613	—
92nd	1971–72	18,561	607	1,429	—
93rd	1973–74	18,872	649	1,487	—
94th	1975–76	16,982	588	1,788	297
95th	1977–78	15,852	634	1,898	527
96th	1979–80	9,103	613	1,876	852

Sources: John F. Bibby, Thomas E. Mann, and Norman J. Ornstein, *Vital Statistics on Congress, 1980* (Washington, D.C.: American Enterprise Institute, 1980), 86, and materials collected by Louis Fisher.

[a]This figure is the number of pages of debate covering the budget resolutions in the *Congressional Record*. The figure for the 94th Congress includes debate on the trial run for FY 1976 and the first two resolutions for FY 1977. The third resolution for FY 1977 was passed in March of 1977 and, therefore, is included in the figure for the 95th Congress.

stantial inference, but it is not unreasonable to believe that the House spent three hundred hours of floor time in the 94th Congress considering the budget resolutions. The 94th Congress devoted nearly three hundred pages of debate in the *Congressional Record* to those resolutions (see table 3.1), and the amount of debate on them has risen sharply in every session since then. How much time is being devoted to the budget is a mystery, but it is clear that House members and their staffs have invested considerable personal, committee, and floor time to the budget. Moreover, much of that time has been new time, that is, it is time that had not previously been allocated by other committees or in other ways to deal with the subject; it is time that is being formally allocated to budgetary and fiscal concerns for the first time.

This growing attention to budgetary matters also has developed at the expense of other matters of public concern. Allen Schick estimated that budget-type votes accounted for two-thirds of the roll calls in the Senate in 1981.[4] The dominance of budgetary deliberations is also reflected in the concentration on those topics by the media and the public. Since very few other major pieces of legislation have moved through the legislative pipeline, the focus of the rest of the nation has been on the budget.[5] As the amount of time spent on budgetary matters has increased, many members have begun to feel that the budget debates dominate congressional activity to an unhealthy degree. One of them explained that frustration: "All we ever do up here any more is the goddamn budget. We came here because we had other things we wanted to get done, but we haven't had the chance. I'm getting tired of it."

That frustration, which is fairly widespread but not dominant, is compounded by discountenance with the continued inability to adhere to the budget timetable established in the 1974 law. The timetable in the law requires Congress to pass the first budget resolution by 15 May, complete action on spending bills by seven days after Labor Day, and pass the second resolution by 15 September. Congress has been reasonably successful in meeting the first deadline, having missed it substantially only for FY 1981, when it failed to pass the first resolution until 12 June, and for FY 1983, when it failed to pass the resolution until 23 June. The first resolution for FY 1984 was passed by the House on 23 March, but Congress did not complete action on it until 23 June. The second resolutions, however, have been much more problematic. Second resolutions in the first three years of operation, excluding the FY 1976 trial run, were passed in September. The next two years, the second resolutions were passed well into the start of the new fiscal year, 28 November, 1980, and 20 November, 1981. FY 1982 was nearly a quarter over before the second resolution for that year was passed, on 10

December. Second resolutions for FY 1983 and FY 1984 never were passed; the first resolutions for those years contained provisions making them binding should Congress not enact a second resolution.

The practice that has developed of revising the second resolution along with the following year's first resolution has increased dissatisfaction with the schedule. These delays have made it difficult for the other committees to get their work done on time. The fiscal year routinely begins under a continuing appropriations resolution, and authorizing committees frequently need to request waivers for authorizing legislation they failed to report on time. The Budget Act, which moved the start of the fiscal year back a quarter, has had little success in dealing with the timetable problems that were partially responsible for its adoption (see Chapter 1).

The difficulties in achieving the timetable have sparked a variety of calls for further reform. The most common suggestion is to implement a two-year budget cycle rather than the present annual plan. One member of the Budget Committee described the situation and explained his recommendation for a two-year budget:

> We can't run budget resolutions through here every six months; that's crazy. First of all, you drive the members nuts and, secondly, you don't make very good decisions because you know in six months that you will change them. (And you wind up burying everything in the third budget resolution anyway.) I think, without question, that this process ought to operate over at least a two-year basis. We ought to do one resolution that covers two years. That kind of stability is absolutely essential right now. The chaos that we're creating ... it's not like it suddenly evaporates; it stays with the members and creates albatrosses around the necks of the budget processes .... I would set a scenario over a two-year period; it could be revised but at least you set it. You take a period of time to analyze the decision, you make the decisions, and then you go on to other issues.

The Committee System

The Founding Fathers gave the House of Representatives predominant control over federal spending largely because the House, of all the institutions that they had created, would be most responsive to the populace. Our first national leaders took this power very seriously and considered it a tool that the House could use to balance the resources of the other institutions. James Madison, in defending the system in *The Federalist, No. 58,* argued that "this power over the purse may, in fact, be regarded as the most complete and effectual weapon with which any constitution can arm the immediate representatives of the people.'' The importance of this pecuniary power has continued to impress House members, and the desire to maintain that power has been a prime motivation behind various rules and committee adjustments throughout congressional history. Certainly the feeling that the power of the purse was slipping away was largely responsible for the enactment of the Congressional Budget and Impoundment Control Act of 1974.

Prior to the implementation of that act, congressional consideration of fiscal policy, tax policy, and spending priorities was fragmented and haphazard. A formal congressional fiscal policy simply did not exist. Tax policy was the province of the Ways and Means Committee; spending was authorized by specialized standing committees; and money was appropriated by the subcommittees of the Appropriations Committee (all based, of course, on the vote of the entire body). No one considered the consequences of these actions in combination with one another. The Budget Committee now has the responsibility of considering all three sets of activities plus their combined effects. While the Budget Committee cannot actually authorize spending, appropriate funds, or write tax laws, it does deliberate on the appropriate balance among all of these components.

The same legislation that created the Budget Committee also introduced a new set of procedures designed to add some linkage to the wide range of budgetary deliberations undertaken by the separate actors within the system and by the body, itself, only seriatim. The new procedures, plus this new set of actors with responsibilities similar to those held by preestablished units, have influenced the way in which the committees of the House conduct their business.

PROCEDURAL CHANGES DUE TO THE BUDGET ACT

Authorizing committees, the Ways and Means Committee, and the Appropriations Committee have all had to make adjustments in their operations as a result of rules changes that were part of the Budget Act. One of the primary changes is that they have a new timetable they must follow. By 15 March they must submit their ''views'' to the Budget Committee. In that report they offer cost estimates for programs under their jurisdiction and identify any initiative they are likely to undertake. Any legislation to provide new authorization must be reported by the committee by 15 May of the year prior to the start of the fiscal year for which it would become effective. Rules changes also require authorizing committees to consider the fiscal impact of the legislation under their jurisdiction. Should any authorization bill exceed the spending level in the second resolution, Section 311 of the Budget Act provides for a point of order that can prevent or delay floor consideration of that bill. These provisions have altered the behavior of the committees and are generally adhered to, but they can be and frequently are waived.[6]

The Appropriations Committee has also had to make adjustments to deal with the new budget procedures. The rules require it to make estimates of appropriations for the coming fiscal year by 15 March and to submit those estimates to the Budget Committee.[7] The Budget Committee considers the estimates while developing the first budget resolution. After the first resolution has been passed, the Budget Committee translates the functional spending figures into allocations for each appropriations subcommittee, using a complicated "crosswalk" procedure. Section 310 of the law requires the Appropriations Committee, to "the extent practicable," to complete action and to present a summary of all appropriations measures prior to reporting any one of them. It is also expected to report those measures in order that action on them can be completed within seven working days after Labor Day, and, of course, the appropriations are expected to be within the limits established by the second budget resolution.

The Ways and Means Committee has been affected both as an authorizing and a revenue-raising committee. As an authorizing committee it is subject to the same constraints as other committees; it must submit its views by 15 March, report new authorizing legislation (including entitlement programs) by the 15 May deadline, and not violate the totals found in the second resolution. As a tax committee, any action that it takes to alter (either up or down) the total revenues to be raised by the federal government must not be considered until after the adoption of the first resolution. Finally, under the law, the Ways and Means Committee must deal more formally and openly with tax expenditures; what constitutes tax expenditures is now defined, and they must be estimated.

RELATIONS BETWEEN THE BUDGET COMMITTEE
AND OTHER HOUSE COMMITTEES

During deliberations on reforming the budget process, one of the primary concerns of the House membership was its potential effect on the committee system. The creation of a new committee with responsibilities that range over nearly the entire scope of congressional activities was certain to lead to conflicts, jurisdictional jealousies, and policy quarrels. The leadership of the established committees did not want to sacrifice their prerogatives to a new set of participants, but they all wanted something from the reforms and they recognized that changes would be meaningless if the new budgeters had no power. Thus, a balance was reached, whereby the Budget Committee would have important powers but would be controllable.

The main source of control over the House Budget Committee is the guarantee of seats on the committee for members of the Ways and Means Committee (five members), of the Appropriations Committee (five members), and of the leadership of both parties (one each). The other primary device for checking the power of the Budget Committee is the limited term of service on that committee for its membership. Members are limited to serving no more than six years (plus an additional term, if chosen chairman) in any ten-year period. The goal of that provision is to encourage members to maintain loyalty to their permanent committees and not to become advocates of the Budget Committee, especially in important jurisdiction battles.

In its first few years of existence, the Budget Committee was more generally perceived as a nuisance than as a major threat. While there were conflicts between it and the other House committees, the checks on the committee served their purpose. At least until the 1980s and the use of reconciliation, the Budget Committee was generally responsive to the initiatives of the other committees and usually left enough room in the resolutions for the remainder of the House to pursue policies at a reasonable level.[8] According to one member; "Until about two years ago [1980], the general reaction was that the Budget Committee was a pain-in-the-rear-end process to have to go through in terms of making recommendations and setting targets, but the Budget Committee was not so omnipotent that it was impacting on everyone's jurisdiction."

The precarious position of the budget process in its early years of operation encouraged the Budget Committee frequently to defer to the remainder of the House. The first few chairmen were in a position in which they often feared either to win or to lose a major conflict. Supporters of the budget process were concerned that, if they succeeded on a major policy battle, the vanquished would play an obstructionist role and work to destroy the process. If they lost a major battle, advocates fretted that the process would be so discredited that it would be quietly laid to rest. Therefore, the committee rarely challenged other committees on anything very important. The reconciliation provisions in the FY 1982 budget (and, to a lesser extent in FY 1981, FY 1983, and FY 1984) represented a different pattern of relationship between the Budget Committee and the remainder of the House. Both the large number of dollars and the range of programs affected by reconciliation for FY 1982 were probably aberrations, but the future is more likely to look like the early 1980s than the 1970s.

Ways and Means Committee.   Relations between the Ways and Means Committee and the Budget Committee have generally been good for a variety of reasons. The groundwork for favorable interactions was laid in the original compromises found in the act. The seats reserved for members of the Ways and Means Committee have provided that committee with an important voice in the budgetary deliberations. Because the Budget Committee considers only a single, overall revenue figure, its jurisdiction is limited on the revenue side of the budget, thereby limiting potential sources of controversy between the two committees.

The relationship between the House Budget Committee and Ways and Means has been much warmer than the Senate Budget Committee's relationship with the Finance Committee largely because of the personalities of the leaders of the four committees. In the Senate, former Budget Committee Chairman Edmund Muskie (and, later, Peter Domenici) was more aggressive than any of the House chairmen, and former Finance Committee Chairman Russell Long has been a vocal opponent of the budget procedures. In the House, the power of then Ways and Means Chairman Wilbur Mills was on the wane when the budget procedures were first used, and his successor, Al Ullman, had served as Budget Committee Chairman and was a supporter of the process. Both chairmen were reasonably cooperative with the Budget Committee and shared many of the same goals. As a result, differences between the two House committees rarely reached the boiling point.

Another factor that helps to account for the cordial relationship between the committees is the Budget Committee's caution in dealing with the expenditure side of the budget that is under the control of the Ways and Means Committee. One Republican member of the Ways and Means Committee explained; "Until the first use of reconciliation the Budget Committee may as well not even been there . . . . [Our] committee didn't even notice the Budget Committee. It wasn't subservient; it wasn't even there."

Reconciliation added to the Budget Committee's influence over the activities of Ways and Means. Other committees were also affected, but Ways and Means has consistently had to make major adjustments under reconciliation—about one-fourth to one-half of all spending cuts have been under its jurisdiction, along with essentially all revenue adjustments. But, even under these circumstances, Ways and Means has not had its jurisdiction seriously abused. The same member described the role of the Budget Committee in reconciliation: "The Budget Committee has not been bullying about it, nor have they tried to force specific changes. They have only said, 'Meet your goal or we'll meet it some way or another.'"

In trying to assess the overall impact of the Budget Committee, a key Ways and Means staff member suggested that the Budget Committee does influence the activities of Ways and Means but does not place a great burden on that committee: "We have basically been able to do what we wanted to. But we have had to consider, just like the rest of the committees, how our agenda fits into a broader agenda . . . . We haven't felt constrained, but we have felt like we need to keep our eye on the ball." Most members of the Ways and Means Committee feel that they have had a relatively free rein in the budgetary deliberations. That perception is fairly accurate, but they have had that flexibility because they have been largely sympathetic to the goals of the Budget Committee and have been cooperative in attempts to reach those goals.

Authorizing Committees. With the exception of the dramatic use of reconciliation in the FY 1982 budget, the Budget Committee has had only a minor impact on the activities of the authorizing committees. The primary goal of the Budget Committee, in its dealings with the authorizing committees, has been to have influence at the margin; the primary means it has used have been to inform, cajole, bargain, and convince. The most obvious variance from that pattern has been the use of reconciliation, but there have been other times when the Budget Committee has gone public, usually on the House floor, in opposition to the activities of other committees. However, those fights have been fairly rare.

The normal pattern has been for the Budget Committee to honor, at a reasonable level, the funding requested by authorizing committees. In considering the Fiscal Year 1977 budget, for example, the committee honored requests by both the Education and Labor Committee and the Commerce Committee to provide start-up funds for major new social initiatives. The Budget Committee voted to include $50 million for the Humphrey-Hawkins full employment legislation and the same amount for a national health insurance program in the first resolution, thereby saving it from challenge on the floor.[9] This support of policy initiatives by the Budget Committee, particularly by the Democratic majority, led then Minority Leader John Rhodes to take a partisan shot at the Democrats by describing their style of budgeting: "To the Democrats in Congress, budgeting requires only an adding machine without a subtract button. Nowhere in the Democrat-engineered budget process does a fiscal policy appear. Instead, they first vote *seriatim* on how much they would like to spend in all governmental programs; they then add up this wish list and take the resulting total and call that the appropriate level of federal spending."[10] Chairman Giaimo essentially conceded that point to Rhodes by simply responding that the Republican-backed spending limitation was unrealistic because the members of the House wanted more spending, not less.

That pattern of accommodation has been typical of the way in which the Budget Committee has interacted with the other committees. At least until the use of reconciliation, the comment by one committee chairman typifies the way that much of the House felt about the impact of the process: "I just doubt that it is affecting my authority, or any chairman's authority, to a great degree; however, it depends on the mood of the country and the demands of the President—on how this budget works."

Disagreements between the Budget Committee and the House authorizing committees that do come to the surface can be put into three analytic categories. The first type of conflict occurs when a committee or an individual fights on the floor for a higher total in a particular function during consideration of the resolution than had been recommended by the Budget Committee.[11] The second type of conflict occurs during consideration of a piece of authorization or appropriations legislation. If the Budget Committee has determined that a particular bill is "budget busting" because it exceeds the limit in the budget resolution, it may fight it on the House floor.[12] A third, analytically separate but overlapping category of conflict occurs when the Budget Committee chooses a particular total for a function and fights to retain it because of the need to strike a balance that will enable the passage of a resolution.[13]

The need to strike a balance is the primary variation from the generally accommodating nature of the activities of the Budget Committee. It has had to reach a balance among the size of the deficit, military spending, and domestic spending. That juggling of priorities is precisely the role it was created to play. However, the committee has had very little room to make independent judgments on committee requests. The vote split on the budget resolutions has normally been very close, which has constrained the behavior of the Budget Committee. According to one member; "You've got to keep putting the coalition together and that coalition is a very, very delicate one. You go too far to one side and they're going to knock you off; you go a little too far on the other side and the other side will oppose you." The bottom line of the Budget Committee's action is whether it can get a majority on the floor—Has it accommodated each committee enough to gain support from its membership without alienating others in the body?

The usually pleasant relations between the Budget Committee and the authorizing committees does not imply that the budget process has left authorizing committees unaffected. The reforms were designed to change the power of those committees, and they have done so. The committees can no longer routinely authorize backdoor spending; reconciliation has forced them to make spending cuts in areas under their jurisdiction which they otherwise would not have made; and they have been forced to consider how their programs fit into a broader picture and to understand that trade-offs are made, either explicitly or implicitly. In addition to these changes, authorizing committees now share jurisdiction with a new set of actors and the

Budget Committee often considers initiatives even before the appropriate authorizing committee does. The powers of authorizing committees are not the same as before the reforms, but for the most part, the House has accommodated these changes in a congenial fashion.

Appropriations Committee. As it entered the 1970s, the Appropriations Committee was characterized as stable and was determined to counter expansionist forces by limiting budgetary growth.[14] But as the 1970s evolved, so did the nature of that committee. Less dominated by its conservative leadership, it was less dedicated to budget cutting. The changes in the Appropriations Committee were partially responsible for the need to reform the way in which Congress dealt with the budget and were also influenced by the Congressional Budget Act. The Appropriations Committee entered the 1970s as the "guardians of the Treasury" and left the 1970s as "claimants" for the public purse.[15]

The Appropriations Committee has been influenced most by the changes in the Congressional Budget Act. Whereas before the act it had dominant control over expenditures, it is now considerably constrained. It must make requests for allocations in the 15 March estimates and then is constrained by the figures in the first budget resolution. Using the crosswalk procedures, the functional category figures are allocated among the various appropriations subcommittees for guidance in preparing their appropriations legislation. The Appropriations Committee has lost—some might claim abdicated—considerable control over federal spending.

The Appropriations Committee has been concerned that it will lose even more of its authority over spending if it does not protect that authority vigilantly. Its greatest concern is that the Budget Committee will deal in budgetary line items. It desires a process whereby the Budget Committee deals very broadly with aggregates and stays away from specific spending judgments, leaving the Appropriations Committee to make all the specific spending decisions. This matter has been a source of some contention because the House Budget Committee, following the House tradition of specificity, has had a tendency to become program-specific in its deliberations. While it has not reached the point where it routinely deals with line items, it is more specific than the Senate Budget Committee.

The tendency to deal with the functional aggregates on a line-item basis is somewhat greater on the second resolution and considerably greater on a third or revised second resolution. The debates on the second resolution tend to focus on whether more (or less) money is needed for specific programs within general functional categories. The lifting of the spending limit on the revised second resolution tends to be very specific, as each increase requires justification on a program-by-program basis. This practice is not satisfactory to the Appropriations Committee (or most authorizing committees) and has periodically been a public source of dissatisfaction. A large number of floor amendments offered on the first resolution for Fiscal Year 1980 sparked Appropriations Chairman Jamie Whitten to complain:

> We are greatly distressed about the increasing tendency of the Budget Committee to construct their recommendations for overall aggregate targets on the basis of individual program line items .... While line item recommendations in the budget resolution process have no actual effect, they obscure the overall macroeconomic responsibilities of the Budget Committee and needlessly duplicate the hearings and deliberations that are the responsibility of the authorizing and appropriations committees .... I am afraid that we are losing sight of the basic objectives of the Budget Act.[16]

RECONCILIATION

The use of reconciliation has been the greatest source of tension between the Budget Committee and the other House committees, but the House Budget Committee has been reasonably moderate in its advocacy of this process. It resisted the use of reconciliation longer than the Senate did and objected more fervently to its use on the first budget resolution. When it has used reconciliation, the Budget Committee has been rather timid about it.

The first serious attempt to use reconciliation, in the second resolution for FY 1980, found the Budget Committee acting as the advocate for the remainder of the House committees, in opposition to its use. The Senate included a reconciliation order in its second resolution for that year. A compromise was reached in conference which sent instructions to trim $3.6 billion to the floor of the House but which permitted a separate House floor vote on that provision. House conferees worked to defeat that provision and, needless to say, succeeded. Chairman Giaimo argued that promises to make cuts of $1.7 billion had been extracted from various committee chairmen and that the informal approach was preferable to forcing cuts through reconciliation. Rep. Paul Simon agreed, claiming that utilizing reconciliation at that point would be like "throwing salt in the wounds of our colleagues who have done a good job."[17]

A year later, however, it was clear that that arrangement had not worked, and the House Budget Committee supported an attempt to force reconciliation for the first time. Tensions between the Budget Committee and other House committees reached their highest point, for a variety of reasons, during this first use of reconciliation. First, the use of reconciliation came on the first budget resolution, which, while probably necessary, angered opponents of spending cuts. Second, the adjustments required were, within the political context, fairly substantial. The initial House resolution called for first-year spending cuts of $6.4 billion and revenue enhancements of $4.2 billion. Third and most important was the concern over turf—who would have the right to set policy in particular substantive areas.

After the Budget Committee had included reconciliation instructions in the first resolution, a large group of House committee chairmen wrote a letter protesting the action and requesting a rule that would permit a floor amendment aimed at removing that provision.[18] The letter highlighted the concerns of the chairmen about turf: "Balancing the budget should be accomplished by the spending committees in light of their evaluation of the priorities of the activities within their jurisdictions. The depth of the cut in any one program category should not be predetermined by the Budget Committee. It may suggest general overall reductions; it should not direct specific program cuts."[19]

The ensuing floor battle also reflected concern over jurisdiction. Congressman Peter Peyser expressed his concerns:

> It appears to me if we follow this recommendation of the Budget Committee, that we are basically totally undercutting the authorizing committees whose function really is to develop these programs as they see fit in line with their research and study to do what is best to accomplish major ends.
>
> Now if we act at this time on this, it is like saying all the work we have done is for nothing and we are following the dictates of a committee which has not had a chance to do the kind of work we have.

Morris Udall was more blunt about his feelings:

> It is a grab for power to do things that authorizing and appropriating committees ought to do; and it should not be done by fiat handed down by the Budget Committee.[20]

The defeat of the floor amendment to remove the reconciliation instructions was the first solid evidence that the budget process could be used to cut spending. Undoubtedly, however, it passed because it enabled the House to enact a resolution that showed a very small surplus. The strong political desire to have a surplus (even if only on paper) so overshadowed other factors that the House took that drastic action over the objections of most of its committee leadership.

After the vote, politics changed and a balanced budget became an unrealistic goal. Without that constraint, the ensuing actions on reconciliation looked more like "politics as usual," as the Budget Committee became more accommodating toward the other committees. House committees failed to achieve the level of adjustments required (but failed by only $200 million), and many of the cuts were not entirely satisfactory to members of the Budget Committee.[21] Yet the official Budget Committee position was that the House committees had "substantially complied," and members of the Budget Committee generally praised the efforts of their House colleagues.[22] The Budget Committee clearly felt that it had pushed as far as it could and gladly accepted the precedent-setting efforts of the House.

Under pressures from the White House, the Budget Committee was forced to recommend even greater spending cuts in the FY 1982 first resolution. The House Budget Committee recommended a fairly moderate budget, which included a deficit of about $25 billion and a reconciliation order to lower authorizations by about $16 billion.[23] The House rejected the Budget Committee's recommendation and two more liberal budgets before accepting the Gramm-Latta substitute. That conservative substitute required the reconciliation of twice as many dollars as the Budget Committee's recommendation. In complying with that provision, most committees returned to "politics as usual." The Budget Committee accepted the package and sent it to the House. On the House floor, the Budget Committee was defeated again; the reconciliation package that passed the House was not the one put together by its committees and approved by the Budget Committee but was a conservative substitute written by dedicated budget cutters in the House and the White House.

The bitter disputes over the FY 1982 budget have had considerable impact on the way members see the budget process and on their feelings toward keeping, reforming, or disposing of it. To understand how the budget process has influenced the House, it is important to remember that those decisive floor fights were between a majority of House members and the minority, who held powerful positions; the Budget Committee did not impose its will on other committees.

The budget battles of the early years of the Reagan administration, including reconciliation, were the result of fundamental policy differences; the means to achieve policy goals were basically irrelevant. After the 1980 election, a majority of both houses of Congress had very specific and ardent views on the federal budget—spending needed to be cut overall, priorities needed to be reallocated from domestic programs to defense programs, and taxes needed to be reduced. In the Senate, the majority controlled positions of leadership, and the program carried through with few problems. In the House, however, an ideological minority (at least on those issues) controlled the leadership and on important committees actually exaggerated its formal majority position. As a result, Republicans and conservative Democrats were not even part of the deliberations of major committees, such as the Ways and Means and Budget committees; Republican budget proposals received little consideration within the usual committee structure. This frustrated majority, then, had to resort to extraordinary means to accomplish its policy goals. The budget resolution and the reconciliation process provided convenient mechanisms for that end. Without the budget process, the majority may have remained frustrated, or they may have found another tool (such as a continuing resolution) to enact their program.[24] Few, if any, approved of legislating by omnibus, but a solid majority opted for that approach as the only one available to them. One Republican member of the Budget Committee described that frustration in detail:

> The House [in the 97th Congress] is made up of two parties on a 5 to 4 ratio with the leadership in the hands of liberals. But two-thirds of the Democratic Party is liberal and one-third conservative; five-sixths of the Republican Party is conservative and one-sixth liberal. The two conservative factions make up a clear majority on the floor. The committees, however, have the same staffs that they have had since 1954—the same people who put together the New Frontier and the Great Society. The committee chairmen, for the most part, are more liberal than they were ten years ago. Clearly, the liberal leadership of the Democratic Party controls not only the leadership and staff, it controls the party ratio and the timing and the Rules Committee—in short, the overall normal process of the House—until you get to the floor and there, of course, the fruits of this normal committee process get rejected.
>
> The Budget Process offers one an opportunity to short-circuit this whole normal procedure. It offers a packaging opportunity in reconciliation and its enforcement procedures to permit the floor to enforce its will on an apparatus that is out of phase with the floor ... and, quite obviously, the budget process was used for that purpose. But, if we did not have a budget process we would have had to invent one.

Reconciliation was used in an extraordinary way in 1981 to circumvent the normal legislative process largely because the usual procedures frustrated a majority—a majority determined to find some device to achieve its policy goals. More normal use of reconciliation is likely to continue primarily as a means for program oversight and for making marginal adjustments in priorities. The use of reconciliation for FY 1984 (over $13 billion in spending was cut over three years) suggests that standard use of reconciliation remains a powerful tool that can have considerable influence on budgetary policy. It will probably continue to be the best method to limit federal spending and reallocate priorities, but its use in the future is more likely to resemble its use in 1983 than in 1981, that is, it will probably be the product of deliberation, bargaining, and compromise among the House committees.

Budget Resolutions on the Floor of the House

The specific requirement of the Budget Act that the House pass two budget resolutions a year has not been easily satisfied. On the floor, the outcome of House action is never certain; resolutions have been defeated, have been passed late, or have seemed irrational.

The House has, for example, defeated one resolution and rejected another conference report. In 1982, after having defeated eight different budgets, the House passed the first resolution for FY 1983 so late that it included a provision to convert the first resolution to a binding second resolution if Congress failed to enact a second resolution by 1 October (which is what happened). The House rejected the FY 1981 conference report on the first resolution because, it seemed, it contained too much defense and not enough domestic spending. Yet it immediately turned around and passed a motion offered by Delbert Latta, instructing conferees to insist on retaining the high level of defense spending that they had just defeated. The floor of the House has not been a happy home for budget resolutions.

The uncertain fate of the budget resolutions is reflected in the vote on each resolution. Of the first sixteen resolutions that passed the House, two of them passed by four votes and two more by just six votes; in fact, seven resolutions survived by thirteen or fewer votes (see table 3.2). Most of the key votes on reconciliation have been equally as close. However, not all of the resolutions have faced difficult floor fights; two resolutions passed by over seventy-five votes. Those easy victories do not obscure the requirement that Congress, by its own rules, must pass two resolutions a year; that passage is never guaranteed and rarely easy. The difficulty of most floor fights colors the deliberations throughout. The Budget Committee, both in its initial deliberations and in conference, the leadership of the House, and individual members all know how important a few votes can be to the outcome. Part of the effect, then, of the budget procedures on the remainder of the House can be traced directly to this pattern of voting on the floor.

Partisanship and the House Budget Resolutions

One reason for the continual closeness of the vote on budget resolutions is that they are highly partisan. The partisan nature of budgeting in the House is unusual for Congress. Throughout the twentieth century partisanship in Congress has declined,[25] and issues that clearly and neatly divide the parties on a continual basis are rare. But vast majorities of Democrats have opposed vast majorities of Republicans on every resolution to date. In table 3.2 the

Table 3.2. Votes on House Budget Resolutions

Resolution	Vote Yes-No	Republicans Yes-No (% Yes)	Democrats Yes-No (% Yes)
1st, FY 1976	200–196	3–128 (2.3%)	197–68 (74.3%)
2nd, FY 1976	225–191	11–124 (8.1)	214–67 (76.2)
1st, FY 1977	221–155	13–111 (10.5)	208–44 (82.5)
2nd, FY 1977	227–151	12–113 (9.6)	215–38 (85.0)
3rd, FY 1977	239–169	14–119 (10.5)	225–50 (81.8)
1st, FY 1978	84–320	2–135 (1.5)	82–185 (30.7)
1st, FY 1978, revised	213–179	7–121 (5.5)	206–58 (78.0)
2nd, FY 1978	199–188	4–129 (3.0)	195–59 (73.8)
1st, FY 1979	201–197	3–136 (2.2)	198–61 (76.4)
2nd, FY 1979	217–178	2–136 (1.4)	215–42 (83.7)
1st, FY 1980	220–184	9–134 (6.3)	211–50 (80.8)
2nd, FY 1980	212–206	0–154 (0.0)	212–52 (80.3)
1st, FY 1981	225–193	22–131 (14.4)	203–62 (76.6)
2nd, FY 1981	203–191	2–146 (1.4)	201–45 (81.7)
1st, FY 1982	253–176	190–0 (100.0)	63–176 (26.4)
2nd, FY 1982	206–200	136–50 (73.1)	70–150 (31.8)
1st, FY 1983	219–206	156–32 (83.0)	63–174 (26.6)
1st, FY 1984	229–196	4–160 (2.4)	225–36 (86.2)

Source: Various *Congressional Quarterly Weekly Reports.*

percentage of each party supporting each resolution is shown. Rarely have 10 percent of the members of the Republican Party supported a Democratic budget, and never have they provided 10 or more percent of the support of any Democratic budget. The three resolutions that were predominantly Republican engendered slightly greater Democratic support, but none of them captured one-third of the Democratic votes. That voting on House budget resolutions is highly partisan is incontrovertible, but it is less clear why those votes divide the parties so clearly and consistently (particularly in light of the bipartisan nature of budgeting in the Senate).

Budget debates have every reason to be partisan; they involve the issues that are fundamentally important to the parties. Fiscal policy, with all of its ramifications for the size of government, tax burdens, deficits, and the trade-off between inflation and unemployment, should divide Democrats and Republicans. The establishment of spending priorities divides the parties as each opts for a different mix of programs, particularly when they balance domestic and defense spending. The budget includes both a dream of where our country should be headed and a blueprint for getting there—if anything will divide the parties, that should.[26] One member of the Budget Committee described that partisanship: "In the House we have always taken the view that the budget is the best way to demonstrate the difference between the parties. If you have an ounce of manhood you couldn't possibly go along with the other guys. Even if you agreed with them, you would have to invent some different kind of policy."

The House pattern, however, contrasts sharply with the Senate's bipartisan budgeting. When asked why the two houses are different, the first explanation offered by virtually everyone is "personality." The original Senate Budget Committee Chairman, Ed Muskie, and the ranking minority member, Henry Bellmon, worked well together; both had been minority party governors; and both were committed to making the budget process work. The two of them largely set the tone for Senate deliberations. On the House side, the majority Democrats were ambivalent about whether they wanted a partisan process, but ranking minority member Delbert Latta was not. Latta consistently resorted to partisan goading of his Democratic opponents. For example, after Chairman Giaimo accepted reconciliation because the promises he had extracted from committee chairmen the previous year had not been fulfilled, Latta took to the floor of the House: "I probably could say, 'We told you so,' but I will not. As a matter of fact, if you take a look at the debate on this subject last year you will find the House Republicans were supporting reconciliation, the Senate was supporting reconciliation and the majority of the House was not."[27] The personalities of key people have undoubtedly played a role in the early stages of the budget process and are likely to have a lasting impact.

The partisan precedent, combined with a number of other differences between the two chambers, suggests that budgeting will continue to be more partisan in the House. One of those differences is the broader and more pragmatic view taken by senators than by representatives. The House has had to fight the trend to get very specific in its deliberations, whereas the Senate has concentrated on the "big picture" more successfully. The more general focus allows some disagreements to remain buried and, thus, not become sources of contention. Partisanship has been limited in the Senate because Senate liberals have been more willing than their counterparts in the House to accept the principle that most budgets can be cut and Senate conservatives have been less inclined than those in the House to push for across-the-board cuts or, in Hill parlance, to "resort to the meat cleaver." In other words, fewer senators have set themselves up at the extremes, so the focus of differences between the two parties has been much narrower.

Two institutional differences have served to limit Senate partisanship. First, the six-year term gives senators a longer perspective on public budgeting and limits the propensity to look for a partisan advantage in every decision. One member of the House explained that, in the House, "The parties will try to demonstrate that the budget is a big point of difference between them in order to make the budget an election issue."

A different member elaborated on the same point: "The Senate, just by virtue of the six-year term, generally tends to be more statesmanlike on issues like budgets and foreign affairs and the House, by virtue of its two-year term, tends to be a little more controlled by mob rule and political motivations."

The second institutional influence on partisanship is the limited terms of the members of the House Budget Committee. That limit decreases the stability of the House committee. The Senate, on the other hand, places a higher priority on cooperation, recognizing that the key actors in the budget process will remain in those positions for an indefinite time.

The Role of Ideological Extremes in the Budget Process

The pattern of voting on House budget resolutions (i.e., close and partisan) has increased the importance of those at the ideological edges of their party. The importance of the extremes is not unique to the budget resolutions, but their positions on budget resolutions are unusually significant because the votes are generally close and the policies established in the budget resolutions are far-reaching.

The partisan nature of the voting has meant that the majority Democrats have been able to count on the votes of most of their colleagues (usually those in the center of the party's ideological spectrum) and the opposition of nearly all Republicans. However, to win, the Democrats have had to hold the votes of most of those on the extremes of their party. But Democrats have had trouble holding onto their most liberal and conservative members (see

Table 3.3. Number of Democrats Who Opposed Their Party on First Resolution Votes, as Classified by Their ADA Scores

Fiscal Years	ADA Scores			
	25 and Below	Between 25 and 50	Between 50 and 75	75 and Above
1976	35	8	6	24
1977	23	5	6	10
1978	21	15	5	17
1979	40	16	5	4
1980	19	4	5	21
1981	9	4	5	44
1982	41	30	10	5
1983	35	16	6	6
1984[a]	23	5	0	2

Source: Various *Congressional Quarterly Weekly Reports.*
[a]Americans for Democratic Action (ADA) scores for FY 1984 are from 1982.

table 3.3). Liberals and conservatives, in very disproportionate numbers, have voted against their party on the budget resolutions. Still, for the first six years under the budget procedures, the Democrats succeeded in reaching enough of those on the edges to win; in 1981 and 1982 they failed to do so and lost to the Republicans. The narrowness of most victories has meant that virtually every member of the winning coalition is important. Democrats have not been able systematically to exclude or to lose any part of their party; when they lost the battle for their conservatives in 1981 and 1982, they lost the war for the budget.

The importance of individual votes has increased the bargaining strength of those on the edges of their party.[28] Democratic leadership, then, has had to make concessions to conservatives in the areas of limiting the deficit and increasing defense expenditures. Liberals have pushed for additional domestic spending. The success of the Democratic leaders throughout the 1970s is a tribute to their extraordinary majorities, as well as to their ability to juggle a variety of demands. The consequence of that success has been increasing pressure on the budget.

This situation has left ideologists in a position to demand policy concessions. That position has escaped the notice of neither the leadership nor the ideologists. One Democrat with experience trying to assemble winning coalitions commented: "It's always the fringe groups that can impact a lot more on what policy decisions are made because they are very much in control of the vote. Fringes ... have a lot more to say about what that [budget] package looks like.''

A liberal Republican who liked his position in the early 1980s boasted: ''In the first Latta budget I got about a billion, 200 million for social programs put in over and above the 1982 freeze ... in the second one, I got about 750 million more for social programs ... education of the mentally retarded, child-maternal health care, higher education ... we had to negotiate back and forth to get those.''

The Budget Process and the House Leadership

The congressional budget process, while providing the House leadership with significant capabilities, has been a consistent source of problems and frustration for the House, particularly for the Democratic leadership. The responsibility for passing the budget resolutions and the authority to enforce those provisions should be a considerable source of power, but passage of the resolutions has never been easy and enforcement has compelled the leadership to take actions that have made their allies unhappy. The Democratic leadership was particularly troubled during 1981 and 1982 when, first, they failed to enact Democratic budgets and, second, had to implement budgets they had opposed on the floor of the House. At that point, the Democratic leadership reached a low point; political observers variously wondered whether it was time for Speaker O'Neill to retire, whether the country had returned to a period of imperial presidency, and whether President Reagan's threat to the congressional power of the purse was greater than Nixon's had been. In short, the House leadership looked nearly powerless before the onslaught of a skilled president.

There are, however, advantages to being at the center of the partisan debate over fiscal and spending priorities. The House leaders of both parties develop a coherent and comprehensive statement of their goals and the means of achieving them. That situation puts them more clearly in the role of national policy leaders than they have been in the past. The constituencies of each party recognize the importance of the House debate and focus much of their attention on the House leadership. It is not coincidental that, in this period, Speaker O'Neill came to symbolize the Democratic party and its policies—even during the Carter presidency.

The task of establishing party positions has fallen to the House because it has been more openly partisan about budgeting than has the Senate. Also, the House of Representatives is the logical place for these deliberations. It, more than any other governmental institution, includes the ideological range of each party. The budgets developed in the House, therefore, represent the priorities of each party—both the central philosophical thrust and the range of programs and interests that appeal to the range of party members. Being the architect of that plan puts the party leadership in the position of playing ''broker'' among competing interests.

The reforms of the mid-1970s, including the Budget Act, provided the leadership with sufficient resources to act as broker among, but not to dictate to, those competing party interests. The leadership has some control over the Budget Committee—it automatically receives one seat on the committee and has considerable ability to influence the appointment of both the members and the chairman. The majority leadership also controls the calendar and jointly appoints (with the Senate leadership) the head of the Congressional Budget Office. The House provision limiting the terms of both committee members and its chairmen prevents individuals on the Budget Committee from developing independent power sources. Finally, the leadership has a set of enforcement procedures affiliated with the budget process. These procedures, particularly reconciliation, insure that decisions that have been made can be executed. On the other hand, the House membership has become increasingly independent of control by the leadership,[29] and the task of reconciling all factions of either party has become nearly impossible.

The task of leadership has become weightier under the Budget Act. Success pays higher dividends, yet it is more difficult to achieve. If the leadership can get the votes, it can implement its program more assuredly— a program that it would not have developed were it not for the Budget Act. The challenge, of course, is getting the votes. One member's views summarize the position of the leadership; ''When you have the votes to win, leadership is made much easier [than in the past] because then it's your decisions, your policies.''

Conclusions

The original goals of the 1974 law, as elaborated by the Rules Committee, provide a basis for drawing conclusions regarding the impact of the act on the House. Those five goals, as developed by former Rep. Richard Bolling, are:

> 1. to enact a workable process; it must meet ''the realities of congressional budgeting and . . . [not] inhibit the proper functioning of Congress'';
> 2. not to prevent Congress ''from expressing its will on spending

policy''; the primary goal is ''to make Congress informed about and responsible for its budget actions'';

3. to keep spending power from becoming concentrated in the hands of a few individuals; the budget committees should ''coordinate the revenue and spending sides of the budget'' but not have the power to dominate budget policy;

4. to insure that the new process would ''operate in tandem with and not override the well-established appropriations process . . . . The purpose of budget reform should be to link the spending decisions in a manner that gives Congress an opportunity to express overall fiscal policy and to assess the relative worth of major functions''; and

5. to avoid complexity by utilizing procedures that ''deviate only the necessary minimum from the procedures used for the preparation and consideration of other legislation.''[30]

Evaluating the Budget Act according to these criteria suggests that it has had at least some success. The first goal requires Congress to pass its resolutions according to schedule and do so without disrupting the remainder of the legislative process. Indeed, Congress has passed the required resolutions (although it succeeded in FY 1983 and FY 1984 only by combining the first and second resolutions), but not always on time. There is also considerable evidence, discussed above, that those resolutions have increasingly come at the expense of normal legislation and normal procedures.

The act's greatest success has been in the area of Bolling's second goal: Congress has been able to work its will on spending matters. The history of the act has shown that Congress can increase spending with relative ease or decrease spending through reconciliation. The House, under the budget procedures, is able to make informed and responsible decisions—if it chooses to do so.

The goal of coordinating budgetary actions but not controlling them has also been achieved with reasonable success. However, future use of the budget procedures may tell a different story. The dominance of a handful of legislators and presidential assistants in 1981 clearly indicates that power can be concentrated. It is unlikely that the House will accept that practice again, but the possibility always remains. A second danger is that the Budget Committee will become increasingly specific and begin to make most of the major spending decisions. Again, it is doubtful that the remainder of the House would accept that practice, but, without caution, there is also that possibility.

The goal that the new procedures should provide linkage but not dominate the appropriations process has been reached with some success. The House still prefers to think of most of its decisions as distributive rather than redistributive, but the process has made that increasingly difficult. The procedures have, however, made the normal appropriations process even more troublesome. It remains nearly impossible to get appropriations measures passed by the beginning of the fiscal year, if at all. This problem, along with some of the failures to achieve the first goal, are responsible for much of the discussion of biennial budgeting. Congress has too much work to do and not enough time under existing procedures.

The budget process resembles other legislative processes because the new procedures were grafted onto the old ones. The budget process obviously differs from other legislative processes, and the remaining House activities have been altered by the process, but the goal was to strike a balance that would permit real budgeting without completely restructuring the House rules of procedure. That balance has been and remains precarious as the House continues to struggle with the strain placed on the institution by the Budget Act.

The act changed the House and the way that the House does business, but it was not a revolution. As one member concluded, the goals and the impact of the act, are limited and have largely been achieved: "The budget process has not been exact, has been imprecise, and only partially effective as a tool. But, I never thought that it was going to be a panacea or a substitute for the will to govern."

The Impact of
Budget Reform
on the Senate

LANCE T. LELOUP

The House of Representatives fills an extremely important role under our constitutional system. But if there was one stroke of genius—and there was more—that came from the minds of those constitutional forebears, it was the Senate, because it is here where men will stand against the storms of political frenzy and in many instances throw the light of public scrutiny upon legislation which would otherwise be detrimental to the Republic. I do not want to see the Senate become a second House of Representatives.

—Senator Robert Byrd

During the great reconciliation battle of 1981, on the House side of Capitol Hill, the storms of political frenzy were raging. The Republican-conservative alliance was in the process of upending the Democratic majority amidst name-calling and bad feelings on both sides. Both the House and the Senate were trying to agree on cuts to existing programs of over $35 billion, and many sacred cows were being sacrificed. But there was less turbulence in the Senate. Reflecting their cherished traditions, the senators attempted to demonstrate—in Senator Byrd's words[1]—that they were not like "the other body."

The Budget and Impoundment Control Act of 1974 attempted to change the way in which Congress deals with the fiscal affairs of the nation. What effect have the changes had on legislative procedures, political power, and national policy? What effects have they had on the Senate, as compared with the House of Representatives? What is there about the Senate in the 1980s that helps in understanding the impact of the budget process, and what is there about the budget process that helps in understanding the Senate of the 1980s? An assessment must begin with a brief look at the modern Senate and at recent transitions. The Senate Budget Committee, designed to implement and enforce the budget process in the Senate, is of particular interest. Because of the importance of the Republican takeover of the 97th Senate and the use of the reconciliation process, the record of budgeting in the Senate from 1975 to 1980 will be compared with the more recent period. Finally, the record of the budget process in the Senate will be used to draw some general conclusions about the problems of Congress and the budget in the 1980s.

Transitions in the Senate

The Senate of the 1950s was the "Citadel,"[2] the "Inner Club," the "Senate Establishment."[3] It was a legislative body with a strong set of norms of behavior, or "folkways."[4] But the Senate was changing. By the 1960s, Randall B. Ripley characterized power in the Senate as shifting from decentralized to individualistic.[5] By the early 1970s the Senate had larger Democratic majorities and had become more liberal.[6] While committees in the Senate have not tended to be as strong or as important as those in the House, they form an important part of the power structure. Under the Johnson rule, every senator was guaranteed a major committee assignment, and many chairmanships were assumed by members with less seniority than in the past. Assessing the power structure of the Senate in the 1970s, Norman Ornstein, Robert Peabody, and David Rhode concluded that power was more individualistic and evenly distributed than it had been previously: "The Senate is a more open and fluid and decentralized body now than it was in the 1950s. Power, resources, and decision-making authority have become more diffuse."[7]

By the 1980s, the Senate had evolved again, with a change in its ideological make-up; the defeat of prominent liberals and the election of a Republican majority for the first time in a quarter century were the most significant changes. But even the 98th Senate was recognizable to the handful of senators who had served in the 88th Senate, twenty years before. It was still a legislative body that respected deliberation, unlimited debate, and independence and was not looking for strong centralized leadership. Although committees were not as dominant in the Senate as in the House, they remained the most important work groups. Committee autonomy and prestige were still respected. Even with tighter party discipline in the Republican Senate, structures and legislative processes were still oriented toward serving individual members' needs.

Budgeting in the Democratic Senate, 1975 – 80

In reforming the budget process, the Senate was able to "add a new and comprehensive budgetary framework to the existing decision-making processes with minimum disruption to established methods and procedures."[8] The most obvious difference between the House and Senate provisions was the weakness of the House Budget Committee. In the House, the Ways and Means and Appropriations committees were able to insure themselves direct representation on the Budget Committee and to limit the tenure of committee members. Committee self-interest, as much as anything else, was behind these provisions. In the Senate, there was no perceived need to institutionalize a weak Budget Committee. The new panel was less threatening than in the House. Nonetheless, one could clearly observe an accommodation to committee interests in the formulation of budget legislation in the Senate. Accommodation and deference to other committees also characterized the implementation of the budget process in the Senate, despite the characterization of the Senate Budget Committee as aggressive and combative by many observers.

The senators were able to adapt to the requirements of the Budget Act better than their counterparts in the House, where the battles were more protracted and the debate more acrimonious. Budget resolutions from 1975 to 1980 consistently passed the Senate by margins of about two to one. Bipartisan support for the budget resolutions was fostered in the Democratic Senate by the cooperation of then Budget Committee Chairman Edmund Muskie and ranking minority member Henry Bellmon.

Senate support for budget resolutions is best demonstrated by examining the history of roll-call voting on the floor of the House and the Senate. Whereas the House votes between 1975 and 1980 were sharply partisan and decided by very close margins, the resolutions were supported by up to half of the Senate Republicans (see table 4.1). No resolutions were defeated on the Senate floor, as occurred in the House. This is not to say that the Senate was without conflict. Senator Muskie actively enforced the budget resolution and challenged various spending bills on the Senate floor. Although the Budget Committee lost these votes as often as it won them, the support for its work in assembling the resolutions was not eroded.

How did the Senate Budget Committee under the Democrats compare with other Senate committees and the House Budget Committee? Although other Senate committees were not formally represented on the Budget Committee, as they were in the House, a form of de facto representation existed as part of a process of accommodation. One accommodation to the Appropriations Committee was informal representation on the Budget Committee. In the 94th Congress, four of the sixteen members of the Budget Committee also sat on the Appropriations Committee. In the 95th Congress, this increased to six of sixteen members. The Senate Appropriations Committee had about twice the proportional representation on the Budget

Table 4.1. Votes on Budget Resolutions, 1975–80

Date	Resolution/Bill	Vote Yes-No	Republicans Yes-No	Democrats Yes-No	Northern Democrats Yes-No	Southern Democrats Yes-No
			House			
05/01/75	1st Res., FY 1976	200–196	3–128	197–68	151–33	46–35
11/12/75	2nd Res., FY 1976	225–191	11–124	214–67	162–31	52–36
04/29/76	1st Res., FY 1977	221–155	13–111	208–44	159–20	49–24
09/09/76	2nd Res., FY 1977	227–151	12–113	215–38	154–16	61–22
02/23/77	3rd Res., FY 1977	239–169	14–119	225–50	176–15	49–35
04/27/77	1st Res., FY 1978	84–320	2–135	82–185	50–132	32–53
05/05/77	Revised: 1st Res., FY 1978	213–179	7–121	206–58	142–39	64–19
09/08/77	2nd Res., FY 1978	199–188	4–129	195–59	139–32	56–27
05/10/78	1st Res., FY 1979	201–197	3–136	198–61	152–25	46–36
08/16/78	2nd Res., FY 1979	217–178	2–136	215–42	154–25	61–17
05/14/79	1st Res., FY 1980	220–184	9–134	211–50	147–33	64–17
09/27/79	2nd Res., FY 1980	212–206	0–154	212–52	157–25	55–27
05/07/80	1st Res., FY 1981	225–193	22–131	203–62	128–54	75–8
11/18/80	2nd Res., FY 1981	203–191	2–146	201–45	133–33	68–12
09/04/80	Reconciliation, FY 1980 (adoption of rule)	206–182	0–143	206–39	142–27	64–12
			Senate			
05/01/75	1st Res., FY 1976	69–22	19–18	50–4	36–1	14–3
11/20/75	2nd Res., FY 1976	69–23	19–15	50–8	41–0	9–8
04/12/76	1st Res., FY 1977	62–22	17–16	45–6	32–4	13–2
09/09/76	2nd Res., FY 1977	55–23	14–18	41–5	27–3	14–2
05/04/77	1st Res., FY 1978	56–31	15–17	41–14	36–3	5–11
09/09/77	2nd Res., FY 1978	63–21	17–13	47–8	33–4	14–4
04/26/78	1st Res., FY 1979	64–27	16–19	48–8	35–4	13–4
09/06/78	2nd Res., FY 1979	56–18	14–12	42–6	30–3	12–3
04/25/79	1st Res., FY 1980	64–20	20–15	44–5	29–4	15–1
09/19/79	2nd Res., FY 1980	62–36	17–22	45–14	28–12	17–2
05/12/80	1st Res., FY 1981	68–28	19–22	49–6	31–5	18–1
11/20/80	2nd Res., FY 1981	50–38	14–20	36–18	24–11	12–7

Source: Congressional Quarterly Weekly Reports.

Committee as the House Appropriations Committee had, with its five guaranteed seats. The appropriations committees had received other concessions in the Budget Act, such as the restrictions on backdoor spending. Informal accommodation to the Senate Appropriations Committee was important because it potentially had the most to lose from the creation of an independent budget committee.

The Senate Finance Committee, by comparison, had only one member on the Budget Committee during the 95th Congress, but accommodation to the Finance Committee was less important because the budget process posed less threat to its autonomy and power. In the formulation of the Budget Act, the Finance Committee had been able to exclude more explicit revenue figures from the resolutions. The publicized "battles" between Muskie and Senator Russell Long (D, La.) between 1975 and 1979 did not alter the fact that the Finance Committee's domain was fairly secure from the start.

Compared with the House committee members, Senate Budget Committee members between 1975 and 1980 tended to have lower seniority. John Ellwood and James Thurber reported that, in the 94th Congress, the average number of years in the Senate was 8.8, compared with an average of 14.8 in the House.[9] By maintaining norms of committee service, a seat on the Budget Committee was more attractive to younger members of the Senate. This contributed to the greater strength of the Senate Budget Committee.

Were ideological differences within the Senate committee less than within the House committee? This would be a logical explanation for the conflict within the House committee, as compared with the Senate committee, when both were under Democratic control. In the 95th Congress, House Budget Committee Democrats were more liberal and Republicans were more conservative than their party as a whole.[10] But ideology does not seem to explain the differences because the same split was found on the Senate committee. Senate Budget Committee Democrats had higher Americans for Democratic Action (ADA) ratings than did all Senate Democrats (about five points higher), whereas committee Republicans had lower ADA ratings than did all Senate Republicans (about sixteen points lower).[11] In spite of an ideological split similar to that of the House committee, other factors intervened to produce a less volatile and more harmonious committee.

By constituting the Senate Budget Committee as a regular standing committee, traditional norms of seniority, committee loyalty, and restrained partisanship were preserved. Members had incentives to prevent the all-out conflict that took place in the House. However, as Richard Fenno suggests, Senate committees tend to be more permeable than House committees; they are not impregnable.[12] Traditional committee norms are only part of the answer. The Senate Budget Committee balanced committee prestige with a recognition of individual member's needs and a decentralized power structure, consistent with the general trends of the Senate in the late 1970s. This appeared both in committee leadership and in committee decision-making processes.

Senators Muskie and Bellmon combined to provide leadership based on bipartisanship and consensus building. There was conflict on the committee and it often developed along party lines, but it resembled what John Manley has called "restrained partisanship."[13] Once the choices were made, the committee presented a united front on the Senate floor and urged members of both parties to support its position. Senator Bellmon expressed this philosophy when opposing cuts in the first resolution for FY 1979:

> [I] voted for an even larger cut in spending during the markup of the resolution and . . . this puts me in somewhat of a dilemma. I have, since the Budget Committee was formed, consistently taken the position that we ought to work as a committee, work our wills, make the best decisions we could, and then, having come to that conclusion, we ought to support that decision as a committee so that when we came to the floor we would not each of us be going in our separate directions and, in this way, weaken the budget process. . . . So, attractive as I find the Senator's amendment to be, I must say that I feel at this time, partially because other committees will not have known in advance about the impact that such cuts might have on the areas of their concern, that the amendment should be rejected.[14]

Roll-call votes within the committee during its first few years are instructive in analyzing decision-making processes. Of the seventy-two recorded roll-call votes between 1975 and 1977, *none* were straight party-line votes. This compares with 14 percent for the House committee. Over half (54 percent) of those votes in the Senate Budget Committee were party votes, in which a majority of Democrats opposed a majority of Republicans. While this is significantly lower than the 78 percent party vote in the House Budget Committee, the figure is still relatively high compared with the votes in other Senate committees. With three conservative Democrats who voted with the Republicans more often than with the majority party, Muskie could not look only to members of his own party for support on crucial committee votes; this further promoted bipartisanship.

Although Senate Republicans had the lowest party cohesion scores of the four caucuses in floor voting, they had higher party support scores in committee votes than did the Democrats. This was a harbinger of a voting pattern that would emerge in the Republican Senate. The amount of voting agreement between the chairman and ranking minority member in this same period contrasted with the pattern observed in the House. Muskie and Bellmon voted together on thirty-six of seventy-two recorded votes, exactly half. Agreement between leaders of the House committee was only 14 percent on all votes cast in committee. In comparison with the House, partisanship on the Senate Budget Committee was clearly more restrained.

Restrained partisanship enhanced the power and prestige of the Senate Budget Committee; it also served individual members' needs far better than did unrestrained partisanship. Each committee member could expect to play a meaningful role on the committee. Given the fluid nature of voting alignments on the committee, members could maximize their bargaining power. This was reflected in higher committee attendance and participation than in the House.

The norm of specialization was generally stronger in the House than in the Senate, and on the Budget Committee it was a norm to be avoided; members were expected to be generalists, not specialists. Since the committee must balance the desires and requests of a variety of competing interests, they need to avoid advocacy for a particular set of agencies, programs, or another standing committee. One member described the differences with the House: "I detect more of a constituency thing on the House side—members pushing for their pet functions. This causes problems when it is brought to the floor. We have much less of this on the Senate side. One of the reasons we have been successful is that the committee is an accurate reflection of the make-up of the Senate. Items fought out in the committee are not fought on the floor."[15] The committee attempted to show the Senate that it was not an advocate of any particular point of view, but rather that it was concerned only with fiscal policy and discipline.

Decision-making processes adopted by the committee in the first six years reflected accommodation to individual members' needs and deference to existing Senate power. For example, the Senate committee was less specific in its subtotals than was the House, thus avoiding consideration of the line items or specific programs within the functional totals.

Accommodation to individual members' needs was apparent in the way a budget resolution was formulated. Unlike Congressman Brock Adams (D, Wash.) and Robert Giaimo (D, Conn.), chairmen of the House Budget committee in the 1970s, Senator Muskie did not begin with a specific chairman's "mark," that is, a set of budget figures that form the basis of discussion. The committee in the Senate considered a total for an entire function, often without any further specification of how the total was to be subdivided among committees. In addition, the Senate committee began deliberations using the current policy estimates (projections of a standpat budget provided by the CBO) as a baseline, while the House Committee used requests in the President's budget as its baseline.

By not establishing a chairman's mark, Muskie permitted committee members to be more fully involved in the process of fixing totals. One of the major complaints of House committee members, especially the Republicans, was that the chairman's figures were presented as a fait accompli and that the committee discussions were usually ignored by the chairman (and a majority of the Democrats). The process of decision making adopted by the Senate Budget Committee from 1975 to 1980 limited the number of complaints from standing committees about incursions on their territory and fostered fuller participation by committee members.

The budget process in the Democratic Senate was a significant departure from past practices, superimposing a new apparatus over the old appropriations-authorization-revenue process. Nonetheless, from formulation and selection of members, to decision making, the committee had carefully made sure that the budget process "fit" the Senate.

Budgeting in the Republican Senate, 1981–85

The upset victory of the Republicans in the Senate elections in 1980, accompanied by Ronald Reagan's landslide victory in the presidential contest, brought significant changes to the United States Senate. The 1982 midterm elections insured that the Republicans would control the Senate through 1985. Out of power for a generation, Senate Republicans initially displayed greater party cohesion, stronger leadership, and greater cooperation with the White House than recent Congresses had done. Although a number of the changes were quite dramatic, some of the characteristics of the budget process in the earlier period remained, and the individualistic nature of the Senate power structure remained largely intact. This was particularly true in the 98th Congress.

There were many new players in the budget drama. The House Budget Committee was headed by James Jones (D, Okla.). Muskie and Bellmon were no longer in the Senate, and the Budget Committee was chaired by Peter Domenici (R, N.M.), with Ernest "Fritz" Hollings (D, S.C.) as ranking minority member. Only three Democrats and one Republican remained from the original Senate Budget Committee. In the 97th Congress, half of the twelve Republicans on the committee were freshmen, while all ten Democrats had served in the 96th Congress. Informal representation of other committees continued in the 97th Congress, again favoring members of the Appropriations Committee. Four Democrats—Hollings, Chiles, Johnston, and Sasser—and two Republicans—Andrews and Kasten—also served on the Senate Appropriations Committee. Although no Democrats in the 97th Congress served simultaneously on Budget and Finance, three of the Republicans were also on the Senate Finance Committee. The overlap of Appropriations and Budget committees and the increase in the number of Finance Committee members on the Budget Committee continued an important trend by facilitating communication and negotiation on the frequently contentious taxing and spending issues.

How did the ideological orientation of the committee change under the Republicans? Recall that the Senate Budget Committee was as ideologically divided "on paper" as the House Budget Committee but much less divisive and partisan in practice. Table 4.2 compares the liberalism / conservatism of the first Budget Committee with the committee in the 97th Congress. The ADA and Americans for Constitutional Action (ACA) ratings are rough indicators of ideology; meaningful comparisons between years are difficult. The most valid comparison is between the average of Republicans or Democrats on the committee and the average for all members of their party in the Senate in a given year. Using this indicator, the ideological divisions are nearly identical to their pattern in the 1970s. Committee Republicans are more conservative than all Senate Republicans, and committee Democrats have ratings very close to the average for all Democrats. What is significantly different is the numbers. There were twice as many Republicans on the committee in the 97th Congress as there had been in the 94th Congress. While there were a few liberals on the Democratic side, such as Metzenbaum, Riegle, Hart, and Biden, the conservatives on the committee formed a substantial majority. The freshman Republicans tended to be conservative, like most of the Republicans elected in 1980. In this way, the committee demonstrated a continuity in the ideological stance of the two parties but simultaneously reflected the electoral turnover, which gave the conservative minority in the 94th Congress a majority on the committee six years later.

What other characteristics of the Senate Budget Committee were altered with the changeover in the Senate? Most noticeably, public bipartisanship, Muskie-Bellmon style, diminished. The excitement of victory did not leave the Republicans in a bipartisan mood. Negotiations focused on President Reagan, Majority Leader Howard Baker (R, Tenn.), Domenici, and other Republican committee chairmen, less so on Hollings and the Democrats. Beneath the Republican show of unity in 1981, some Democratic cooperation was in evidence. The Senate had not yet become another House of Representatives on budget matters.

Three key votes on the Reagan economic program in 1981 provide important clues about the continuity and change in the Senate during the first year of Republican control. For example, the Republicans voted as a bloc in support of the president's economic programs (see table 4.3). Formerly the least cohesive of the four caucuses, they displayed a cohesiveness similar to that of their Republican colleagues in the House. The Democrats became slightly less cohesive but still tended to support the budget measures by a two-to-one margin.

Republicans on the Budget Committee unanimously supported all three of the key votes listed in table 4.3. Seven of ten Democrats opposed the

Table 4.2. Liberalism and Conservatism in Senate Budget Committee, 94th and 97th Congresses

| | *Senate Budget Committee—94th Congress*[a] | | | | |
| *Democrats* | | | *Republicans* | | |
Name	ADA	ACA	Name	ADA	ACA
Muskie (Maine)	80	8	McClure (Idaho)	0	100
Mondale (Minn.)	75	0	Domenici (N.M.)	5	87
Cranston (Calif.)	75	4	Dole (Kans.)	10	87
Biden (Del.)	75	17	Buckley (N.Y.)	5	82
Magnuson (Wash.)	70	9	Bellmon (Okla.)	10	76
Aboureszk (S.D.)	60	14	Beall (Md.)	20	42
Moss (Utah)	55	17			
Chiles (Fla.)	45	48			
Hollings (S.C.)	40	28			
Nunn (Ga.)	20	62			
Average	59.5	20.7	Average	8.3	79
Average, Senate Democrats	54.3	23.2	Average, Senate Republicans	25.7	63.3

| | *Senate Budget Committee—97th Congress* | | | | |
| *Democrats* | | | *Republicans* | | |
Name	ADA	ACA	Name	ADA	ACA
Hollings (S.C.)	39	43	Domenici (Chair, N.M.)	17	71
Chiles (Fla.)	50	38	Armstrong (Colo.)	11	100
Biden (Dela.)	67	18	Kassenbaum (Kans.)	37	63
Johnston (La.)	33	29	Hatch (Utah)	17	96
Sasser (Tenn.)	67	23	Boschwitz (Minn.)	28	96
Hart (Colo.)	61	36	Tower (Tex.)	6	91
Metzenbaum (Ohio)	83	12	Andrews (N.D.)[b]	—	—
Riegle (Mich.)	84	15	Symms (Idaho)[b]	—	—
Moynihan (N.Y.)	47	15	Grassley (Iowa)[b]	—	—
Exon (Nebr.)	21	39	Kasten (Wis.)[b]	—	—
			Quayle (Ind.)[b]	—	—
			Gorton (Wash.)[b]	—	—
Average	59.4	25.15	Average	21.5	85.9
Average, Senate Democrats	58	26	Average, Senate Republicans	29	73

Source: Congressional Quarterly Weekly Reports, 1976, 1981.

[a]Only one nonfreshman joined the committee in the 95th Congress—Johnston (D, La.) — ADA = 15, ACA = 56.

[b]Denotes freshman.

Republican majority's first resolution, but only two of ten opposed the tax bill in late July. As the Republicans did when they were in the minority, the Democrats on the Budget Committee displayed a fluid pattern of voting in 1981.

By 1982, the traces of bipartisanship seemed to have disappeared altogether in the Senate. Facing huge deficits, additional cuts in domestic

Table 4.3.   Key Senate Votes on Reagan's Economic Plan

Date	Measure	Vote	Republicans	Democrats	Northern Democrats	Southern Democrats
5/12/81	1st Budget Resolution, FY 1982 — committee report, as amended	78–20	50–2	28–18	14–17	14–1
6/25/81	Omnibus Reconciliation Bill of 1981	80–15	52–0	28–15	13–15	15–0
7/29/81	Economic Recovery Tax Act of 1981 — committee report, as amended	89–11	52–1	37–10	24–8	13–2

Source: Congressional Quarterly Weekly Reports, 1981.

spending, and a myriad of unpleasant choices, Senate Democrats were increasingly opposed to the Republican figures and were relegated to offering a series of floor amendments to the first resolution. Much of the first resolution was drafted by the Republican caucus behind closed doors.[16] The Republicans were able to modify the plan that was reported by the Budget Committee without a floor vote, using a rule that allows a majority of a committee to change legislation that has not been amended on the floor.[17] This flirtation with "king caucus" in the Senate in 1982, completely closing out the Democrats, was in sharp contrast to the Muskie-Bellmon years and even to the pattern of 1981.

The votes on the first concurrent resolution for FY 1983 revealed the most partisan voting pattern on a budget resolution in the Senate since the process was instituted. Except for two or three defections on both sides, it was straight party-line voting (see table 4.4). The debate was more rancorous as well, with Hollings decrying the Republican plan and claiming Domenici "does not have the troops" to get the plan passed.[18] The process was changed in a number of other significant ways. Conferees agreed to use the clearly unrealistic but more palatable House numbers in the final report rather than the CBO estimates of the Senate version. This represented a retreat from the normal Senate insistence on accuracy and a diminution of Senate influence over the increasingly fragmented House. The conferees also agreed to make the first resolution binding if the second resolution was not passed by 1 October, a de facto elimination of the second half of the budget process.

Table 4.4. Senate Votes on Budget Resolutions, 1982

Date	Measure	Vote	Republicans	Democrats	Northern Democrats	Southern Democrats
5/21/82	Senate Concurrent Resolution 92— 1st Budget Resolution, FY 1983— committee report, as amended	49–43	46–2	3–41	1–28	2–13
6/23/82	Senate Concurrent Resolution 92— 1st Budget Resolution, FY 1983— conference report	54–45	51–3	3–42	1–29	2–13

Source: Congressional Quarterly Weekly Reports, 1982.

The budget process in the House was under attack in 1982. Appropriations Committee Chairman Jamie Whitten sponsored an amendment to the first resolution that would have allowed appropriations bills to clear Congress even if they exceeded targets in the budget resolutions. Although this amendment was initially adopted in the House, it was not included in the final version. It did indicate, however, the nature of the wholesale assault on the budget process and the problems in Congress as a whole. The changes in the Senate in 1982 were significant. Partisanship, disagreements over assumptions, and reliance on the caucus were all new to the upper chamber. For 1982, at least, the Senate did appear to be another House of Representatives on budget matters. But it was not to last.

The first session of the 98th Congress ushered in yet another changing, and sharply contrasting, pattern of Senate voting on the budget. On the surface, this is surprising. The composition of the Senate changed little after the 1982 midterm elections, with the Republicans maintaining a 54–46 majority. Baker was still majority leader, Domenici was still Budget Committee chairman, and Reagan was still president. Yet in 1983, Republican unity had disappeared, and commentators were noting that the Republicans were in ''disarray.'' In table 4.5, the votes on the first budget resolution for FY 1984 contrast with the previous year's votes (see table 4.4). Senate Republicans were clearly divided over a budget resolution that was at odds with the desires of the president. What had happened?

Historically, party unity has declined after the immediate surge of loyalty following the takeover by a party long out of power. But the unpredictable and fluid nature of voting alignments in the Senate primarily reflected the

Table 4.5. Senate Votes on Budget Resolutions, 1983

Date	Measure	Vote	Republicans	Democrats	Northern Democrats	Southern Democrats
5/19/83	Senate Concurrent Resolution 27— 1st Budget Resolution, FY 1984 — Gorton substitute, final passage	50–49	21–32	29–17	24–8	5–9
6/23/83	House Concurrent Resolution 91— 1st Budget Resolution, FY 1984 — conference report	51–43	19–31	32–12	25–6	7–6

Source: Congressional Quarterly Weekly Reports, 1983.

salience of policy concerns over party, committee, or institutional loyalty. The Reagan budget in 1983, with its huge deficits, failed to address the pervasive concerns of many Senate Republicans. Although this may have served the president's political and economic objectives (Reagan suggested he would prefer no budget resolution to the Senate version), it represented a failure of presidential legislative leadership. Two years earlier, the budget process had been the vehicle of presidential leadership. Seen largely as irrelevant in 1983, with the White House content to wait until after the 1984 elections to deal with structural deficits, senators and the budget process floundered.

Enforcing the Budget Process in the Democratic Senate: The Dominance of Accommodation

The Senate Budget Committee under the Democrats was aggressive and expansionist, as contrasted with that of the House. Muskie and Bellmon were willing to challenge other powerful committees in the Senate when the budget targets were in danger. Was this the most typical relationship? Evidence suggests that, in fact, accommodation to the standing committees was the norm. The question is not whether there were "conflicts," "power struggles," or "budget battles" in the Senate; it is a matter of emphasis, not revision. To assess the thesis of accommodation, the relationships between the Senate Budget Committee and the standing committees will be reviewed in more detail, with an examination of conflicts as well as more routine actions.

THE AUTHORIZING COMMITTEES AND THE BUDGET COMMITTEE

One of the first big tests for the Senate Budget Committee occurred in 1975 when Muskie challenged John Stennis and the Armed Services Committee over a military construction bill. Even many members of the Budget Committee were surprised when the Senate sided with Muskie. A few early episodes such as this helped to create an image of the Budget Committee and its leaders as aggressive protectors of the process. Given this orientation, one might have imagined that many members of the spending committees were unhappy with the budget process and Budget Committee. But this was not the case during the first six years.

The authorizing committees were generally satisfied with the budget process. There was some grumbling about the 15 March reports and the 15 May deadline for reporting authorizing legislation because the time constraints faced by the committees required a change in their behavior. However, members were satisfied in the vast majority of cases. They got what they wanted in terms of money and programs.

The 15 March views and estimates submitted by the standing committees revealed strong advocacy for higher spending. Their roles in the spending process came into direct conflict with the role of the Budget Committee. But as rational decision-makers, they adapted to the system. Their requests were expansive in order to ensure that their particular programs got a "place" in the first resolution.[19] The Budget Committee regularly reduced these requests, but not beneath a level acceptable to the standing committees. An apparent adversary relationship turned out to be cooperative role playing. When the Budget Committee's cuts were too deep, an unhappy committee could challenge and get its money restored by the full Senate.

Section 402 of the Budget Act allows the 15 May deadline to be waived under special circumstances; the waiver provisions were used quite extensively in the 1970s. In the Senate, authorizing committees must report a waiver resolution, which is referred to the Senate Budget Committee for its recommendation to the full Senate. These requirements were not implemented until 1976, and during the next three years 101 waivers were requested. Only a few of these requests were not recommended favorably by the Senate Budget Committee, although in several other cases the requests became moot.[20]

One might have expected that the number of requests for waivers would have declined as the Senate adjusted to the budget timetable. In 1976, twenty-one waivers were requested, increasing to forty-three in 1977 and thirty-eight in 1978. Were the requests for waivers justified? Table 4.6 lists the most common reasons given by the authorizing committees for reporting legislation after the deadline. The two most prevalent reasons, delay caused by the administration and unforeseen needs, appear consistent with the justification for the section 402 waiver procedures. Other reasons, however, reflect delays that should be correctable through better planning, such as work load, staff problems, and unfamiliarity with procedures.

Certain committees in the Senate used the waiver procedures more frequently than others. Approximately 70 percent of the waivers were requested by eight Senate committees (see table 4.7). Foreign Relations headed the list, with eleven requests. Both Foreign Relations and the Select Committee on Energy had a greater problem with administration-caused delays. Others, such as Environment and Public Works, Agriculture, and Judiciary, have less valid reasons for frequent waiver requests.

Why did the Senate not enforce the waiver provisions more rigorously in the first few years? The reason was that the cost of antagonizing authorizing committees was not worth the benefit of cleaning up the ''loose ends'' of the process. That the House was somewhat more guarded in granting waivers, despite its relative weakness, suggests again that the Senate Budget Committee was very accommodating to the legislative committees. Reconciliation would change that trend.

THE APPROPRIATIONS COMMITTEE AND THE BUDGET COMMITTEE

Early in its existence, the Budget Committee challenged the Appropriations Committee and obtained approval from the Democratic caucus for the right to have joint jurisdiction with Appropriations in handling presidential rescissions and deferrals. Ellwood and Thurber have argued that the comparative advantage to Muskie and the committee was quite small but that it was important for them to assert their authority and establish their existence.[21] Was this typical of their actions toward the Appropriations Committee?

Former Appropriations Chairman John McClellan was originally skeptical but soon became a strong ally of Muskie and the Budget Committee. Despite the challenge by Muskie over impoundment jurisdiction, the Senate Appropriations Committee was not threatened with line-item estimates by the Budget Committee. Muskie commented: ''We do not go into the

Table 4.6.   Reasons for Waiver of Budget Act, 1975–78

Reason	No. of Cases
Delay caused by administration	23
Emergency, unforeseen needs	20
Committee work load, inadequate time, other priority legislation	19
Committee reorganization, adjournment, staff problems	13
Other congressional delays	12
Committee error, unfamiliar with procedures	5
No reason given	4
Other	6
	$N = 102$

Source: Senate Budget Committee; compiled from records of requests to waive section 402 of the Budget Act and the reasons, as categorized by the Budget Committee.

program detail that the Appropriations Commiteee does. If we were to do the actual allocation by appropriation bill, we would be doing the Appropriations Committee's work. That is not our responsibility.''[22]

The Senate Appropriations Committee had more to gain than its House counterpart because the new process enabled the committee to approach parity with the House. Joel Havemann concluded that the budget process assisted McClellan in consolidating his power as chairman by giving him

Table 4.7.   Budget Act Waivers—Frequency by Senate Committees, 1975–78

Committee	Waivers Requested
Foreign Relations	11[a]
Energy (Select)	10[b]
Environment and Public Works	9
Agriculture	9[c]
Judiciary	9
Indian Affairs (Select)	8
Banking and Currency	6
Armed Services	6
	63
Others (4 or fewer each)	34[c]

Source: Senate Budget Committee; compiled from committee records of requests to waive section 402 of the Budget Act.

[a]One request received an unfavorable recommendation from the Senate Budget Committee.

[b]One request was not acted upon by the Senate Budget Committee.

[c]Three requests from individual members, not committees.

more control over the subcommittees.[23] For these reasons, the relationship emerged as an alliance.

The members of both the Budget and Appropriations Committees indicated that the dominant pattern was one of cooperation. One member, who was on both committees, commented: "From the start, there has been a mutual respect between the two committees [Budget and Appropriations]. . . . I think that Appropriations actually appreciates our efforts to hold down spending—it relieves some of the pressure on them."[24]

A Democrat on the Appropriations Committee echoed this sentiment:

> We get along with them [Budget Committee] very well and have had very few problems. At first some of my more senior colleagues were resentful—felt a little threatened but we have moved away from this after the first year. This has been a meaningful change accomplished together, and I believe we [on Appropriations] have improved our performance.[25]

Few appropriations bills were challenged by the Budget Committee on the Senate floor. Members of the Appropriations Committee have constituted up to 40 percent of the Budget Committee, which helped to insure that their interests were protected. The committee has also acted as an advocate in the process. Appropriations subcommitee chairman William Proxmire, self-proclaimed budget cutter and sponsor of the "Golden Fleece" award, described how experience taught him to behave:

> I made a low estimate and lived to regret it. I fought for the estimate, but I lost. Ever since then I have been a little gun-shy and I have attempted to come in high rather than low. . . . They [the estimates] can contain everything including the kitchen sink. It is easier and safer to suggest a high figure so that in the end one will look good by coming in under it rather than submitting a lower figure which may be exceeded.[26]

The appropriations subcommittees in the Senate were able to ensure that the vast majority of their spending goals were achieved. Despite some overt cuts, the budget resolutions over the first five years expanded to meet the desires of the appropriations and authorizing committees.

THE FINANCE COMMITTEE AND THE BUDGET COMMITTEE

There was less cooperation between the Finance Committee and the Budget Committee during the period of Democratic majorities in the Senate. Senator Muskie's observations on the control exercised by Finance were only half-humorous:

> The Finance Committee now controls the entire revenue side of the budget, which is 50 percent of it, and then if you look at the spending side,

medicare, medicaid, social security and so on—You add it altogether,
yes, and I expect it is close to 75 percent of the whole budget which goes
through the Finance Committee. We don't focus on it, we let it grow,
and I don't blame Russell [Long] for not wanting the budget process; he
has got 75 percent of the budget now, why should he give to anybody
else any part of it? [laughter].[27]

The expansion of tax expenditures allowed the Finance Committee to
enlarge its policy domain after the implementation of the budget process,
even though its discretion was reduced in other ways by reforms in the early
1970s. The Budget Act requires the Budget Committee "to devise methods
of coordinating tax expenditures, policies and programs with direct budget
outlays," but the act did not equate tax expenditures with direct outlays. The
Budget Committee lists tax expenditures, but these expenditures are not
approved in the resolutions. There is no provision for Congress to control tax
expenditures directly or to integrate revenue decisions with other budget
choices.

When he was committee chairman, Russell Long resisted any attempts to
bring his committee's actions under closer scrutiny and centralized control.
Senator Muskie described the root of the problem:

Our problem with Finance is that there is only one number in the budget
resolution that affects revenues, and that is the overall revenue floor. If
we adjust that to accommodate some total of tax expenditure reform, as
we did two years ago, $2 billion, you see Russell [Long] is astute enough
so he can put together a totally unanticipated package of offsetting
changes in the revenue code that would fit under the $2 billion restric-
tion . . . Russell [Long] plays the game superbly. He is defending his
committee's jurisdiction and no committee in the Senate has expanded its
jurisdiction over more substantive program areas . . . than Finance.[28]

In the first budget resolution in 1976, the Senate Budget Committee
included a figure of $2 billion in revenue to be gained from tax reform. Long
opposed it on two grounds. First, he pointed out that tax reform legislation
usually does not take effect immediately, and second, he argued that the
Budget Committee had no right to instruct the Finance Committee.[29] Muskie
and the committee held their position and took the fight to the Senate floor,
where Long prevailed in a number of votes.

Other conflicts took place during these first few years. The Finance
Committee met the totals of the first resolution for FY 1978, but contrary to
Budget Committee suggestions. The Budget Committee urged the Senate to
change the Finance Committee's bill. Senator Lloyd Bentsen argued for the
Finance Committee:

If it [the Budget Committee] can deal with specificity and detail as to
which taxes should be raised and which taxes should be lowered, then it

has taken over the responsibility of the Senate Finance Committee. . . . If
that happens, you are going to see this same pattern followed in the Appropriations Committee and finally, in the other authorizing committees,
and you will have seen the destruction, I think, of the budget reform
act.[30]

The Senate upheld the position of the Finance Committee in a close vote
because enough other committees (and a majority of committee chairmen)
were concerned about encroachments by the Budget Committee.

The Senate Budget Committee, in the 94th through the 96th Congresses,
played an active and occasionally assertive role in enforcing the budget
resolutions. Some of its actions can be attributed to the normal desire of a
committee to protect and expand its power and jurisdiction. Both Dennis
Ippolito and Allen Schick generally arrive at similar conclusions concerning
the impact of the budget process on Senate committees. Ippolito concludes
that the Finance Committee refused to accept any formal recognition of the
Budget Committee's expanded claims.[31] He calls the budget committees
"adding-machine committees that take the demands of spending committees and impose as much restraint on them as the current congressional mood
allows."[32] Schick strongly emphasizes the role of accommodation in multiple dimensions of the budget process and suggests that "the trick for the
Budget Committees is to accommodate without surrendering all meaningful
enforcement."[33] The experiences in the 97th Congress, however, pose a
challenge to the accommodation thesis.

Enforcing the Budget Process in the Republican Senate: The Temporary Decline of Accommodation

The congressional budget process had its first significant impact on the
budget priorities of the United States in 1981. Ironically, given the desire by
reformers in the early 1970s to clip the budgetary wings of the president, the
budget process was used by President Reagan to achieve his economic
priorities.[34] Working through the overlooked reconciliation process, the
president, Republican leaders in the Senate, and a Republican-conservative
coalition in the House were able to make major changes in the federal
budget.

The very nature of enforcement of the budget process went through a
metamorphosis when the Republicans gained control of the Senate. From
challenges to other standing committees, turf disputes, and questions over
granting waivers, the reconciliation packages forged by the Budget Com-

mittee and the Republican leadership moved to wholesale rewriting of authorizations and appropriations. Because the exercise was so different in the 97th Congress, some comparisons of relations between the Budget Committee and the standing committees are no longer relevant. In general, relations have been more strained. There has been less accommodation, but enforcement has been more meaningful.

The reconciliation provisions are found in section 310, (c), (d), and (e) of the Budget and Impoundment Control Act. In the original language of the statute, the budget resolutions may determine that spending authority contained in the laws, bills, and resolutions of a committee is to be changed. If more than one committee is involved, the Budget Committee receives recommendations and reports a bill to the full chamber. Debate in the Senate on any reconciliation bill or resolution is limited to twenty hours. Dormant for the first five years of the budget process, it was not used in the Senate until 1980, resulting in a bill late in the year that produced cutbacks of about $8 billion. Originally intended to be used at the end of the process in conjunction with the second resolution, reconciliation was chosen by the Reagan administration as the vehicle to achieve its desired budget cutbacks at the *beginning* of the congressional budget process in 1981. This adaptation of the reconciliation process was not done by amending the Budget Act but simply by providing for it through a concurrent resolution. Although a number of legal and parliamentary issues have been raised concerning the use of reconciliation, the real issues are political. Despite the very significant changes brought about by reconciliation, the House and Senate achieved those changes in a different manner.

The first resolution passed in May of 1981 mandated cutting over $35 billion from existing programs. After a month of arguing, haggling, and bargaining into the wee hours of the morning, the Senate arrived at a package that, if not enthusiastically endorsed, was acceptable to a majority. Senator Edward Kennedy commented on the package of cuts adopted by the Committee on Labor and Human Resources, where he served as ranking minority member of a committee chaired by conservative Senator Orrin Hatch:

> These are significant victories that make our reconciliation package a major improvement over the administration's original proposals. They have been achieved with bipartisan support on the committee. They have been accepted by the administration, the majority leader, and the chairman of the Budget Committee.[35]

The House, too, had a month of cutting and struggling with the reconciliation package, but, in contrast with the grudging acceptance by the senators, the stunned Democratic leaders and committee chairmen saw their work completely thrown out and replaced by a hastily assembled substitute, largely dictated by the Reagan administration. Compare the comments of Representative Kika de la Garza, chairman of the House Agriculture Committee, to those of Senator Kennedy:

> I resent the fact that the Committee on Agriculture of the House of Rep-
> resentatives and their members, their power and their jurisdiction have
> been usurped by a member of this House [Representative Phil Gramm (D,
> Tex.)] and some unelected member of the administration [Budget Director
> David Stockman] and in some corner or some dark alley or hallway or
> heaven knows where they meet, they wrote and maybe are still writing
> what is going to be our package for agriculture. I resent and I challenge
> the right of anyone to do that.[36]

While reconciliation may have had a significant effect on the congressional committee system, on the emphasis of lawmaking over representation, and on legislative-executive power in national politics, in 1981 the Senate appeared to have done less damage to its norms, procedures, and legislative processes than had the House. The "tyrannical majority," in the words of Robert Byrd, did not rule in the Senate. There was still more accommodation to the standing committees than in the House.

The reconciliation process, almost by definition, means a decrease in accommodation to the desires of the legislative committees. Still, the Senate managed to get through a process distasteful to all committee chairmen by letting each committee help "wield its own scapel." The cuts were painful and may have contributed to the partisan atmosphere that prevailed in 1982. The budget process in the Senate had come a long way from the early days when Senators Muskie and Bellmon took the floor in sequence, urging support, keeping down the number of amendments, and arguing about the importance of the process. In 1982 the Democrats offered a long list of amendments to the budget resolution, while the Republicans generally held together to defeat them. Arguments about "protecting the budget process" would have seemed ridiculous in that situation. Yet only a year later, the voting alignment seemed to have come full circle, with both parties divided and the leaders simply trying to find anything that would pass. What do these confusing patterns and trends allow one to conclude about budgeting in the Senate?

Conclusion

Republican party unity proved ephemeral. In 1983 the Republicans were divided and disorganized. The deficit reduction package called for in the budget resolution remained a promise unfulfilled when the Senate adjourned in late 1983. The failure to pass a second resolution, combined with action on reconciliation, raised serious doubts about the budget process as it approached its tenth anniversary. Many Senate committee chairmen voted against the first resolution in May and June and could not be counted on for leadership in implementing its provisions. While the failure to take action on the budget in 1983 could be seen as a return to Senate accommodation and deference, that conclusion misses the more important point. The continued decline in the process reflects pervasive institutional weakness and a lack of political will in both the House and Senate, which budget reform has failed to correct.

Enforcement of the budget process in the Republican Senate of the 1980s was significantly different from that in the Democratic Senate of the 1970s. With greater presidential leadership and sharp partisanship, the procedures were more potent. The question becomes, What happens without presidential leadership or partisanship? Party unity in the 97th Congress is the exception rather than the rule. The ability to structure members' loyalties requires a special set of circumstances, which is difficult to achieve. Dependence on the president in 1981 and 1982 left the Senate in far worse shape when the president failed to respond to fundamental concerns of senators in 1983. The problems of the budget process in the Senate in the 1980s are far less problems of the particular procedures of the Budget Act than of the fundamental operation of a fragmented Congress and weak political parties in the United States. By 1984, it did not appear that the Senate could act independently on the budget without presidential guidance.

Is Congress any more capable of gaining "control" over the budget than it was in 1974? What can one conclude about the Senate in particular? Budget reform has left the Senate more equal to the House in budgeting, but that is little to "crow about." Yet, if budget reform has not been a smashing success, neither has it been a failure. The Senate of the mid 1980s looked much as it did a decade earlier: individualistic and decentralized, maintaining the norms of accommodation and deference. It remains distinctive from the House, but both share difficulties in getting budgets passed. The problem is not with the procedures established by the Budget Act, although some tidying up, such as eliminating the second resolution and making the first resolution binding, would help. Procedures alone cannot change behavior; they can only facilitate policy making when the leadership and will exist. Budget resolutions, a tight timetable, and reconciliation are all improvements over the pre-1975 appropriations process, despite the mixed record of the ensuing years. Retreating from the budget process now would leave Congress in an even worse position. The process still offers the potential for collective decision making, even if the force to achieve that must come from a mobilization of political resources outside of Congress.

5

Budget Reforms
and Interchamber
Relations

JOHN W. ELLWOOD

H ow has the Congressional Budget Act of 1974 affected interchamber relations? Some overviews of the congressional process
have compared the two chambers to highlight their differences.[1]
Some of the best studies of congressional committees have compared House
and Senate committees with the same policy jurisdictions.[2] Finally, a small
body of scholarly literature has grown up around conference committees.
Until recently, conferences have been closed to the public, so most of these
studies have used input-output models to address the question of "who
wins" rather than the nature of conference decision making.[3]

In addressing the question of whether the 1974 Act has affected interchamber relations, this chapter will concentrate on three topics: (1) whether
the act has caused a shift of power from the House to the Senate, (2) whether
the act has led to greater interchamber communications and planning, and
(3) the pattern of conference committee decision making that has been
established for budget resolutions.

Shift of Power to the
Senate on Taxing and Spending

It is difficult not to conclude that the Congressional Budget Act has
caused a shift of power from the House to the Senate on budgetary questions.
Traditionally, House dominance on spending and taxing legislation has
come from two sources: the initiation of taxing and spending legislation in
the House and the greater legislative detail of House committee work, due to
the knowledge and specialization of House members who sit on fewer
committees and subcommittees than their counterparts in the Senate.

INITIATION OF LEGISLATION

Under the Constitution, revenue bills must be introduced and passed in the House before they come to the Senate floor. Appropriations bills have traditionally followed the same procedure. As a result, the House has determined the main parameters of spending and taxing legislation. In fact, House dominance was so great that its conferees would let the Senate "win" a majority of confrontations in conference in order to gain general Senate acceptance of the major aspects of the bill.[4] The effect of sequencing on appropriations decisions is well summarized by Richard Fenno in his classic study of the appropriations process:

> Throughout the book we have noted the impact of the appropriations sequence upon appropriations decision-making. We have observed that with each successive step in the sequence, the amount of money at stake in the decision grows progressively smaller .... Dominance in conference must not be confused with dominance of the larger process. In that respect, it is the House rather than the Senate which makes the more consequential appropriations decisions. The Senate makes no change at all in nearly one-third of the House decisions.[5]

The House sequencing advantage has been eliminated because of budget resolutions and the recently implemented reconciliation process. Between 1975 and 1982, the Senate acted before the House either in reporting the budget resolution out of committee or in voting initial floor passage ten out of fifteen times. In the other five cases, the Senate enacted within a week of the House.

This pattern is not surprising since the major function of each budget committee is to adjudicate among the "claimants" within its chamber for the limited budgetary resources that are available in any given year.[6] Thus, each budget committee puts together its budget resolution *de novo* with respect to the other chamber. Although the output of the budget committees prior to conference is responsive to various cues—such as the current services budget, the president's budget, the 15 March reports from other committees, and assessments of the likely passage of legislation— information on the activity in the other chamber is not among the vital information that is weighed. Thus, at a minimum, it is possible to say that the differences between House and Senate versions of budget resolutions represent independent chamber positions rather than the traditional model of the Senate acting as an appeals court for agencies or groups denied resources by the House.

As the budget process has developed over time, the lack of sequencing has periodically given the Senate an opportunity to constrain the House by acting first. In calendar year 1981, the Senate approved its reconciliation instructions (S. Con. Res. 9) on 2 April, a week before the House Budget Committee took up the first budget resolution (and three weeks before the Senate Budget Committee took up its first resolution). This pattern was not accidental; it was urged on the Senate Budget Committee by the House Republican leadership and the Reagan administration as a way of increasing the pressure on House Democrats.[7] Early Senate action on reconciliation also provided the Republican minority and their Conservative Democratic Forum allies in the House with a set of internally consistent budget numbers when it was time to draft their version of the House reconciliation instructions (referred to as Gramm-Latta I).

To the extent that one considers reconciliation bills as money and tax legislation, the budget process has enabled the Senate to initiate legislation that, prior to calendar year 1980, appeared to be prohibited by the Constitution and tradition. Thus, in calendar year 1980, the Senate approved its version of the Omnibus Reconciliation Act of 1981 (S. 2885) on 23 July, whereas the House did not approve its version (H. R. 7756) until 4 September.[8] As finally approved, this legislation included changes to the tax law reported out by the Ways and Means and Finance committees, which raised federal revenues by $3.6 billion in FY 1981. Having gone that far, in calendar year 1982 the Senate actually considered a major piece of tax legislation, the Tax Equity and Fiscal Responsibility Act of 1982, before action on it was taken in the House.[9] At a minimum, reconciliation is a mechanism for the Senate to initiate revenue and appropriations legislation.[10]

This change seems to portend a dramatic shift of power to the Senate. Walter Oleszek, writing prior to the passage of the Congressional Budget Act, reported that Senator John McClellan's "oft-repeated proposal for a Joint Committee on the Budget . . . [was] never enacted by the House— mainly because that body . . . [viewed] the measure as an intrusion by the Senate into its prerogative of initiating appropriation bills."[11] The development of the budget process suggests that those fears were well founded.

COMMITTEE POWER AND RESOURCES

With three exceptions, the budget committees of the House and Senate have the same duties and jurisdictions. The Senate Budget Committee has joint jurisdiction over legislative changes to the Budget Act and temporary waivers to the provisions of the act. In the House, both these jurisdictions lie with the Rules Committee.

The third difference is the permanent status of Senate Budget Committee membership versus the mandated membership (five members each from the House Appropriations and Ways and Means committees and a member from each political party's leadership) and limited tenure of the House Budget Committee. James Thurber and I have contended that this last difference is a major cause for the aggressiveness of the Senate Budget Committee and the desire of the House Budget Committee to avoid direct conflict with other House committees.[12]

The greater aggressiveness and power of the Senate Budget Committee within the Senate as against the House Budget Committee within the House has been well documented.[13] The Senate Budget Committee has been able to achieve passage of its resolutions by close to a two-thirds majority while the House Budget Committee has had great difficulty in gaining a majority within the House for any set of numbers. Moreover, the Senate Budget Committee has had a successful record in turning back floor amendments to its resolutions, whereas Gramm-Latta I and II are only the latest and most dramatic examples of the House Budget Committee ''being rolled on the floor.''

In addition, the Senate Budget Committee has championed nearly every expansive interpretation of the Budget Act.

1. During the first two years of the budget process, the House Budget Committee wanted to report resolutions in the millions of dollars (thus following appropriations committee practice); the Senate Budget Committee wanted to round off the resolutions to a tenth of a billion dollars.

2. During the second year of implementation, the Senate Budget Committee wanted to include ceilings and floors for the Transition Quarter (the three-month period that occurred as the government shifted from a fiscal year beginning 1 July to one beginning 1 October) as part of the first concurrent resolution for FY 1977; the House Budget Committee resisted this attempt to guarantee that other committees of Congress would not load spending into this three-month period.

3. In calendar year 1978, as part of its FY 1979 budget cycle, the Senate Budget Committee adopted multiyear budgeting to control spending growth. In calendar year 1979, as part of the FY 1980 cycle, multiyear numbers were included in Senate resolutions.

Because they face reelection every two years (and because their staffs believe that multiyear budgeting is misleading and possibly conservatively biased), the House Budget Committee resisted the adoption of multiyear budgeting until the implementation of the reconciliation process made it necessary.[14]

4. The Senate Budget Committee first initiated reconciliation as part of the second concurrent resolution for FY 1980. Although Senate floor passage of the reconciliation instructions occurred only because many senators knew that the House members would never go along with them, House Budget Committee conferees opposed reconciliation on the grounds that its imposition would "break faith" with the authorizing committees of the House, which had promised to adopt legislative savings. Thus, until calendar year 1980, the House Budget Committee sought to control spending through bargaining agreements with the other committees of the House, while the Senate Budget Committee sought to expand its statutory authority to mandate control of expenditures on other Senate committees.

5. During the first attempted implementation of reconciliation in the fall of calendar year 1979, House Budget Committee conferees argued for a narrow interpretation of the coverage of reconciliation, one that would have eliminated it as a tool for controlling the growth of existing entitlements. Section 310 of the Budget Act specifies that budget resolutions can include reconciliation instructions directed at (1) new budget authority, (2) prior-year authority, and (3) new spending authority. In Section 401(c)(2), new spending authority is further defined as (1) contract authority, (2) borrowing authority, and (3) entitlement authority. The first two forms of spending authority have largely been controlled or eliminated by the backdoor provisions of the Budget Act. The last, however, covers major programs that made up the fastest growing part of the federal budget during the 1970s.

The House Budget Committee took the position that, under Section 310, reconciliation could only be directed against "new" entitlements, that is, entitlements enacted for the first time during the session covered by the budget resolution containing the instructions. The Senate Budget Committee took the position that reconciliation could be directed against entitlement provisions enacted into law in prior Congresses. Regardless of the merits of this interpretative dispute—and the House position does appear to be correct if one reads the act narrowly—the Senate Budget Committee position enabled the budget committees to gain greater power over the programs that were causing most of the federal government's budgetary growth.

Traditionally, House committee members have had more information than their Senate counterparts. The greater size of the House allows for greater specialization on the part of its members. This specialization, reinforced by fewer committee assignments and, frequently, by longer service on a given committee (or subcommittee), enables congressmen to have a greater grasp of legislative detail than do senators. This has supposedly been a major advantage for the House in conferences. More importantly, it has reinforced the ability of the House Appropriations and Ways and Means committees to determine the shape of spending and taxing legislation by shaping legislative detail.

This pattern has been reversed in the budget process. As previously mentioned, the Senate Budget Committee is a regular standing committee of the Senate, so senators can stay on the committee as long as they wish. But members of the House Budget Committee can serve for only six years out of a ten-year period (in certain circumstances, eight out of ten for the chairman.)[15]

Having watched members of the two budget committees interact in conference over a five-year period (calendar years 1975–80), my view is that, on budget resolutions, each side is about equally well prepared. This equality of knowledge of legislative detail is reinforced by the nature of budget resolutions. At one level, the art of budgeting involves technical detail beyond the interests of either congressmen or senators. Deflators, spend-out rates, and budget authority allocations are exotica that can be left to staff. At another level, however, budget resolutions raise questions that appeal to the broad interests of senators. The resolutions are macro-instruments. They set *overall* spending and taxing levels. They affect priorities by forcing choices of allocation across committee jurisdictions. Such issues and questions appeal to senators who are used to dealing with "the big picture" across policy domains. The traditional strengths of the House — emphasis on legislative detail through specialization on a relatively (for Congress) narrow policy area—are not so useful.

Over time, the House Budget Committee has devoted considerable effort to following the legislative detail of the House. House Budget Committee staffers deride the inability or unwillingness of the Senate Budget Committee to keep track of Senate legislation. (In the early years of the process, the Senate scorekeeping system lacked a capability to compare the budget resolutions with the budgetary effect of what had actually passed the Senate.) Members of the Senate Budget Committee (and particularly its staff) take the position that the House Budget Committee's attention to detail is a poor application of resources, given the main purpose of the congressional budget process, namely, the setting of macroeconomic policy (fiscal policy) and the coordination of budgetary action.

Interchamber Communications

Prior to the interviews for this chapter, I hypothesized that, because budgeting requires coordination and summation of the parts, the budget committees would be forced to engage in more interchamber coordination than is the norm for Congress. The norm, of course, is almost no coordination or communication among committees except at conferences over differing versions of bills. My interviews have forced me to reject this hypothesis—at least for the period prior to the implementation of reconciliation (that is, prior to calendar year 1980 or the FY 1981 budget cycle).

Interchamber contact is best discussed at three levels: interaction among the budget committee staff responsible for various budget functions; interaction among high-level budget committee staff, such as staff directors, chief counsels, chief economists, and heads of the budget numbers units; and interaction between representatives and senators.

BUDGET ANALYSIS

In my interviews, various staff members of the budget committees claimed that they spent less than 1 percent of their time with their counterparts on the other budget committee. Excluding interaction during conferences, the budget analysts on each committee staff appear to engage in the greatest amount of interchamber contact. A major duty of the analysts is to monitor the progress of legislation and budgetary issues that affect their account(s) and / or function(s). The overwhelming amount of this monitoring is focused on the progress of legislation within one's own chamber; but, because budget staff members are hired for program expertise as well as political abilities, they have a tendency to call each other and discuss issues on an ''analyst-to-analyst'' basis.

HIGH-LEVEL STAFF

During the first few years of the budget process, there was considerable contact between staff directors and chief counsels over process issues. When the committees were being organized, the Congressional Research Service ran several war games or mock runs to see how the process would work. At these runs the two initial staff directors, Walter Kravitz and Douglas Bennet, and the two initial chief counsels, George Gross and John McEvoy, discussed and tried various approaches to making budget resolutions. This relatively high level of contact continued during the first years of the process, centering on interpretations of the many vague clauses of the Budget Act. However, as the process became more routine, this contact declined.

COMMITTEE MEMBERS

With the traditional exception of conferences, prior to the implementation of reconciliation, almost no contact occurred between members of the two budget committees. High-level staff members expressed the frustration of bringing together the chairmen of the two committees, only to have them stare at each other with nothing to say.[16]

THE ROLE OF THE CONGRESSIONAL BUDGET OFFICE

John Manley and others have pointed out that one of the virtues of the Joint Tax Committee is its role as a conduit of information and communications between the two taxing committees.[17] The Congressional Budget Office (CBO) seems to perform this function for the budget committees, although to a lesser degree.

On issues involving budget numbers and economic forecasts and assumptions, CBO is the one office that knows the position of each budget committee. Therefore, rather than calling his counterpart directly, it is not unusual for a budget committee staffer to call CBO in order to find out what is happening in the other committee.

There are three basic advantages in dealing through CBO rather than directly with counterparts on the other budget committee. First, deference is central to politics and bargaining. From the perspective of the Hill staffer, a CBO staff member occupies a lower order on the deference scale than does the equivalent staff member on the other budget committee. One can (try to) demand that a CBO staffer do something according to one's wishes; a similar demand of an equivalent budget committee staffer quickly escalates to a situation in which each side is speaking in the name of its chairman.

Second, CBO provides a useful bargaining agent for the two committee staffs. It provides fairly neutral information that (because of the previously mentioned deference ordering) can be relied upon in most cases. Third, forcing CBO to act as the bargaining agent for disputes between the staffs of the two committees is a way of limiting conflict, since each side can present its demands to CBO rather than to the other, and if pressed, each side can tell CBO to solve the problem.

Two examples illustrate this pattern. Throughout their history, the two budget committees have disagreed on how to score the budgetary actions of each house against the targets of the budget resolutions. CBO (which is required by the Budget Act to do the scoring) initially tried to get the two committee staffs to meet in the same room to reach a compromise. Attempts were even made to have chairmen Adams and Muskie meet to resolve the dispute. Those efforts failed, and eventually CBO was ordered to solve the problem. Its solution was two scorekeeping reports.

A second example occurred when the budget for FY 1983 was considered. The House and the Senate differed on what should be included in the defense function current policy baseline. The House wanted CBO to use the traditional methodology; the Senate claimed that, since Congress had adopted a multiyear defense plan, that plan should also be considered as a part of the baseline. Obviously, the game each side was playing was to structure the agenda for the coming debate on defense by either raising or lowering the base from which the debate would occur.

Rather than deal with each other, the two sides communicated through a CBO intermediary. Eventually each side said that its chairman insisted his approach be used. CBO resorted to its traditional solution—it produced three baselines for the defense function (those for the CBO, the Senate, and the House).

The important point for this discussion is that, during this process, a great deal of interchamber communication and coordination took place without the two parties ever confronting each other directly. A solution was found and conflict was minimized.

LEVELS OF INTERCHAMBER COMMUNICATION SINCE THE
IMPLEMENTATION OF THE RECONCILIATION PROCESS

One reason that the levels of interchamber contact and communications are low—but normal by congressional standards—is that the budget process allows each chamber to have its own programmatic assumptions for the agreed upon set of numbers. As many observers have pointed out, a conference has never been stalemated over dollars—it is too easy to split the difference. The issues that stalemate conferences and cause interchamber conflicts are different programmatic goals, assumptions, and so forth. Prior to reconciliation, budget resolutions directly affected only funding levels, and even in this regard they represented "moving targets" rather than fixed levels.

Reconciliation, however, involves lawmaking, as opposed to the procedural coordination of budget resolutions. Not only must the numbers agree, but the changes in each program or tax law have to be the same. This obviously reduces each side's degree of freedom.

It is not surprising then, that the implementation of reconciliation led to a dramatic increase in interchamber communication. One should not underestimate the scope of reconciliation; in legislative process terms, it is truly massive. The Omnibus Reconciliation Act of 1980 (P.L. 96–499) involved fifteen House and thirteen Senate committees. The act affected 266 budget accounts and over 250 authorizations. If Congress had followed the traditional practice of handling each reauthorization with a separate piece of legislation, the content of Public Law 96–499 would have accounted for about one-fourth of the average work load of recent Congresses.

Such massive legislative activity required extensive coordination and communication. Robert Keith reports that, in the conference, "about 30 congressional committees were represented and more than 250 legislators were appointed as conferees. In order to make the task manageable, the conference was divided into 58 subunits. Members of the legislative committees served only on the subunits handling issues within their committee's jurisdiction, but budget committee members served on all subunits."[18]

The budget committees went to great lengths to monitor each reconciliation conference subunit. Boiler rooms were established in each budget committee so that the progress of each subunit could be monitored. Attempts were made to guarantee that a budget committee member (or at least a staff member) was in attendance at each subunit at all times. Each member carried a beeper so that he could be contacted, should his presence be needed at a particular subunit.

Part of the increase in interchamber contact certainly was due to the majority status of the Republicans in the Senate and their minority status in the House. The Republicans have traditionally had a technically weak minority staff on the House Budget Committee. Therefore, when the House minority formed an alliance with the Conservative Democratic Forum's "boll weevils," they lacked the capacity to put together an internally consistent conservative alternative. As part of the effort leading up to what became Gramm-Latta I,[19] the House minority turned to the Republican Senate Budget Committee staff for help. Early in the session Republican staffs from the House and Senate met and planned to use early Senate activity on reconciliation in order to create pressure on House Democrats.[20] As part of this plan, the Senate Budget Committee took up and passed its reconciliation instructions almost a month before it was scheduled to mark up the first concurrent resolution. When the House Budget Committee met to mark up its resolution, reconciliation had already been invoked by the Senate.

When faced with the need to put together a substitute set of reconciliation instructions, the House minority again turned to the Senate Budget Committee staff. Both sides seem to agree that just about all the numbers in Gramm-Latta I were provided by the Senate.

As the summer progressed, the level of interchamber communication increased. At the height of the reconciliation conferences, the top staffs of the two budget committees held hour-long meetings at the beginning of each day in order to keep each other apprised of what was happening. The chairmen of the two committees also met periodically.

Why was the degree of interaction on the reconciliation bill so extraordinary? Obviously, the influence of an administration that knew how to play legislative politics was one factor. The different statuses of the parties in each chamber was another. But one can at least postulate that reconciliation came very close to executive budgeting. Dollar goals were set and monitored, and members were frequently faced with zero-sum choices. Although many false reductions were counted as real cuts, in the exercise the parts did have to agree with the whole. Much of the flexibility of the budget resolution process was removed. In this environment, it could be posited, the coordination inherent in executive budgeting came to the fore.

Decision Making in Budget Resolution Conferences

As with all congressional legislative activity, the height of interchamber communication and interaction in the budget process is associated with conferences. This section, therefore, analyzes the results and decision-making patterns of thirteen budget resolution conferences that were held from calendar year 1975 through calendar year 1981.

Concurrent resolutions on the budget must be passed by both chambers in identical form before they become effective. Since the House and Senate versions of budget resolutions have differed (with one exception), and since neither chamber has been willing to accede to the other's version, conferences have been required in all but one case (the Senate version of the second concurrent resolution for Fiscal Year 1982 was accepted by the House). Although most major legislation requires a conference, only about 10 percent of the bills enacted by Congress follow this route.[21]

ORGANIZATION OF CONFERENCES

Members of congressional conferences (referred to as conferees or managers) formally represent their chamber and / or committee. Thus, voting within conferences occurs on each side; the conferees of one house vote among themselves to make an offer to the other house, which must then vote whether or not to accept the offer.

During the period under study, the Senate Budget Committee was represented by ten conferees—six from the majority party and four from the minority party. The House Budget Committee was generally represented by fifteen conferees—nine from the majority party and six from the minority party. In the case of budget resolution conferences, managers have been chosen on the basis of their seniority on the budget committees.

Unlike the pattern of the appropriations process, where, by tradition, the Senate Appropriations Subcommittee chairman acts as the chairman of the conference committee and the conference is held on the Senate side of the Capitol, the chairmen of the two budget committees have alternated as chairman of budget resolution conferences, which are held in the most convenient available room. This arrangement reflects the equal status of the Senate in the budget process. Budget conferences have lasted from a day to several weeks, but the average conference has taken three days.

PATTERNS OF DECISION MAKING: PREPARING FOR THE CONFERENCE

The manner in which the two budget committees approach conferences reflects their styles of decision making. Prior to conferences, the staffs of the two committees meet to settle technical disagreements when possible and to identify those issues to be negotiated by the conferees.

In the case of the Senate Budget Committee, an intelligence memorandum is then prepared for the chairman. This document is the culmination of a monitoring effort that has been under way since the budget committees began to mark up their respective resolutions. It lists the issues of dispute and gives the staff's judgment concerning which issues can be negotiated before the conference. It also contains what amounts to a legislative history of the passage of the other chamber's resolution. Key votes in committee and on the floor are identified and analyzed.

The staffs of both committees then prepare "marks" of what they would like to achieve in the conference. The House Budget Committee "mark" is modified and approved at a caucus of the Democratic House conferees. It is also approved by the Democratic leadership of the House (one member of the leadership is required to sit on the House Budget Committee and thus is a conferee).

During the first years of the budget process, the Senate Budget Committee mark was prepared solely for the use of Chairman Muskie. As such, it was an individual rather than a collective mark. While each senator received a briefing book, setting out the disputed issues in each function and also arguments for the Senate position, only Muskie's book included extra pages with the suggested marks for the functions and arguments to back up the policy positions of the marks.

As Senator Muskie moved toward a closer working relationship with ranking minority member Henry Bellmon, the staff-suggested mark was shared with the minority staff. When possible, a negotiated chairman–ranking minority member mark was formulated. Thus, the Senate Budget Committee's mark, over time, became a committee leadership mark. This distinction between a party leadership mark in the House and a committee leadership mark in the Senate is consistent with the overall decision-making patterns on budget questions in the two chambers.[22]

The first three columns of table 5.1 set out the average dollar differences between House and Senate budget resolutions in thirteen conferences that were held from calendar years 1975 through 1980. The Senate generally wanted higher levels of expenditures than the House for the national defense, international affairs, natural resources and environment, and commerce and housing credit functions. The House wanted to spend more on transportation, community and regional development, veterans' benefits, and the human resource functions (functions 500 and 600).

Over the first six years of the budget process, these differences largely canceled each other, with the House resolution being higher than the Senate resolution by an average of $1.7 billion in budget authority and $700 million in outlays.[23] In these terms, the net margin of disagreement between the two chambers was very small—only 0.9 percent for budget authority and 1.9 percent for outlays.

The size of the disagreement grows when the differences are viewed in absolute terms, however. When the signs of the disagreement are ignored, the chambers differed by an average of $17.6 billion in budget authority and $9.1 billion in outlays. This represents a relative disagreement of 3.3 percent in budget authority and 1.9 percent in outlays.

The magnitude of the disagreement between the chambers is larger for the first concurrent resolution than for the second, with the absolute difference in budget authority declining by 25 percent between the resolutions (from $21.0 billion for the first resolution to $14.3 billion for the second) and the absolute difference in outlays dropping by 41 percent (from $11.5 billion for the first resolution to $6.8 billion for the second).[24] This pattern is consistent with the notion that the second budget resolution is largely a ratification of the decisions made by Congress since the passage of the first budget resolution in May.

The last three columns of table 5.1 set out the means of the Senate Budget Committee chairman's marks for budget authority and outlay. The data are presented as percentages of the distance from the midpoint between the

Table 5.1. Averages (means) of Differences between House and Senate Budget Resolutions and of Senate Budget Committee Chairman's Mark for Budget Resolution Conferences

Function	House Resolution Minus Senate Resolution (in billions of dollars)			SBC Chairman's Conference Mark: Percentage Deviation from Split-the-Difference Point		
	Budget Authority	Outlays	Total	Budget Authority	Outlays	Total
050 National Defense	$ −2.0	$ −1.2	$ −1.6	15.9%	30.7%	23.3%
150 International Affairs	−0.2	0.0	−0.1	37.2	36.4	36.8
250 General Science, Space, and Technology	0.0	0.0	0.0	35.9	30.8	33.3
270 Energy	0.0	0.1	0.0	66.6	−55.6	5.5
300 Natural Resources and Environment	−0.5	−0.1	−0.3	17.2	6.3	11.8
350 Agriculture	0.0	0.2	0.1	15.4	21.2	18.3
370 Commerce and Housing Credit	−0.1	−0.2	−0.2	14.3	−6.3	4.0
400 Transportation	1.1	0.3	0.7	23.5	58.0	40.7
450 Community and Regional Development	1.2	0.1	0.7	49.8	20.1	34.9
500 Education, Training, and Social Services	1.1	0.7	0.9	45.6	46.1	45.8
550 Health	−0.3	0.0	−0.1	5.3	3.4	4.3
600 Income Security	0.7	−0.2	0.3	−5.7	32.9	13.6
700 Veterans' Benefits and Services	0.2	0.2	0.2	31.8	30.1	31.0
750 Administration of Justice	0.0	0.0	0.0	53.8	25.0	40.0
800 General Government	0.0	0.0	0.0	38.5	15.4	26.9
850 General Purpose Fiscal Assistance	−0.2	−0.2	−0.2	15.4	23.1	19.2
900 Interest	−0.2	−0.5	−0.3	−2.2	−2.2	−2.2
920 Allowances	0.7	0.2	0.6	102.2	86.8	94.8
950 Undistributed Offsetting Receipts	0.1	0.1	0.1	53.8	53.8	53.8

Source: Author's calculations from unpublished data and conference committee reports on budget resolutions held from calendar years 1975 through 1980.

Senate and House resolutions to the Senate resolution. For example, the average position of the Senate mark for budget authority for the national defense function was 15.9 percent of the distance from the midpoint to the Senate resolution. Negative numbers indicate a willingness of those preparing the mark to settle between the midpoint and the House resolution figure. The higher the positive percentage, the greater the desire to achieve the numbers contained in the Senate-passed resolution.

If the mark is interpreted as the Senate's initial bargaining position, it is not surprising that it comes between the midpoint and the House position in only five of the thirty-eight categories. But assuming the mark represents a true goal of the chairman (a goal that was achieved in many instances), the Senate's position is quite aggressive.[25]

The variance in the chairman's conference mark is associated with four factors: (1) a desire to maintain the Senate's position on what are perceived to be the most crucial issues, (2) a general desire by the more conservative Senate Budget Committee to achieve lower spending levels, (3) the realization of the need to support powerful Senate conferees who, because of their other committee assignments, desire higher spending levels for given functions, and (4) a desire to maintain a "truth in budgeting position" for those functions for which spending levels are driven by estimates rather than policy choices. These factors, it turns out, reappear as major determinants in explaining decision-making patterns in the conference.

The most aggressive Senate positions are taken on functions 920 and 950. The expenditures levels for these functions are driven by estimates of what is likely to happen in the future on such questions as the sale and leasing of offshore oil rights, the likelihood and magnitude of federal pay increases, and the prospect of natural disasters that will require additional federal support. Owing largely to the influence of Senator Bellmon, the Senate Budget Committee, from its inception, took a fairly conservative approach to these functions.[26] Defense of the numbers in these functions became a process issue for the committee staff. This is not to say that the Senate conferees were unwilling to use these estimated functions as a way of controlling conflict within the conference; adjustments in these estimates have provided a key ingredient to conference compromise.

What appear to be tough Senate positions for functions 250, 350, 750, and 800 really reflect the limited size of the function and / or the lack of dispute between the two committees on these categories.

The remaining functions—those that drive the budget in both programmatic and expenditure terms—involve an interplay of the desire to save money, the desire to uphold the Senate's position on important issues, and the need to placate powerful senators. Thus, some of the most aggressive

Senate positions are found for the three functions—400, 450, and 500—that are most important to the House coalition. These functions contain the distributive projects (pork barrel) so vital to congressmen. They are the functions for which the House resolution tends to exceed the Senate resolution by the greatest amount. As such, the Senate marks for these functions reflect two factors—the desire to uphold the Senate position on some of the issues most important to each side and the desire to save money.

The health, income security, and veterans functions present interesting exceptions to this pattern; exceptions that illuminate the more subtle forces at work in the conference. The willingness of the Senate to give in to the House on the health function reflects a desire to save money and a need to placate the Senate's most powerful conferee, Senator Warren Magnuson. For most of the period under study, Senator Magnuson was chairman of the Senate Commerce Committee, the committee that controlled the authorization for most programs in the function (with the exception of the two big uncontrollable entitlements, Medicare and Medicaid). He was also chairman of the HEW-Labor Subcommittee of the Senate Appropriations Committee. Thus, he was in a position to influence the authorization and funding of most health legislation. The Senate Budget Committee's decision making in committee, on the floor of the Senate, and in conference tended to support the desire of the senator from Washington for higher spending levels for most health programs.

The unwillingness of the chairman's conference mark to accommodate the House position on veterans' benefits reflects the relative lack of power of another budget committee member, Senator Alan Cranston. As chairman of the Senate Veterans Committee, Cranston fought for higher veterans expenditures in the Senate Budget Committee, on the Senate floor, and in budget resolution conferences. Although his position did tend to be adopted in conference, his relative lack of influence was reflected in his inability to gain passage for his amendments in committee markup or on the floor. This lack of Senate power was also shown in the unwillingness of those who put together the chairman's mark to set aside the norms of supporting the Senate position and saving money in order to placate the senator from California.

The peculiar pattern for the income security function results from differing assumptions. This function, which represents over one-third (34.3 percent in FY 1981) of all budget outlays, comprises the very large entitlement programs that have been enacted since the New Deal to help the elderly and the poor. These programs—Social Security and other retirement programs, Supplemental Security Income for the elderly poor, food stamps, Aid to Families with Dependent Children (AFDC), and housing assistance—are "relatively uncontrollable" in the sense that their funding levels cannot be adjusted annually by the appropriations process.[27] Because less than 2 percent of the outlays in this function can be controlled by the appropriations committees, the budget resolutions for this function, prior to the implementation of the reconciliation process, were based on estimates.

Over time, House resolutions have tended to be based on more optimistic economic assumptions. This was particularly true during the Carter years. Many of the largest entitlements in this function, such as Social Security, are funded by taxes earmarked for trust funds. Budget authority figures for trust funds represent the money going into the fund, while outlays represent payments from the fund. Optimistic economic assumptions imply, therefore, that the money going into the fund will increase—more people working more hours will pay more wage taxes—and outlays will decrease— fewer people will choose early retirement. Thus, the more optimistic economic assumptions of the House help to explain why the House has higher budget authority and lower outlay estimates in its resolutions than does the Senate. To the extent that programmatic differences separated the two chambers, the House, seeking expansion of nontrust fund programs, sought higher budget authority rather than outlay levels.

The final, and from the Senate's perspective, frequently the most important differences between the two chambers were in connection with the national defense and international affairs functions. These were the only areas for which the Senate consistently called for higher spending than did the House. The national defense function represents the only case for which the Senate Budget Committee consciously raised its numbers under the assumption that a compromise with the House would lower the final figures. The national defense function also represents an area in which the chairman, in many cases, preferred lower funding than did a majority of his committee members and conferees. Thus, the national defense mark represents the interaction of desires to win on the most important disputes and to compromise in order to save money as well as a realization that, on this issue, "cut insurance" was included in the Senate mark.

PATTERNS OF DECISION MAKING: IN THE CONFERENCE

Budget resolution conferences have developed a fairly consistent decision-making pattern over time. The conference opens with a general discussion of the economic assumptions and the revenue target (or floor in the case of the second resolution). If compromise cannot be reached, topics are postponed until the function totals are set.

A unique aspect of bargaining with budget numbers is the large number of interactive constraints that are operating. The prime constraint on the bargain is the acceptable limit of the deficit (or the need for a surplus, as was the case in the spring of 1980). There is usually no economic or policy logic for this acceptable limit. In 1975, for example, conservative members of Congress claimed that there was no way they could support a resolution with a deficit above $40 billion. Whatever the acceptable limit is, however, it constrains all other budgeting.

Economic assumptions also provide a constraint. Optimistic growth assumptions (usually accompanied by higher inflation assumptions) imply lower outlays and higher revenues and thus, a smaller deficit. Non-congressional economic forecasts generally place outer limits on these assumptions, thus constraining the conferees.[28]

Function totals can occasionally affect economic assumptions, as opposed to the traditional causal pattern. Because expenditures for the major entitlements, which make up the human resources functions, are sensitive to economic changes, the setting of the expenditure totals for these functions helps the conferees to reach a compromise on the economic assumptions. A policy dispute is turned into a technical exercise by allowing programmatic bargains to determine economic assumptions rather than (following the traditional analytic approach) letting economic assumptions determine the program levels. Although analytically poor, this approach does have the virtue of helping the two sides reach an agreement. Thus, it is not unusual for the economic assumptions to be set after the compromises for the other numbers have been reached.

The conferees generally take up and quickly reach agreement on the smaller, less controversial functions. These compromises are frequently negotiated by the staff before the conference. The pattern of compromise for these functions has normally been to accept the lower number in order to free as much additional monies—within the acceptable deficit constraint—as possible for the more difficult compromises to come.

The conferees then attempt to settle the more difficult function differences. Initially, they take up the functions in no particular order. Rather the order is determined by the presence or absence of interested conferees. During the period under study, for example, consideration of the health function was delayed until Senator Magnuson could be present, and consideration of the community and regional development function did not take place without Majority Leader James Wright.

While occasional compromises are reached for individual functions, budget conferences have always climaxed with the negotiation of packages of functions. In table 5.2, the functions included in the final compromise packages for each conference between Fiscal Years 1976 and 1981 are listed. As one might expect, the functions that are most frequently part of the final package are those for which the two chambers are in widest disagreement—functions 050, 270, 450, 500, and 600.

TWO CASE STUDIES: PATTERNS OF BARGAINING

In tables 5.3 and 5.4, the series of counteroffers leading to final conference agreements for the first concurrent resolutions for Fiscal Years 1976 and 1977 are outlined. Their patterns are quite typical of the bargaining stages in budget conferences. Before turning to the specifics of each sequence, it is important to keep in mind one procedural and two political constraints that limit the flexibility of budget resolution conferees. First, under the rules of the House and of the Senate, the conferees may not go beyond the scope of the resolutions passed by the two chambers. In budget conferences this implies that the budget function agreements should be within the range established by the two resolutions.

Two major political constraints also limit the conferees. The first is the size of the deficit. The limiting effect of the deficit creates another constraint—the potential inability to use distributive politics in limiting conflicts by increasing the size of the "pie." Congress is an institution that is at its best when it can turn redistributive issues into distributive ones. The relatively flat distribution of power and the subcommittee system have the virtue of maximizing access points into the political process for many interests. Such a system is not suited to resolving zero-sum conflicts. For this reason, Congress rarely handles issues in redistributive terms. Rather, it seeks to make many interests happy by trying to give as much to as many groups as possible without making it appear that there are any losers.

The danger of budgeting for this type of decision making is that, if the budget aggregates are allowed to act as constraints on the parts, it becomes increasingly difficult to avoid redistributive politics. The conference sequences of tables 5.3 and 5.4 illustrate how the conferees, under a deficit constraint, still sought to maintain a distributive decision-making process.

In examining the final sequence of counteroffers that led to agreement on the FY 1976 resolution (see table 5.3), one is struck by the narrowness of the margin of disagreement. Very small differences in the alternative packages appear to be crucial. What is being argued is not money levels—the estimating uncertainties at the time of the first resolution are larger than the ranges of disagreement—but rather the political symbols and cues associated with the inclusion or exclusion of given programs.

Table 5.2. Functions Included in Packages That Resulted in Final Conference Agreement

Function	FCR[a] FY76	SCR[b] FY76	FCR FY77	FCR FY78	SCR FY78	FCR FY79	SCR FY79	FCR FY80	SCR FY80	FCR FY81	Total
050 National Defense		X		X		X		X	X	X	6
150 International Affairs						X					1
250 General Science, Space, and Technology										X	1
270 Energy						X		X	X	X	4
300 Natural Resources and Environment			X					X			2
350 Agriculture			X					X			2
370 Commerce and Housing Credit						X					1
400 Transportation				X						X	2
450 Community and Regional Development	X		X	X		X	X				5
500 Education, Training, and Social Services	X	X	X	X	X		X	X	X	X	9
550 Health		X	X				X				3
600 Income Security	X			X	X			X	X	X	6
700 Veterans' Benefits and Services					X						1
750 Administration of Justice											0
800 General Government											0
850 General Purpose Fiscal Assistance								X			1
900 Interest									X		1
920 Allowances	X		X			X					3
950 Undistributed Offsetting Receipts		X				X					2

Source: Author's calculations from data in the unpublished transcripts of the budget resolution conferences.

[a] FCR = first concurrent resolution.

[b] SCR = second concurrent resolution.

Table 5.3. Sequence of Counteroffers Culminating in Final Conference Agreement for First Concurrent Resolution, Fiscal Year 1976 (in billions of dollars)

Function	Initial Positions			Final Series of Counteroffers				Agreement
	House Passed FCR[a]	Senate Passed FCR	SBC[b] Mark	First Senate Offer—Rejected by House	House Counter-offer—Rejected by Senate	Domenici Motion—Rejected by Senate Conferees	House Counter-offer—Rejected by Senate	Bellmon Motion—Accepted by Senate and House
450 Community and Regional Development Outlays	$9.0	$6.6	$8.2	$8.6	$8.8	$8.3	$8.7	$8.65
500 Education, Training, and Social Services Outlays	20.4	19.4	19.4	19.4	19.9	19.9	19.9	19.85
600 Income Security Outlays	124.9	126.1	126.1	125.3	125.3	125.3	125.3	125.30
920 Allowances Outlays	1.5	1.1	1.3	1.5	1.3	1.3	1.2	1.20
Package Subtotal Outlays	155.8	153.2	155.0	154.8	155.3	154.8	155.1	155.00
Deficit	70.0	67.2	NA	68.6	69.1	68.6	68.9	68.80

Source: Author's calculations from data in the unpublished transcripts of the conference on the first concurrent resolution for FY 1976.

[a]FCR = first concurrent resolution.

[b]SBC = Senate Budget Committee.

Table 5.4. Sequence of Counteroffers Culminating in Final Conference Agreement for First Concurrent Resolution, Fiscal Year 1977 (in billions of dollars)

Function	Initial Positions			Final Series of Counteroffers						Agreement
	House Passed FCR[a]	Senate Passed FCR	SBC[b] Mark	Moss Offer No. 1	Bellmon Offer No. 1	Moss Offer No. 2	House Counter-offer	Senate Counter-offer	House Counter-offer	Senate Counter-offer
300 Natural Resources and Environment										
Budget Authority	$14.80	$18.00	$16.90	$18.00	$18.00	$18.00	$16.40	$18.00	$17.00	$17.00
Outlays	15.70	15.60	15.70	15.70	15.60	15.70	15.70	15.70	15.70	15.70
450 Community and Regional Development										
Budget Authority	6.50	7.40	7.40	7.40	7.40	7.40	10.00	7.40	7.40	7.40
Outlays	6.20	7.80	7.80	7.80	7.80	7.80	8.40	7.80	7.80	7.80
500 Education, Training, and Social Services										
Budget Authority	24.12	22.40	24.60	24.60	24.60	24.60	24.60	24.60	24.60	24.60
Outlays	23.00	21.20	23.00	23.00	22.40	23.00	23.00	23.00	23.00	23.00
600 Income Security										
Budget Authority	156.76	163.70	159.90	—	—	+1.00	—	—	—	—
Outlays	139.23	140.10	139.30	—	—	—	—	—	—	—
920 Allowances										
Budget Authority	4.99	0.60	0.80	0.80	0.80	0.80	0.80	1.80	2.80	2.85
Outlays	2.96	0.70	0.80	0.80	0.80	0.80	0.80	1.00	1.30	1.15
Package Subtotal										
Budget Authority	50.41	48.40	49.70	50.80	50.80	51.90	51.80	51.80	51.80	51.85
Outlays	47.86	45.30	47.30	47.30	46.60	47.30	47.90	47.50	47.80	47.65
Revenues	363.00	362.40	362.70	362.50	362.40	362.50	363.00	362.50	362.70	362.50
Deficit	52.44	50.20	51.00	50.50	49.90	50.50	50.55	50.65	50.75	50.80

Source: Author's calculations from data in the unpublished transcript of the conference on the first concurrent resolution for FY 1977.

[a]FCR = first concurrent resolution.

[b]SBC = Senate Budget Committee.

121

Some of the counteroffers are rejected by the side of the author making the motion before they can be tendered to the other chamber's conferees. Thus, Senator Domenici's motion, which represented the Republican position, was rejected by the Senate conferees.

The sequence of counteroffers in table 5.3 represents the Senate moving toward the House position. In doing so, the Senate conferees sought to avoid the high degree of conflict that would have resulted from redistributive bargaining; instead, they sought funds from functions for which funding levels were, at that stage in the budget cycle, almost totally determined by forces beyond the control of Congress. In order to accomplish this feat, the conferees settled the smaller, less contentious functions in favor of whichever side had the lower estimate. Then they made adjustments in those functions most determined by estimates—interest, allowances, and undistributed offsetting receipts—in order to free funds to reestablish the distributive pattern of the final compromise.[29]

The Senate began the bargaining, having "saved" $800 million by previously agreeing to lower estimates for the income security function. The House countered by asking for $700 million more in the two crucial functions—450 and 500. This increase was cushioned when the House lowered its estimates for allowances by $200 million, thus limiting the aggregate increase to $500 million. The Domenici motion, although rejected by his own side, was crucial because it signaled that the Senate Republican conferees were willing to accept the House number for public service employment. The House, having won that disagreement, then compromised by lowering its previous offer for the crucial public works function, 450, by $100 million and lowering the allowances estimate by an additional $100 million. The final offer of Senator Bellmon reallocated $50 million from the House money for public works to the Senate's preferred public service employment stimulus.

This pattern of limiting redistributive conflict by lowering estimates for other functions is repeated in the FY 1977 sequence (see table 5.4). In this case, the Senate took the initial position that the House's stimulus funds in the allowances function should be redistributed to the program functions. As one surveys the offers, one sees a general pattern of the Senate moving toward the House's position. Once again, the margin of disagreement was quite small, and the conferees sought to manipulate estimates—in this case, revenues—to free a little extra money for distributive bargaining. This sequence even included a side payment when Senator Moss (acting as Senate chairman in Muskie's absence) offered an additional $1 billion in budget authority for the income security function in return for the House's acceptance of distribution of its funds previously contained in allowances.

The Senate opened with an offer quite similar to its conference mark (the only exception being the higher budget authority level for function 300). Senator Bellmon then offered the Senate Republican alternative, aimed at lowering the deficit below $50 billion. This offer was rejected by the Senate conferees. Moss then restated his offer, which had been rejected verbally but not formally by the House conferees, with the "sweetener" of the income security side payment. The House conferees counteroffered by distributing their stimulus package across the functions. This had the effect of providing a basis for negotiations because, although the House had not compromised on its desired level of funding, it had shown the Senate what its package would look like against the Senate numbers.

The Senate then counteroffered by saying, in effect, "we will give in to your desire to have a stimulus pot in allowances if you lower your outlay level by $400 million." However, the Senate counteroffer also reduced the budget authority for stimulus programs in the House's counteroffer by $1.6 billion. This was done in order to maintain the Senate's desired funding level of $18 billion for function 300, the category containing EPA waste-water sewer grants, a program sponsored by Senator Muskie.

The House counteroffered again by shifting $1 billion of the $1.6 billion in budget authority that the Senate wanted for the EPA grants to the allowances function. The Senate had agreed to the House's concept of a pool of allowance funding for stimulus programs if the House came two-thirds of the way to the Senate's funding level for EPA waste-water treatment grants. At that point, the budget authority numbers were set; what remained was the final, and successful, Senate attempt to trade a $150 million outlay reduction in the House stimulus package for a $50 million increase in that package's budget authority.

The sequence of counteroffers in table 5.4 illustrates the classic side-payments pattern of one side granting (or seeking) increases in budget authority in return for getting its way on outlays. This is the traditional manner of avoiding redistributive conflict in budgetary disputes within the executive branch. Outlays are constrained by the deficit. But budget authority—for construction programs, for example—takes several years to turn into outlays. This is particularly true for waste-water treatment grants. In the counteroffers for function 300 in table 5.4, the outlay estimates never changed, although the budget authority levels varied by $3.6 billion. This is because the Treasury will only make payments for these grants upon completion of the various construction contracts, and such contracts take several years to complete. Thus, the Senate could increase funding for its favorite program while agreeing to higher levels of outlays for the House stimulus program without dramatic increases in the deficit.[30]

The final pattern that emerges from the sequences of offers and counter-offers set out in tables 5.3 and 5.4 is that, at the crucial moment, the Senate conferees were willing to drop their opposition to the House practice of going beyond a hundredth of a billion dollars in order to split the difference and reach agreement. In each sequence, the final Senate offer was made at a tenth of a billion dollars.

WINNING IN CONFERENCE

We now consider which chamber tends to win on which issues in budget resolution conferences (see table 5.5). Final conference numbers for each budget function are grouped into five categories. If the final result equals or exceeds (in the direction from the midpoint to the House number) the House resolution number, the result is coded *1*. If the result is between the midpoint (the point that represents a ''split-the-difference'' result) and the House resolution number, it is coded *2*. If the conference agreement is at the split-the-difference midpoint, it is coded *3*. If the result is between the midpoint and the Senate goal, as reflected in the SBC chairman's mark, it is coded *4*. Finally, if the result is greater than the SBC chairman's mark, it is coded *5*.[31]

Table 5.5 contains the percentage distribution for each function for thirteen conference agreements. It also contains a mean score for each function. A mean of *3* indicates equal numbers of House and Senate victories, numbers greater than *3* imply a pattern of Senate victories, and numbers less than *3* suggest a predominance of House victories. Table 5.5 separates the results for budget authority and outlays, inasmuch as some interesting differences appear when the data are so displayed. Since no differences are evident between the patterns of winning on the first and second budget resolutions, these are combined into one table.

The data in table 5.5 indicate that the Senate conferees won more than their share of disputes on the level of funding in budget resolutions. Leaving aside the smaller, less controversial functions—750, 800, and 850—the House consistently won only three budget authority disputes—agriculture, income security, and veterans' benefits—and two outlay disputes, agriculture and veterans' benefits.

The Senate conferees not only won the functions about which they cared the most—national defense, natural resources and environment, and commerce and housing credit—they also appear to have consistently bested the House conferees in two areas near and dear to the House, the pork-barrel function of regional and community development and the education, training, and social services function.

The degree of Senate conference dominance is so great that, for the national defense, international affairs, natural resources and environment, commerce and housing credit, and community and regional development functions, the final conference agreement reached or exceeded the Senate's goal, as measured by its chairman's mark, more often that it was on the House side of the midpoint.

WHY THE SENATE TENDS TO WIN IN BUDGET CONFERENCES

Prior research on the nature of appropriations and revenue bill conferences has stressed the importance of sequencing on outcomes. Fenno, Manley, and Strom and Rundquist have all suggested that what appear to be Senate victories are actually bargains whereby the House conferees agree to Senate amendments in return for Senate acquiescence to the House-drawn bills.[32] This traditional explanation is not applicable to budget resolution conferences, since each chamber's resolution is developed independently of the actions of the other house.

To understand the Senate pattern of conference success, it is helpful to think of conferences as examples of small-group bargaining. As many writers have pointed out, the goals of such bargaining are limited. "Conferees want to sustain the position of their respective chambers on the bill, and they want to receive a result acceptable to a majority of both chambers."[33]

Within this limited arena of conflict, however, each side brings to the bargaining sessions assets and liabilities, which, according to Fenno, can be grouped into two categories: external and internal. The major external influences are (1) the degree of unity of the parent chamber on the issues before the conference, (2) the degree of unity and power of the full committee, (3) possible intervention by the executive branch, (4) possible intervention by interest groups, and (5) limits on the nature of the bargaining process created by the rules of each house and the nature of the issues under dispute. Internal influences can be grouped into five categories: (1) the degree of unity within each group of conferees; (2) the interpersonal bargaining styles and skills of the conferees, especially the two chairmen; (3) the needs and demands of individual conferees who are perceived as "powers" within their own chamber; (4) the varying desire of individual conferees to "win"; and (5) the limits of time. The Senate managers tend to win in budget conferences because they have advantages in almost all of these categories.

External Factors. The basic external asset that the Senate managers brought to conference negotiations during the period under study was the

Table 5.5. Winning in Conference: Conference Agreement Compared to House and Senate Resolutions and to Senate Conference Mark

Function	Percentage Distribution of Budget Conference Results					Total	Mean Score
	At or Beyond House Resolution	From Mid-point to House Resolution	At Mid-point: Split the Difference	Midpoint to Senate Conference Mark	Conference Mark to Senate Resolution		
Budget Authority							
050 National Defense	8%	8%	31%	31%	23%	101%	3.5
150 International Affairs	0	23	8	31	38	100	3.8
250 General Science, Space, and Technology	0	0	77	8	15	100	3.4
270 Energy	14	14	14	29	29	100	3.7
300 Natural Resources and Environment	0	0	38	23	38	99	4.0
350 Agriculture	15	8	62	0	16	101	2.9
370 Commerce and Housing Credit	14	0	43	14	29	100	3.4
400 Transportation	8	23	8	38	23	100	3.5
450 Community and Regional Development	23	0	0	15	62	100	3.9
500 Education, Training, and Social Services	15	31	8	31	15	100	3.0
550 Health	23	0	31	23	23	100	3.2
600 Income Security	25	33	25	8	8	99	2.4
700 Veterans' Benefits and Services	31	8	23	31	8	101	2.8
750 Administration of Justice	15	15	31	0	38	99	3.3
800 General Government	15	8	54	0	23	100	3.1
850 General Purpose Fiscal Assistance	23	0	54	8	15	100	2.9
900 Interest	31	0	31	15	23	100	3.0
920 Allowances	0	17	8	17	58	100	4.3
950 Undistributed Offsetting Receipts	8	0	31	23	39	101	3.9

Table 5.5. (*continued*)

Outlays

050 National Defense	15	0	31	15	38	101	3.6
150 International Affairs	8	0	46	8	38	100	3.7
250 General Science, Space, and Technology	0	0	77	0	23	100	3.5
270 Energy	14	8	14	57	14	99	3.6
300 Natural Resources and Environment	15	15	15	31	23	101	3.5
350 Agriculture	31	14	31	8	15	100	2.6
370 Commerce and Housing Credit	0	14	43	14	29	100	3.6
400 Transportation	8	0	15	31	46	100	4.1
450 Community and Regional Development	15	8	23	8	46	100	3.6
500 Education, Training, and Social Services	23	23	0	31	23	100	3.1
550 Health	23	0	46	8	23	100	3.1
600 Income Security	8	15	15	15	46	99	4.0
700 Veterans' Benefits and Services	23	15	38	15	8	99	2.7
750 Administration of Justice	8	15	69	0	8	100	2.8
800 General Government	23	8	38	15	15	99	2.9
850 General Purpose Fiscal Assistance	15	0	54	8	23	100	3.2
900 Interest	31	0	31	15	23	100	3.0
920 Allowances	0	8	0	25	66	99	4.6
950 Undistributed Offsetting Receipts	8	0	31	23	39	101	3.9

Source: Author's calculations from unpublished data for the thirteen budget conferences from calendar years 1975 through 1980.

fact that their resolutions had been passed by a two-thirds majority whereas the House resolutions were frequently enacted by fewer than five votes. Furthermore, the Senate vote had generally been bipartisan; whereas in the House it had been highly partisan. Until 1981 over three-quarters of the Senate's Democrats and about half of the Republican members voted for budget resolutions. In the House, the majority for passage has to come from Democrats since Republican support is frequently limited to fewer than five votes.

This pattern of Senate unity and House division is also found within the two budget committees. The typical pattern is for two-thirds of the Republican members to vote for and support the Senate Budget Committee's resolutions. Except in a few cases, in which a liberal Democrat withholds support in protest, all SBC Democrats have voted for budget resolutions. In the House, Republican members of the Budget Committee consistently vote against their committee's resolutions in the committee and on the floor.

In conference this meant that Senator Muskie could lead from a position of strength. He could threaten (and in one case invoke) what many writers on conferences consider the ultimate threat—returning to the Senate for instructions.[34] As Fenno has pointed out:

> When the conferees cannot come to a decision without taking their disagreement back to the House and Senate for help or instructions, they become engaged in a new pattern of decision-making. The nature of the game changes from one in which the conferees were free to bargain subject to their own intergroup relationships to one in which the conferees become bound to positions fixed outside the conference room. In the latter case, we have the proto-type of dependent decision-making in conference committee.[35]

Lacking political support in their own chamber, the House managers were never able to use the threat of asking for instructions as a lever to obtain Senate concessions. House threats in conference were pleadings for help in getting the conference compromise through their chamber, while Senate threats were made from positions of electoral strength.

The precarious nature of the House coalition made it possible for the executive branch to influence the House managers. In the spring of 1980, for example, the Carter administration successfully opposed a conference agreement on the House floor because it felt that the conferees had included too high a budget authority target for national defense funding.

The House coalition was also so precarious that various interests could exercise great power, relative to the acceptance of the conference outcome. In the fall of 1979, Rep. David Obey led an effort that caused the rejection of the conference agreement because he and a number of liberal interest groups felt that the agreement had slighted funding for human services programs.

Thus, House conferees, because of their external weaknesses in the House Budget Committee and on the House floor, bargain from a position of relative disadvantage.

Internal Influences.   The weak position of the House extends to the make-up of the conference. Because the Republican managers have refused to sign the conference agreement (or to support it on the floor of the House or in the Budget Committee), the House Democrats have found themselves to be a minority within the conference. Although voting in conference takes place within delegations from each chamber, the debate is rather free flowing. The House Democrats have continually faced a situation in which their Republican colleagues have supported the Senate position but then refused to support compromises based on that position. The House conferees have also found themselves isolated from their Senate Democratic colleagues, who have formed bipartisan conservative, pro–budget cutting coalitions with Senate Republicans. In Congress, it appears that coalitions based on committee norms are stronger than those based on party loyalty. This fact has undermined the House manager's position in conference.

The requirement for rotation of the members of the House Budget Committee has also weakened the House's position by negating the traditional House advantage of greater knowledge of legislative detail. Allen Schick points out that the pattern of conference decisions turned in the Senate's favor at the beginning of the 95th Congress, when almost half the Democrats on the House Budget Committee were replaced. Schick quotes a frustrated Rep. Robert Leggett, "The fact of the matter is that the members on the Senate committee are constantly and continually gaining in stature and position and aggressiveness, and this makes it extremely difficult for us to bargain with them when we are junior members and they have this high degree of seniority which they are continually gaining."[36]

The nature of the issues before the conferees has also favored the Senate. The budget process, unlike legislation of revenues and appropriations, does not put a premium on knowledge of legislative detail. The comparative advantage of the budget committee is budget stabilization (macroeconomic) and allocation (priorities) policy. This emphasis on the "big picture" runs counter to traditional House norms.

Given the weak House position during the period under study, the Senate was led by an ideal chairman in Muskie. Different members bring varying bargaining skills and styles to conference committee confrontations. Members vary in terms of their style of advocacy, willingness to compromise, stubbornness, bluster, use of threats, and patience.[37] Senator Hollings, for example, is generally described as a superb cloakroom politician. He has little desire to prolong a conference and is willing to reach quick compromises by using his interpersonal skills in private. Congressman Giaimo, while privately willing to compromise, acted as an extreme advocate in public sessions in order to support and unify his fragile coalition.

Muskie's style was one of extreme patience. He sought to exploit time. Although he had a chairman's mark, he rarely suggested offers either to his side or to the House conferees. He preferred to wait until all the proposals were put on the table and then suggest a compromise. His interpersonal skills, relative to those of someone like Hollings, were weak. His strength came from his general intelligence and his apparent willingness to wait "forever."

A strategy of waiting for the other side to give in was ideal as long as the Senate dealt from a position of strength. Given the greater unity on the Senate side in committee and on the floor, the longer the conference went on, the greater the danger that external forces would make it impossible for the House managers to get the House to agree to the conference report.

Faced with Muskie's apparent willingness to wait forever, the House had to resort to arguments that stressed its weak position. Constant references were made to the need to "keep faith" with various House committees. The House conferees frequently claimed that, unless they could say they had won on an issue, the House would reject the agreement and the budget process would be destroyed. The difficulty with such arguments is that, over time, they lose their effectiveness. This was especially true after the budget process had survived a House rejection of a conference agreement, as it did in the spring of 1979.[38]

Conclusion

A major hypothesis of this chapter is that the procedures of the Congressional Budget Act have increased the power of the Senate in monetary matters. In the past, the required sequencing of money bill action allowed the House to set the terms of debate, with the Senate acting merely as an "appeals court" to the House decision. Since 1974, however, budget resolutions have been developed simultaneously in the two chambers; thus, the basic outlines of budget resolutions have been influenced as much by Senate action as by that of the House.

Once budget resolutions go to conference, the Senate tends to win most of the issues in dispute, including those that it considers most important. Several factors appear to account for this result. First, because budget resolutions set aggregate totals for spending and receipts, the traditional House advantage of greater expertise is reduced. Second, the House has handicapped its position by requiring that the membership of the House Budget Committee be rotated periodically. Finally, at least during the 1970s, the bipartisan support in committee and on the floor put the Senate conferees in a stronger position than their House counterparts.

Since 1974, Congress has been affected by two waves of budget reform. The first came about with the enactment of the Congressional Budget Act. The second occurred when Congress implemented a reconciliation process in calendar year 1980 as part of the passage of the first concurrent resolution for FY 1981. Whereas the first wave of budget reform attempted to influence the enactment of legislation through internal targets, the second wave set up a process that mandated legislative changes to meet certain monetary goals by particular dates.

The implementation of reconciliation in association with the timetable of budget resolutions has meant that the Senate can now act before the House on tax bills and legislation affecting the appropriation of budget authority. In the environment of the early 1980s, when the two chambers have been controlled by different parties, the ability of the Senate to act before the House has given the Republican leadership a major tool for forcing Democratic action.

The reconciliation process, coupled with split party control, has also led to an increase in interchamber interaction. The first wave of budget reform did not affect the level of interaction between the chambers. Periodically, there was somewhat more staff interaction, but that was the exception. However, the massive undertaking of compiling a reconciliation package has forced greater communication between the chambers. Although most of the increase in the level of interaction has resulted from the need to handle the complexity of the reconciliation process, part of it has been attributable to the split party control of Congress, as the minority Republicans in the House sought help and counsel from the majority members and staff in the Senate.

The patterns described in this chapter lead to a number of questions that cannot be fully assessed here. Will the shift in power toward the Senate be permanent? Can the House overcome the effects resulting from the deterioration of the sequencing norms through rules changes (e.g., abolishing the rotating membership of the House Budget Committee); changes in decision-making style (e.g., concentrating more on the "big picture"); or political changes (e.g., building bipartisan coalitions to support its budget action)? And, most important, can Congress cope with a process that requires a dramatic increase in coordination?

The two waves of budget reform have made the political life of the average member of Congress more difficult. Within Congress, the daily routine has become much more complex as budgeting has come to dominate the calendar. Budgeting requires coordination. As the first wave of budget reform was supplemented by the second, congressional budgeting became more like executive budgeting—the parts and the whole had to balance, and decisions that in the past had been handled in a distributive fashion had to be addressed in a redistributive manner. Thus, we are left with the inevitable question that always arises in discussions of congressional budgeting: Can Congress live with the constraints that are inherent in the true exercise of budgeting?

6

Reform, Congress, and the President

DENNIS S. IPPOLITO

The power of the purse is generally considered to be the major bulwark of congressional authority, "underpinning all other legislative decisions and regulating the balance of influence between the legislative and executive branches of government."[1] But while the reach of its taxing and spending powers is clearly substantial, Congress has often been frustrated in its attempts to exercise those powers consistently and effectively. Part of this frustration can be attributed to periodic conflicts among taxing, authorizing, and appropriations committees. In addition to these internal tensions, Congress has, at various times, encountered executive encroachments upon its prerogatives and endured unfavorable comparisons between its budget process and procedures and those of the executive branch.

As a result, there have been several attempts to reorganize congressional budgeting in order to resolve internal problems and counter the developing power of the executive branch. The most recent, the Congressional Budget and Impoundment Control Act, established a congressional budgetary process designed to counter presidential influence over fiscal policy, spending priorities, and budget implementation. According to an exuberant congressional proponent, the 1974 budget reform legislation was "one of the most monumental reassertions of congressional prerogatives in this century."[2] Richard Neustadt concluded that, among the many congressional initiatives of the early 1970s, "in the budget process Congress has reached for a tool which—if it musters leadership to handle—does create a sort of parity with any President, across the board of governmental programs."[3]

For those who expected a dramatic shift in budgetary influence from the White House to Capitol Hill, the actual impact of the 1974 Budget Act has probably been disappointing. Indeed, the Reagan administration's skilled maneuvering of the congressional budget process in the spring of 1981 suggested that presidential control of budget policy might have been facilitated rather than checked by congressional budget reform. Without the

133

procedural assistance provided by concurrent budget resolutions and reconciliation bills, for example, it is difficult to imagine such quick and
wholesale implementation of any president's budget program. The obvious
conclusion, it might appear, is that budget reform has made Congress more,
rather than less, vulnerable to presidential domination. There is, however, a
different and perhaps more accurate interpretation of the background and
impact of the 1974 reform initiative, which suggests that the executive-
legislative power balance was not and is not especially disadvantageous to
Congress. Prior to 1974, Congress had substantially expanded its control
over spending policy. That control has been preserved and strengthened by
congressional checks on impoundment. The continuing and as yet unre-
solved problem for Congress is to reconcile an independent budgetary
process with political and economic pressures for spending control.

The Background of Budget Reform

If impoundment controls—Title X of the 1974 Congressional Budget
Act—can legitimately be explained as a direct congressional response to
executive usurpation, the budget reform provisions contained in that measure hardly represent a parallel case. Those claims were often advanced
during congressional debates and accepted by analysts such as Joel Havemann, who said that prior to 1974 "Congress could do little more than tinker
with the President's proposals . . . could not possibly substitute its own
economic policies or spending priorities . . .[and had] yielded its power of
the purse to the President."[4] Those claims are, at best, exaggerations that
reflect the rhetorical excesses of the Nixon years. Over the preceding two
decades, Congress had enacted major changes in spending policy and
priorities and, more recently, has insulated a substantial share of the budget
from presidential influence. The final version of the Budget Act had
considerably more to do with the distribution of power among authorizing,
appropriating, and taxing committees in Congress than with executive-
legislative relationships. The most important feature of the new budgetary
process was that congressional discretion remained intact. The initial view,
that budget reform should facilitate spending control, was discarded in favor
of a process allowing Congress to take whatever spending or taxing actions it
wanted, as long as it used comprehensive procedures.

SPENDING PRIORITIES

The 1974 Congressional Budget Act requires Congress to set budget
totals and divide spending among the functional categories through use of

concurrent budget resolutions. This procedure enables Congress to set formal spending priorities, and it occasioned considerable enthusiasm among congressional liberals in 1974. Senator Alan Cranston, for example, declared that ''budget reform by itself can play an important role in upgrading the capability of Congress'' by allowing legislators to determine national priorities.[5] In the House, Congressman Jonathan Bingham echoed the view that Congress had somehow been excluded from decisions on spending priorities and welcomed the opportunity for ''meaningful debates on national priorities at the beginning of each Congress.''[6]

Congress had, however, already engineered the most profound change in spending priorities of the modern era—the ''welfare shift,'' which transformed federal budget policy between the mid-1950s and mid-1970s. During this period, Congress presided over rapid growth in total federal spending, a sharp decline in the defense share of the budget, and a corresponding increase in the allocation for social welfare programs. Congress managed this transformation during Republican and Democratic administrations, although it did so without formal statements about priorities.

The outlines of the welfare shift are shown in table 6.1. Between FY 1955 and FY 1975 (the last ''prereform'' budget), defense spending declined as a proportion of total outlays from almost 60 percent to approximately 25 percent; payments to individuals (primarily income assistance and income security programs) increased from less than 20 percent to over 45 percent of the total budget. The relative priorities accorded defense and social welfare were reversed, and the reversal was sharpest during the Nixon administration.

This change in spending priorities was accomplished by reserving the bulk of real spending growth for individual benefit programs. Defense spending in FY 1975 was more than 10 percent below its 1955 level, when measured in constant prices.[7] Payments for individuals, however, rose by nearly $100 billion in constant prices over the same period, thus accounting for some 80 percent of all the real growth in the federal budget. Of particular interest is the apparent inability of Republican presidents, especially Nixon, to arrest this trend. During the later Eisenhower years (FY 1955 through FY 1961), payments for individuals almost doubled in real terms; for Nixon, faced with a Democratic-controlled Congress throughout his tenure, real spending growth averaged almost 12 percent annually.[8] In the Kennedy-Johnson years, the comparable rate was less than 7 percent.[9] When the Democratic party controlled the White House and Congress, social welfare spending rose appreciably, and when a Democratic Congress faced a Republican president, social welfare spending rose even more rapidly. There may be more than one plausible interpretation for this phenomenon,

Table 6.1. Defense Outlays and Payments for Individuals as a Percentage of Total Outlays, Fiscal Years 1955–75

	Percentage of Total Outlays	
Fiscal Year	Defense	Payments for Individuals
1955	58.2%	19.0%
1960	49.0	24.8
1965	40.1	27.3
1970	40.2	32.3
1975	26.4	46.4

Source: Derived from *Budget of the United States Government* (Washington, D.C.: Government Printing Office, selected fiscal years).

but it hardly suggests that Congress was ceding budget supremacy to the president, at least in terms of spending policy, and certainly not during the Nixon presidency. When Nixon took office, "human resources" spending was slightly over $60 billion, or roughly 35 percent of total outlays; despite Nixon's sometimes impassioned opposition, these figures increased substantially each year, and by FY 1975, human resources spending was nearly $170 billion, or more than half of total outlays.[10]

UNCONTROLLABLE SPENDING AND APPROPRIATIONS

A second dimension of the balance in executive-legislative influence involves the growth in uncontrollable spending in the years prior to budget reform. By FY 1967, for example, relatively uncontrollable outlays represented some 60 percent of total spending. In FY 1975, the level was over 73 percent. The composition of the uncontrollable portion of the budget also changed over this period. Outlays from prior-year contracts and obligations accounted for 40 percent of total uncontrollable spending in 1967, compared with 45 percent for individual benefit programs. By FY 1975, the latter had climbed to well over 60 percent, whereas contracts and related costs had dropped to approximately 20 percent. By the mid-1970s, open-ended programs associated with social welfare accounted for almost half of all federal spending. Since this spending was automatic unless statutory changes in specific programs were made, presidential influence on budget policy was restricted. Congressional majorities were required to change existing law, which hardly placed the president at an advantage. The president could still use vetoes and veto threats, as well as less coercive techniques, to counter spending he opposed, but only for the shrinking portion of the budget governed by annual, discretionary appropriations.

If we examine congressional actions on presidential appropriations requests, the conventional wisdom regarding presidential budget dominance appears even more suspect. Between FY 1955 and FY 1969, congressional action on presidential appropriations requests was fairly predictable; some 90 percent of all regular appropriations bills were reduced below levels recommended by the president.[11] The result was an annual average reduction of approximately $3 billion.

In the early 1970s, however, Congress used the appropriations process much more selectively. There were consistent and substantial cuts in several areas. Between FY 1970 and FY 1975, Congress annually cut defense appropriations requests by an average of $3.8 billion in budget authority and $1.6 billion in outlays.[12] Annual reductions in appropriations requests for military construction and foreign operations were, on the average, approximately $900 million in budget authority and $200 million in outlays. At the same time, Congress regularly increased presidential budget requests in other areas. Taken together, the labor-HEW, HUD–independent agencies, agriculture, environment, and consumer protection appropriations bills enacted into law exceeded presidential recommendations by an annual average of $1.1 billion in budget authority and $300 million in outlays. Congress was able, then, to enforce selected appropriations cuts and, despite presidential vetoes, selected increases. Appropriations politics did not reveal presidential dominance.

By the time Congress was considering budget reform, a number of significant changes had already occurred in the presidential-congressional balance of power, with respect to spending policy. A shrinking portion of the annual budget was dependent upon discretionary appropriations, thus limiting the president's leverage. Congress was able to control discretionary appropriations in order to advance the long-term reversal in budget priorities between defense and social welfare, despite the determined opposition of the Nixon administration. Presidential vetoes were useless in countering congressional defense cuts and of limited effectiveness in preventing Congress from increasing spending in other areas. Congress had discarded its traditional guardianship role with respect to spending and restricted the president's ability to influence spending growth and priorities. Within Congress, this signified a shift of power away from the appropriations committees to the authorizing committees. As a result, short-term spending control was considerably more difficult for Congress to achieve, but the difficulties for a president with budget-cutting objectives were even more formidable. The Nixon vetoes and impoundments were signals of executive weakness, not strength.

The piecemeal and uncoordinated approach that Congress traditionally used in making annual budget decisions did concede an advantage in fiscal policy debates to the executive branch. Since Congress did not make formal decisions about the balance between total spending and total revenues prior to FY 1976, presidential totals had, as Aaron Wildavsky put it, an engaging, if undeserved, "magic": "Presidents naturally make up in assurance what they lack in knowledge. Although the executive's total is not entirely plucked out of the air, neither is it turned out down to the last decimal by some infallible sausage machine of modern economic science. The total so authoritatively proclaimed by one man is in fact a product of the fair guesses and wild surmises of many within the executive branch."[13]

The fact that presidential totals went unchallenged by Congress did not mean they were terribly influential in determining fiscal policy. Nor did it mean that the president's expenditure or revenue totals were governed by fiscal policy considerations. Indeed, the relative decline in discretionary spending prior to 1974 made it difficult to manipulate short-term spending, regardless of fiscal policy objectives.

The first unified budget, combining trust fund receipts and expenditures with regular receipts and expenditures, was presented for FY 1969. The executive branch had previously submitted three separate budgets— administrative, consolidated cash, and national income accounts. The administrative budget usually received the greatest emphasis, although there were occasional attempts to focus on alternative budgets when they showed lower deficits. With several sets of possible figures each year, the fiscal policy effects of the president's overall budget were difficult to identify. More important were specific presidential initiatives on taxing or spending legislation; over these Congress retained full discretion.

In addition, presidential totals were not self-executing. Estimating errors and inaccurate economic assumptions, as well as congressional actions, often frustrated presidential fiscal policy goals. The problems were especially noticeable on the spending side. Using administrative budget estimates, for example, spending was underestimated eleven out of fourteen times from FY 1955 to FY 1968, with the average annual error exceeding $4 billion. Revenue underestimates occurred as frequently as overestimates, with the annual error averaging almost $5 billion. The average projected balance between spending and revenue was in error by more than $5 billion annually.

From FY 1969 to FY 1975, when unified budgets were submitted by the executive branch, these problems continued. Outlays were usually more than presidential estimates, with the errors ranging from minor to substantial (see table 6.2). Revenue estimates were faulty in both directions, and surplus and deficit projections were often well off the mark. Under these circumstances, it is difficult to see how presidential totals could determine or control fiscal policy. Congress could and did retain sufficient discretion on both the spending and taxing sides to influence fiscal policy. What it could not do was develop and defend alternatives to presidential totals. This inability, regardless of its actual impact on fiscal policy control, created political difficulties for members of Congress during the Nixon presidency. Administration spokesmen repeatedly charged that Congress's piecemeal handling of the budget and the consequent absence of binding spending ceilings amounted to fiscal irresponsibility. By requiring Congress to establish overall spending and revenue totals in its annual budget resolutions and, at the same time, allowing Congress to change those totals without great difficulty, the authors of the Budget Act hoped to reduce Congress's vulnerability to presidential criticism. The argument that this would some-how correct a decided imbalance in fiscal policy between the two branches was misleading.

IMPOUNDMENT

If much of the antiexecutive rationale behind budget reform was hyper-bolic, the impoundment disputes with President Nixon were serious and quite genuine. Impoundments had occurred as early as the Jefferson admin-istration and had been used, with varying frequency, by the Roosevelt (FDR), Truman, Eisenhower, Kennedy, and Johnson administrations. Congress had, in fact, given President Johnson reasonably broad impound-ment authority to enforce an FY 1968 spending ceiling. In several important respects, however, the Nixon impoundments were distinctive and presented a unique challenge to Congress. They were substantially larger than those of earlier administrations, amounting, according to some estimates, to almost 20 percent of controllable expenditures.[14] They were aimed almost exclu-sively at domestic programs the president opposed and had unsuccessfully recommended for reduction or termination and were, for the most part, intended to be permanent. Between 1969 and 1973, tens of billions of dollars appropriated for more than one hundred programs were impounded. When the president went so far as to promise that impoundments would be instituted even if presidential spending vetoes were overridden, there was little doubt that Congress's power of the purse was being challenged in an unprecedented manner.

Table 6.2. Presidential Estimates and Actual Results, Fiscal Years 1969–75 (in billions of dollars)

	1969	1970 (Johnson)	1971	1972	1973	1974	1975
Outlays							
Original Budget	$186.1	$195.3	$200.8	$229.2	$246.2	$268.7	$304.4
Actual Budget	184.5	196.6	211.4	232.0	247.1	269.6	326.1
Change	− 1.6	+1.3	+10.6	+ 2.8	+ 0.9	+ 0.9	+21.8
Revenues							
Original Budget	178.1	198.7	202.1	217.6	220.8	256.0	295.0
Actual Budget	187.8	193.7	188.4	208.6	232.2	264.9	281.0
Change	+ 9.7	−5.0	−13.7	− 9.0	+11.4	+ 8.9	−14.0
Surplus (+) or Deficit (−)							
Original Budget	− 7.9	+ 3.4	+ 1.3	−11.6	−25.5	−12.7	− 9.4
Actual Budget	+ 3.2	− 2.8	−23.0	−23.4	−14.8	− 4.7	−45.2
Change	+11.1	− 6.2	−24.3	−11.8	+10.7	+ 8.0	−35.8

Source: Derived from *Budget of the United States Government* (Washington, D.C.: Government Printing Office, selected fiscal years).

Despite this, Congress could not immediately fashion an appropriate response. The House and Senate passed separate versions of impoundment control legislation in 1973, but conferees were unable to resolve serious conflicts over procedures. The certainty of a presidential veto added to the partisan and ideological difficulties in the two chambers. Finally, the impoundment control and budget reform initiatives were joined. The linkage brought together liberals opposed to budget reform and fiscal conservatives opposed to impoundment checks. In addition, there was recognition that the initiatives were genuinely complementary. As members of the House Rules Committee, which sponsored the linkage, stated, budget reform without impoundment checks "would leave Congress in a weak and ineffective position. No matter how prudently Congress discharges its appropriations responsibility, legislative decisions have no meaning if they can be unilaterally abrogated by executive impoundments."[15]

REFORM OBJECTIVES

The background of budget reform suggests two very different objectives. First, the necessity of countering presidential power was evinced chiefly in the impoundment section of the Budget Act, and the controls that Congress created under Title X were formidable. The second objective associated with budget reform had to do with the internal organization and politics of Congress, but the substitution of procedural for substantive criteria was quite evident.

The initial reform package sponsored by the Joint Study Committee on Budget Control was designed to facilitate spending reductions. However, neither the House nor the Senate was finally willing to accept this view. In the House, the Rules Committee eliminated many of the restrictive procedures in the Joint Study Committee package. The Senate Rules and Administration Committee, which prepared the final set of revisions on the Senate side, followed a parallel course. By the time budget reform had passed through the legislative process, it had become a very different creature. Congress would adopt comprehensive budgets to establish fiscal policy and spending priorities, but procedures would be flexible, additional budget resolutions would be readily available, and the overall process would not be biased in favor of spending reductions.

With regard to presidential-congressional relations, budget reform maintained (and, given impoundment controls, expanded) Congress's discretionary control over spending policy. As it had in the past, Congress could use this power to promote higher or lower spending—as well as larger or smaller deficits—than the president had requested. What course Congress took depended on the majority preferences of its members rather than on any particular conception of its role as "guardian of the Treasury" or spending advocate. If major political upheavals did not occur in Congress, post-1975 budget policy was likely to follow closely its prereform path. Moreover, the new process promised, at least for a time, the additional benefit of protecting Congress from criticisms about antiquated procedures and fiscal laxity.

Congress and the President

The implementation of congressional budget reform that commenced with the FY 1976 budget does not appear to have substantially altered the balance of budgetary power between Congress and the president. Disputes between the two branches over fiscal policy and spending control typically show no clear winner but rather reflect the continued inability of both sides to determine short-term spending. Indeed, when Congress and the executive branch have agreed on spending policy, they have still been unable to achieve the desired results. The insulation of a good portion of the budget from presidential influence also carries an institutional price for Congress.

SPENDING POLICY

The rate of spending growth for the FY 1976 – 82 period averaged over 12 percent annually, compared with a 10 percent annual rate for FY 1970 through FY 1975. In addition, it was usually at variance with both congressional and executive projections (see table 6.3). During the Ford presidency, congressional spending targets were set well above presidential requests. FY 1976 spending growth was almost exactly what Congress had projected, but in FY 1977, the rate of growth was actually closer to the original Ford budget. For FY 1978 through FY 1981, the spending levels in the Carter administration and congressional budgets were almost indistinguishable, but the effects of this agreement were mixed. Spending growth in FY 1978 was well below the Carter / congressional projections. In the Carter and congressional budgets for FY 1980 and FY 1981, however, the errors in the opposite direction were enormous. The same was true for the Reagan and congressional budgets for FY 1982. This volatility indicates that, under present conditions, neither Congress nor the president can consistently exercise effective short-term control over spending. Whatever policy disputes or agreements there might be can simply be overwhelmed by

Table 6.3.   Projected and Actual Spending Growth, Fiscal Years 1976–82

	Percentage Increase in Outlays		
Fiscal Year	Presidential Budget	Congressional First Resolution	Actual Results
1976	7.1%	12.5%	12.4%
1977	7.6	12.8	9.9
1978			
Ford	9.3	14.4	11.9
Carter	14.1	—	—
1979	10.9	10.6	9.5
1980	7.7	7.7	17.4
1981	6.3	5.8	14.0
1982			
Carter	11.9	6.1	10.8
Reagan	5.3	—	—

Source: Derived from *Budget of the United States Government* (Washington, D.C.: Government Printing Office, selected fiscal years).

estimating errors and unanticipated changes in the economy. At one time, both the Ford and Carter administrations were committed to the Reagan goal of reducing overall spending to approximately 20 percent of GNP, yet neither achieved any significant progress toward that goal. The continued expansion of the uncontrollable portion of the budget, along with likely trends in defense spending, suggest that this goal is equally elusive now.

If one is hard-pressed to find evidence that budget reform has strengthened Congress's ability to control spending, there are indications that spending priorities have shifted slightly. The shifts, however, have not been particularly pronounced in terms of defense versus nondefense spending, at least for that portion of the latter devoted to individual benefit programs (see table 6.4). The defense share of the budget has increased since its low point in FY 1978, but not at the expense of payments for individuals. Rather, within the nondefense portion of the budget, there has been a marked decline in the largely discretionary "all other" category. This was well under way when the Reagan administration took office, and the president's program is predicated upon a continuation of this trend. The projected increases in the defense share for FY 1983 and FY 1984 — to almost a 30 percent level—are accommodated almost entirely by reduced shares for interest and discretionary nondefense programs. In addition, the Reagan program depends upon long-term reductions in the absolute costs for the latter.

Table 6.4. Composition of Budget Outlays, Fiscal Years 1975–82

Fiscal Year	Defense	Nondefense		
		Payments for Individuals	Net Interest	All Other
1975	26.4%	46.4%	7.1%	20.0%
1976	24.5	48.4	7.3	19.7
1977	24.3	48.0	7.5	20.2
1978	23.5	46.0	7.9	22.6
1979	24.0	46.3	8.7	21.0
1980	23.6	47.0	9.1	20.3
1981	24.3	48.2	10.4	17.0
1982	25.7	47.8	11.6	14.8

Source: Budget of the United States Government, Fiscal Year 1984 (Washington, D.C.: Government Printing Office, 1983).

The defense–social welfare dimension of the budget priorities debate is still extremely important, but it does not represent the exclusive focus of current budgetary problems. If budget priorities are shifted toward substantial budgetary growth, as has been the case in the past, then "either / or" competition between defense and nondefense programs can be minimized. If, however, these shifts must be accommodated along with low rates of budgetary growth, direct competition is unavoidable.

The real test for the congressional budget process is the simultaneous redirection of budget growth and budget priorities. And the major constraint that Congress faces is not superior presidential influence but the increasing momentum of automatic spending. If Congress's power of the purse appears shaky, the cause lies in past spending commitments that Congress has already made.

FISCAL POLICY

The congressional budget process put into place by the 1974 Budget Act would, it was promised, allow Congress to coordinate spending and revenue decisions and thereby set independent fiscal policy. This expectation, which represented a generous endorsement of Congress's policy-making capabilities, has lately given way to confusion and controversy. There is no serious question about Congress being able to pursue a fiscal policy course independent of the executive branch. Instead, there are concerns about conventional fiscal policy solutions, the suitability of annual budgets for determining macroeconomic policy, and most important, the degree of control the congressional budgetary process can impose on spending and deficits.

The differences between congressional and executive branch fiscal policy preferences during the Ford administration emerged quickly and followed predictable lines. Congressional budget resolutions projected higher spending levels and larger deficits than President Ford had recommended; Congress also relied more heavily on spending stimulus than on tax cuts, in contrast to the Ford proposals. There was some congressional sensitivity to the deficit issue, which initially led to tentativeness in asserting a distinct policy approach; more importantly, spending shortfalls in FY 1977 and FY 1978 resulted in actual deficits that were closer to the original Ford budgets than to the corresponding congressional budgets. A clear-cut winner in the Ford-Congress fiscal policy disputes was hard to establish because budget totals were affected by economic factors over which neither side had much control.

Despite these difficulties in 1975 and 1976, Congress remained confident about its fiscal policy capabilities, and the election of Jimmy Carter promised a less critical atmosphere in which to apply fiscal stimulus. There was, in fact, general agreement between Congress and the executive branch during the entire Carter presidency. Unfortunately, fiscal policy implementation and its results proved troublesome. Spending shortfalls gave way to massive and embarrassing overspending; simultaneous high inflation and high unemployment complicated fiscal policy choices. Strategies that Congress and the administration originally thought would work eventually appeared to be economically and politically risky, but spending pressures prevented policy adjustments.

The FY 1978 and FY 1979 budgets came in well below the deficit projections set by Carter and Congress, due to spending overestimates and revenue underestimates. Subsequent budgets, however, shattered any illusions about spending control and fiscal policy. President Carter's FY 1980 budget, self-described as "lean and austere," emphasized his "commitment to hold the deficit to $30 billion or less and to move in the direction of a balanced budget."[16] The first congressional budget for FY 1980 was even more optimistic, reducing the projected deficit to $23 billion. In the fall, Congress was forced to raise its spending and deficit projections, although it managed to keep the latter under $30 billion by employing economic assumptions and spending estimates that were more hopeful than realistic. The inevitable result was a third resolution for FY 1980 — which Congress had earlier pledged to avoid—that raised the outlay ceiling by $40 billion and doubled the deficit projection.

By the time the "binding" FY 1980 budget had been abandoned, however, attention was being diverted to the balanced budget being planned for FY 1981. Under pressure from House and Senate Democratic leaders, Carter revised his original FY 1981 budget to show a surplus, and the budget committees followed with balanced budget plans. Moreover, the budget committees launched a concerted effort to tighten spending control by incorporating reconciliation instructions into the first concurrent resolution for FY 1981. It quickly became apparent, however, that the 1981 budget would be far from balanced, regardless of the reconciliation initiative. Congress preserved the figment of a balanced budget by postponing action on a second resolution until after the election, which showed that institutional credibility was less of a concern than electoral politics. However, even this tardy adjustment was far from sufficient. FY 1981 spending turned out to be much higher than estimated, and the deficit matched the 1980 level.

The FY 1982 budget followed a similarly disconcerting path. President Reagan persuaded Congress to adopt a first concurrent budget resolution for FY 1982 that reduced total spending well below the level projected by the Carter administration. Once again, reconciliation was tied to the spring budget resolution, and this time Congress moved quickly to pass a massive reconciliation measure. This was followed by an even more dramatic tax cut. However, the subsequent euphoria was short-lived. The economic assumptions upon which the Reagan and congressional budgets had been based soon proved to be faulty. As a result, spending was greatly underestimated, revenues were overestimated, and the FY 1982 deficit reached an unprecedented $110.7 billion. Similar errors appeared in the Reagan and congressional budgets for FY 1983.

When budget figures change constantly and dramatically, it is difficult to talk about "deliberate" fiscal policy or to argue that fiscal policy governs, rather than results from, spending pressures. During the Carter years, the early prescription for a strong spending stimulus gave way to attempted restraint. Despite the impressive unity between Congress and the executive branch, the spending increases and deficits that emerged hardly amounted to restraint. The obvious similarities between the planned Carter and congressional budgets for FY 1980 and FY 1981, along with the indistinguishable Reagan and congressional budgets for FY 1982—and the extent to which they have all missed the mark—strongly suggest that spending / deficit problems will not disappear soon, regardless of the partisan and ideological shifts in Congress.

The congressional fiscal policy experiment should not be dismissed as a failure, but it has not been the institutional boon many lawmakers once expected. It does appear that the decision-making process has been marginally strengthened, with members of Congress now routinely considering the economic implications of taxing and spending decisions. Congress is also probably more accountable, since it must set forth its fiscal plans—something it could avoid doing prior to the requirement for annual budget resolutions.

Unfortunately, a better process does not insure better policy, and neither Congress nor the executive branch has an impressive record of managing the budget or the economy. There is a common shortcoming—an inability to implement fiscal policies that substantially restrain spending pressures. It should be noted that Congress has not simply used fiscal policy arguments to rationalize spending and deficits. Efforts to reverse a spending-generated stimulus have been overwhelmed by unanticipated growth in mandatory spending programs, notably indexed entitlements, and by the general reluctance in Congress to restrain these programs. Despite recent budget "cuts," spending, not fiscal policy, continues to dominate the congressional budget process.

IMPOUNDMENT

Perhaps the most conspicuous success of the 1974 Budget Act has been in the one area in which congressional prerogatives were being genuinely challenged—impoundment. President Ford, for example, continued the Nixon pattern of widespread policy-based impoundments until the last months of his administration. Over two and a half years, Ford proposed 150 rescissions, most of which were policy based, and 330 deferrals, a substantial number of which were also policy based.[17]

Congress refused to enact approximately 90 percent of the requested rescissions and also disapproved nearly $10 billion in proposed deferrals for FY 1975 and FY 1976.[18] It was especially zealous in guarding its domestic spending priorities and social program preferences. Reaction was particularly negative among legislators of both parties when impoundments were directed against congressional add-ons—appropriations in excess of presidential recommendations. As a result, Ford's attempted use of impoundments as item vetoes was largely unsuccessful. Technical procedures were sometimes exploited to delay spending, but congressional spending preferences were never seriously threatened, as they had been by Nixon.

Under Carter, the deferral process generated few controversies, with no congressional disapprovals in FY 1977 and only isolated ones thereafter. Rescission procedures, however, were indirectly challenged by Congress in battles over weapons systems and water-resource projects, as the administration sought to cancel programs in advance of congressional review through termination or curtailment of projects.[19] These actions were not formal impoundments, but, according to some legislators, they gave the executive branch unwarranted additional influence over the final congressional decisions. For the most part, however, Congress was able to employ its controls over policy-based rescissions effectively.

Initially, the Reagan administration aggressively employed rescission and deferral procedures and had considerable success doing so. As part of the FY 1981 supplemental appropriation passed in June 1981, for example, Congress rescinded $14.3 billion in previous appropriations, only slightly less than the $15.1 billion requested by the administration. With the exception of selected programs administered by the Departments of Labor, Health and Human Services, and Education, the specific reductions approved by Congress conformed very closely to those proposed by President Reagan. Congress also agreed to defer almost $5 billion in FY 1981 spending until FY 1982, thus actually increasing the total that had been requested by the administration.

Indeed, reductions of this magnitude were necessary to accommodate the FY 1981 supplemental appropriation within the spending ceiling set by the revised budget resolution that had been passed in May. That ceiling was nearly $50 billion above the target established by the first concurrent budget resolution for FY 1981, suggesting that fiscal realities provided much of the impetus for Congress's acceptance of this unprecedented rescission initiative. During FY 1982, the Reagan administration used selective deferrals to restrain spending in the apparent hope that Congress would enact appropriations cuts or eventually agree to rescission requests. However, only limited changes were finally adopted in response to spending reduction requests.

The relevant point is that Congress has refused to weaken or eliminate the impoundment controls created by the 1974 Budget Act. Regardless of the fate of Reagan's past or future rescission requests, there has been an overwhelmingly negative congressional response to proposals that would broaden the president's discretionary spending authority. The 1983 Supreme Court decision in *Immigration and Naturalization Service* v. *Chadha* has thrown the one-house veto procedure for deferrals into question, but the more important rescission checks remain in place. As long as the executive branch cannot unilaterally and permanently cut spending, the integrity of the congressional budget process remains adequately protected.

RECONCILIATION

When the House and Senate budget committees decided to employ the reconciliation procedure for the FY 1981 budget, there were, as might be expected, angry complaints from other committees, especially in the House. However, the complaints were directed at the budget committees, not the executive branch. When reconciliation was again used in the spring of 1981, this time more sweepingly and successfully, the executive branch received the broader and certainly the more scathing criticism. For example, the chairman of the House Rules Committee, Richard Bolling, denounced reconciliation as the "most brutal and blunt instrument used by a president in an attempt to control the congressional process since Nixon used impoundment." The Reagan administration, according to Bolling, had engaged in "the most excessive use of presidential power and license."[20]

There is no doubt that the Reagan budget program benefited, at least in the short term, from the comprehensive reconciliation procedure. Authorizing committees were circumvented in a fashion difficult to imagine, utilizing a piecemeal approach. The reconciliation umbrella sheltered a number of programmatic changes and even nonbudgetary initiatives that Congress was unlikely to pass otherwise. The subsequent reaction against reconciliation was sufficiently widespread to raise concerns about the future of the budget process and the power of the budget committees. Nevertheless, another successful, although more limited, reconciliation effort was completed in 1982.

It may be that Congress's occasional embrace of reconciliation is an abdication to the executive branch. Whether to place the onus for this on the budget process and the budget committees is a much more complicated judgment. The justification for neutralizing the process in 1974 was to allow congressional majorities to express their "will on spending policy." Prior to 1980 that will kept reconciliation from being successfully invoked, even in the second budget resolution. Thus, spending committees were under little serious pressure to achieve "legislative savings" goals incorporated in budget resolutions. The creators of the 1974 Budget Act envisioned that the second budget resolution would be binding, except in extraordinary circumstances. However, third budget resolutions have been routinely used to raise spending ceilings and to accommodate discretionary and nondiscretionary spending increases. After the FY 1980 and 1981 spending debacles, it should not have been surprising to find growing congressional concern about the autonomy that spending committees had preserved under the budget process.

If reconciliation truly makes Congress vulnerable to executive branch dominance—and this in itself is debatable—those who wish to preserve congressional independence must develop an alternative that allows Congress to enforce its judgments about acceptable spending totals as well as its preferences about desirable programs. This tension is an inherent feature of "coordinated and comprehensive" budgeting, and there is no reason to expect that it will always be resolved in favor of individual programs rather than totals. No purpose is served by having congressional budget resolutions that are not credible.

Conclusion

The central argument of this chapter is that budget reform has not significantly altered the balance of budgetary influence between the president and Congress. That balance of influence was not particularly disadvantageous to Congress prior to 1974 nor is it disadvantageous today. Impoundment is no longer an unchecked presidential weapon, and the potential reach of presidential vetoes is restricted by the seemingly inexorable expansion of nondiscretionary spending. Thus, the legislative power of the purse is, in terms of executive-congressional relations, the dominant feature of federal budgeting.

The insulation of the budget from presidential influence has not been without institutional costs for Congress. Automatic spending can frustrate congressional as well as executive budgetary goals. Spending growth is harder to control, budget priorities are more resistant to change, and fiscal policy determination can be frustratingly imprecise.

The real problem that Congress faces today is internal: how to resolve tensions between spending and control committees so that congressional policy judgments about spending are consistent and credible. Budget reform has not provided this resolution and, in its present form, is unlikely to do so. It is to this weakness, rather than the illusory specter of presidential omnipotence, that Congress should devote its attention.

President Reagan's budget "victories," which appear considerably less impressive now than they did when enacted, do not represent any substantial diminution in Congress's budgetary powers. They are, in large part, situational, growing out of the shared concerns of many members of Congress that spending growth has continued at unacceptably high levels. When these concerns are sufficiently widespread, Congress may appear to be vulnerable to presidential pressures. This vulnerability exists, however, because Congress has been unable to utilize its independent budget process to develop and implement an effective spending-control plan, not because the president wields superior budgetary powers.

EVALUATING
CONGRESSIONAL
BUDGET REFORM

7

The Congressional Budget: How Much Change? How Much Reform?

ROGER H. DAVIDSON

T he congressional budget process, its present formal structure dating from 1974, is both a puzzle and a paradox. It is a puzzle because few people understand how it works and fewer yet understand how it will work in the future. No one reading the provisions of the 1974 Budget Act was quite prepared for its application in 1980, or in succeeding years. And who, watching the reconciliation process at work since then, would dare to predict exactly what it will be like in six months or six years? Like the budget itself, the process is a moving target.

The paradox flows from the puzzle. Nearly everyone who witnessed the birth of the 1974 act, and those who subsequently wrote or commented on it, believed it was a momentous innovation on Congress's part. Even if the results were not immediately realized, it was argued, they were potentially far-reaching and beneficial; this argument was employed in rallying legislators to uphold "the process" during its first, controversial years. For those who were skeptics, President Reagan's ingenious use of the process as the vehicle for his initial legislative program would seem to be irrefutable evidence of the power of the new arrangements.

While few would deny the altered atmosphere on Capitol Hill, many observers seem unwilling to credit this phenomenon to the budgetary mechanisms themselves. Nor is there consensus on the benefits of the 1974 act, much less its long-range legacy.

Evidence of this dilemma is not hard to discover. President Nixon, unwittingly perhaps, became the "midwife" of the revised congressional budget process when he declared war on congressional spending. In a radio address during the 1972 campaign, he declared:

> Let's face it, the Congress suffers from institutional faults when it comes
> to Federal spending. . . . Congress not only does not consider the total

---

The views expressed in this chapter are the author's and do not necessarily reflect those of the Congressional Research Service.

financial picture when it votes on a particular spending bill, it does not
even contain a mechanism to do so if it wished.[1]

Ten years later, another Chief Executive characterized the budget process in
even less flattering terms:

> The United States Government's program for presenting a budget, or
> arriving at a budget, is about the most irresponsible, Mickey Mouse
> arrangement that any governmental body has ever practiced. It's called
> the President's budget, and yet there is nothing binding about it. It is
> submitted to the Congress and they don't even have to consider it.[2]

From these words, one would not have guessed that President Reagan was
fresh from a series of stunning victories that hinged on this very budget
mechanism. The thrust of his comment was the more limited one of selling
his proposal to grant the President item veto power, but his indictment of the
system was broad gauged.

Scholarly observers have been no less puzzled when assessing the
situation. The best informed analysts harbored few illusions about the
defects of pre-1974 budgetary procedures. In reviewing the old system,
Lance LeLoup echoed the sentiments of many observers on and off Capitol
Hill:

> Legislative committees as well as the Appropriations Committee initiated
> spending commitments. Congressional actions in a given year had alarm-
> ingly little impact on what the government actually spent that year. The
> budget was almost constantly in deficit. Congress was unable to approve
> appropriations in a timely fashion, leaving agencies in budgetary limbo
> for many months.[3]

Has the new system transcended the problems of the old procedures? At least
one thoughtful critic, Louis Fisher, thinks not. Claiming that LeLoup's
assessment "describes quite well the system that now prevails," Fisher
delivered the following indictment:

> The Budget Act of 1974 held out the promise of better coordination be-
> tween the tax and appropriations committees, with the budget committees
> providing the necessary link. Little of the coordination has oc-
> curred. . . . The new process looks better, in terms of formal mechanics,
> while delivering intolerable results. It is not even clear that the budget
> committees have an identifiable purpose, other than attracting votes to
> pass budget resolutions.[4]

Whether or not these assessments are accurate, they signify the extent of
uncertainty over the Budget Act's achievements. Could it be that all the
efforts surrounding this innovation have come to naught?

In examining the meaning and impact of the Congressional Budget and Impoundment Control Act of 1974, it is important to consider the attributes of innovations on Capitol Hill. What forces drive the search for innovations in congressional structure or procedures? How are innovations designed to cope with or respond to these forces? And what other changes took place in the 1970s which affected the launching and implementation of the new budgetary procedures? In other words, the 1974 act must be placed in its proper context.

The Forces for Change

In order to understand the circumstances that produced the present budget procedures, one must look at how changes take place in organizations. From the time of Woodrow Wilson to the present day, commentators have agreed that Congress is a relatively nonhierarchical institution whose prevailing mode of decision making is bargaining. This assessment flows from Congress's character as an elective assembly and suggests that congressional innovation is a complicated and subtle process. There is a growing body of literature about innovation in large-scale organizations, and several analysts have tried to apply these finding to Congress.[5]

Let us start from a simple premise: like all organizations, Congress strives to preserve its autonomy and its span of influence. In the constitutional framework of blended powers, which the late Edward S. Corwin termed "an invitation to struggle," Congress competes with other institutions, including the White House, executive agencies, the courts, and even private organizations.[6]

In the struggle for self-preservation, an organization must do two things. It must adjust to external demands, and it must cope with internal stresses. These are the outside and inside pressures for innovation—what might be called the demand-pull and cost-push of organizational equilibrium. Alone or in tandem, these forces can challenge an organization to reassess its traditional ways of doing things. Congress faces challenges of both types and has responded to each with distinctive sorts of innovations.

Vexing and ever-shifting challenges emanate from the external environment. These may take the form of changing public expectations, fast-moving events, economic problems, world crises, competing institutions, or simply an expanding work load. Many people question whether Congress is capable of mastering complex, technical, and interdependent problems. Detailed and delicate economic adjustments are just one of the sets of responses Congress is expected to make. Many groups stand as "consumers" and potential critics of congressional action, among them wage earners, corporate stockholders, investors, and clients of federal programs.

Another set of pressures for change wells up inside an organization, primarily from membership turnover, factional shifts, work-group rivalries, and changing norms. Senators and representatives make their own claims upon Congress as an institution— claims that must be satisfied sooner or later if the organization is to attract high-level talent, provide a work place where this talent can be utilized, and command loyalty from the participants. Individual members have a variety of goals. Virtually all members want to be reelected; some seem to have no other interest. But most members want to contribute, shape public policy, see their ideas come to fruition, and work in dignity. In a body of 540 politicians, such needs are bound to cause frictions. Other internal stresses are ricochet effects from external demands; for instance, lobbyists' pressures (external pull) may produce personal or committee scrambles for policy leadership (internal push).

Any organization must hold these external demands and internal stresses in balance if it is to survive. Congress must try to respond to expectations held for it by presidents, administrators, lobbyists, economic elites, the press corps, and others, or it must shape those expectations into more manageable dimensions. In grappling with fiscal policy, for example, Congress has organized itself to deal with detailed, line-item issues, but not infrequently it sets targets and allows the president discretion to modify those figures, as happened with the 1981 reconciliation bill. An organization must also provide its participants—mainly members and staffs—with outlets for meeting their own goals, which include not only reelection but also policy inputs and meaningful participation.

Reorganization is one way of relieving these external and internal pressures. People sometimes refer to reorganization as reform, perhaps hoping to gain acceptance for the proposed change. However, *reform* is a loaded word. It denotes change for the better, but whether change is really reform depends upon one's point of view. One person's reform is another's stumbling block. Moreover, with the passage of time, even the most useful innovations may become obsolete. History is strewn with examples of one generation's "reforms," which only make the next generation's problems worse. Therefore, the term *change* or *innovation* is preferable.

The two kinds of pressures for change, outside and inside, produce distinctive types of innovation. Elsewhere I have termed these *adaptation* and *consolidation.*[7] Adaptation refers to shifts in practices or work habits designed to respond to external demands or pressures. Consolidation refers to adjustments in procedures or power relations that are designed to relieve internal tensions. These two types of innovation often arise from different sources and produce divergent effects upon the organization. At other times, as in the case of recent budgetary processes, adaptive and consolidative changes are intertwined in the same set of actions.

For organizational success, innovations must maintain an equilibrium between outside and inside forces. Some innovations have the happy result of helping an institution cope with both sets of forces at the same time. Just as often, however, outside and inside pressures pull in opposite directions, forcing difficult, costly, or even impossible choices. An organization may adapt well to outside demands, but only at painful cost to its participants, or it may handle its internal affairs smoothly, only to be more and more anomalous within its larger environment.

Let us consider two recent and related examples. The Federal Aviation Administration's (FAA) air traffic control system has, by most reports, been successful in coping with outside demands (rising but fluctuating air traffic needs), but only at enormous human cost to its personnel, the flight controllers. When the flight controllers struck in July 1981, at the same time, the FAA had to make adaptive changes, by restructuring the permitted number of flights, and consolidative changes to deploy its personnel more effectively. The striking workers had a union, the Professional Air Traffic Controllers Organization (PATCO), that, from all accounts, served its members' personal needs well—by offering camaraderie and social benefits—but lost touch with shifting external demands (for example, the attitudes of other unions and the general public, not to mention the budgetary struggles then taking place in Washington).

When examining budgetary innovations of the 1970s and the 1980s, it is instructive to recall the accelerating outside and inside momentum for change. These forces also suggest a way of evaluating the consequences of change. In structures and procedures, Congress must not only respond to economic conditions but must also cope with its delicately balanced internal forces.

Changing Budgetary Processes

It is not surprising that Congress's cherished power of the purse is and has been a prime target for innovation. It is at this point that Congress intersects with the nation's economy and the benefit programs geared toward numerous clienteles. Internally, the power of the purse stands at the heart of

legislative bargaining, and the taxing and spending committees have historically been powerful and prestigious.[8]

Modern observers may be startled by the frequency and magnitude of
historical shifts in fiscal procedures on Capitol Hill. The now venerable
appropriations committees, for example, were not created until after the
Civil War. Within a generation, however, funding decisions were scattered
among authorizing committees. Still later, in the 1920s, these decisions
were reconsolidated in the appropriations panels when a landmark change in
executive budgeting was instituted. A consolidated legislative budget and
joint budget committee were included in the Legislative Reorganization Act
of 1946 but were soon abandoned because key committee leaders were
opposed to them. Passage of the 1974 Budget Act was only one of several
important shifts in fiscal policy making in the 1960s and 1970s. Finally, the
use of reconciliation since 1980 represents a major step within — or
beyond — the original framework of the 1974 act.

Fiscal innovations on Capitol Hill have historically resulted from com-
binations of external and internal developments. W. Thomas Wander has
examined such innovations from the Civil War to the present, in light of the
simple theory of change explained above.[9] His findings, along with some
further refinements, are summarized in table 7.1. As can be seen, a
combination of forces was at work in virtually all instances of innovation in
fiscal procedures.

The most obvious environmental factors in such innovations are economic difficulties, especially those brought about by wartime spending. It is
no accident, therefore, that major procedural shifts were proposed or
implemented after the Civil War, World Wars I and II, and the Vietnam
War. A second external push for change lies in "major change in the
relationship between the President and Congress with respect to control of
federal budgetary decisions."[10] These forces are no doubt intermingled,
inasmuch as wars tend to centralize presidential power and, at the same
time, generate pressures for fiscal retrenchment and legislative resurgence.

Internally, budgetary changes reflect the continuing struggle among
members and committees for leverage over policies. These conflicts are
hard to contain because of Congress's basic character as an open, nonhierarchical place, characterized by bargaining. If nature abhors vacuums,
Congress seems to abhor centralized power; individuals or committees that
come to monopolize power inevitably set up counterforces for breaking up
or bypassing that power. Thus, control has bounced back and forth several
times among taxing, spending, and authorizing panels.

The Congressional Budget and Impoundment Control Act of 1974 (P.L.
93–344) is the legacy of the confluence of both external pressures and

Table 7.1. External and Internal Forces for Budgetary Change

	Forces for Innovation	
Innovation	External	Internal
Creation of appropriations committees (1865–67)	Civil War costs	Ways and Means power
Dispersion of appropriations in House (1877–85)	Federal surpluses	Appropriations Committee's dominance
Dispersion of appropriations in Senate (1899)	Federal surpluses	Appropriations Committee's dominance
Appropriations consolidation: House (1920), Senate (1922)	World War I and executive pressures	Chaos in committees
Creation of legislative budget, joint budget committee (1946)	World War II; executive budget centralization	—
Dilution of appropriations revenue committee controls (1970s)	Constituency pressures for "full funding" of programs	Factional shifts in Congress; structural decentralization
Budget and Impoundment Control Act (1974)	Nixon impoundments; economic "stagflation"	Internal committee conflict: "seven-year budget war"
Use of reconciliation (1980s)	Continued economic stagnation; Reagan budgets	Continued budgetary dispersion in Congress

Source: Author's compilations, and W. Thomas Wander, "Patterns of Change in the Congressional Budget Process, 1865–1974," *Congress and The Presidency* 9, no. 2 (1982), 23–49.

internal tensions. External factors began with economic "stagflation," fueled by Johnson-era strategies for funding the Vietnam War. As public spending was squeezed, President Nixon challenged the Democratic Congress, making the budget process a major issue in his 1972 presidential campaign. He also impounded monies appropriated by Congress, challenging the legislative branch to do something about it.[11] Although the administration lost every court challenge to the impoundments, Nixon held the political high ground. As Allen Schick commented, "Bit by bit the spending power has gravitated from the legislative chamber to executive suites, and the power that once was the hallmark of legislative independence is a pale shadow of its original design."[12] If Congress was to protect its prerogatives, it had to change its ways of budget making.

The 1974 budget innovations, then, were designed to halt the flow of power from Capitol Hill to the White House. "In what could be one of the

most significant reassertions of congressional prerogatives," declared Congressman B. F. Sisk (D, Calif.), "the Congress has the opportunity to stop
the arrogation of power of the Nation's purse strings."[13] While this reflected
the majority view of what Congress was trying to do, a few members
suspected it might invite further presidential encroachment. Congressman
Michael Harrington (D, Mass.), said the new procedures would make
matters worse, not better. He spoke of the "irresistible" political pressures
on Congress to "underbid" the executive branch:

> This pressure, a result of the desire of most Members to avoid the tag of
> being "fiscally irresponsible," would make the possibility of a budget
> ceiling set higher than that proposed by the President most unlikely. This
> would enable a President to set an unreasonably low Federal budget—
> with most of the loss coming, as it almost always seems, to social
> programs—without any real fear of being challenged by Congress. What
> is more, at each step in the process Congress would again be exposed to
> a politically vulnerable situation.[14]

However, this was a voice in the wilderness; for most members, the 1974 act
promised a renewed bulwark against executive encroachment.

While the publicized part of budgetary innovation in 1974 was the
face-off between President Nixon and Congress, a less prominent but no less
dramatic conflict was taking place within Congress. Schick called this the
"seven-year budget war." The ingredients, tensions between authorizing
and funding committees, were typical of internal congressional conflicts.
Most authorizing panels are tilted toward the interests and clienteles they
serve—the result of selective membership recruitment and prolonged contact with the groups most directly affected by this legislation. Many
congressional work groups are not microcosms of the parent houses but are
biased in one way or another. From a painstaking compilation of committee
rosters, one student concluded that more than half of all House committees
were "plainly unrepresentative" of the parent chamber when the decade of
the 1970s began.[15] These recruitment patterns, reinforced by long-term
associations with clienteles of the committees, yield decisions heavily
predisposed toward the very interests under the committees' purview. As
one representative observed, "It has generally been regarded . . . that the
members of the committees should almost be partisans for the legislation
that goes through the committee and for the special interest groups that are
affected by it."[16]

To the extent that panels boost the programs they sponsor, vigorous
questioning of those programs may be discouraged by members and outside
clienteles. Raising questions, it is argued, will only weaken a program's
support and hamper the implementing agencies. Thus, former Agriculture

Committee Chairman W. R. Poage (D, Tex.), once turned aside the suggestion that his committee launch a thoroughgoing review of the Department of Agriculture:

> About all we would accomplish, as I see it, is to create hard feeling, a loss of confidence on the part of our farmers that the Department of Agriculture could render them a service, because we can be so critical of the Department . . . that there won't be any farmer in the nation that will have any confidence.[17]

Oversight is often shunned, not only because it is regarded as unglamorous and unrewarding but also because it threatens work-group norms and interpersonal comity.

In the years following the Great Society legislation, the program committees were able to pry their favorite programs away from the Appropriations committees by various backdoor spending techniques. One form of backdoor spending is contract authority, which allows agencies to enter into contracts before they receive appropriations. Another is direct Treasury borrowing authority, which allows agencies to obligate and spend funds that they borrow directly. Finally, an enormous category of backdoor spending is the mandatory entitlements, laws requiring payments to any person or government meeting certain standards established by law.[18] This removed increasing segments of federal spending from the annual funding process and, hence, from the scrutiny of the appropriations process. After World War II, most requests for federal spending went through the appropriations panels; by the late 1970s, only about a quarter of the annual spending went through these committees. As one observer concluded, "the authorizing committees had gained control over the bulk of federal spending."[19] Even in annually funded programs, more and more authorizing panels specified dollar amounts, thus generating pressure for "full funding" of the program.

The role of the appropriations and taxing committees, in maintaining control of the authorizing committees' activities, was also impaired by the reforms of the 1970s. These included weakened power for the chairmen, broadened (which, in the Democrats' case, meant more liberal) membership, and open meetings. For appropriations subcommittees, membership became self-selected rather than chosen by the chairman and ranking minority member, thus enhancing the role of program advocacy in the subcommittees. In 1975 Ways and Means was mandated to create subcommittees, although basic tax measures remained in the full committee. Once their measures reached the floor, these committees were subject to external challenges; in the House, rules governing debate were more open, votes were easier to obtain, and informal prohibitions against floor chal-

lenges were weaker than in the past. The result of these and other innovations of the 1970s was to transform the appropriations panels from
"guardians into claimants" and also to weaken the role of the taxing
committees.[20] This had the effect of removing the conservative, budget-
oriented balance wheels that were central to the 1960s policy-making system
and were described so vividly by Fenno and Wildavsky.[21]

These 1970s reforms radically transformed Congress. They opened up
the House and Senate and their committee rooms to diverse influences,
rendering the policy-making process more open and permeable than it has
been before.[22] The effects of the reforms were similar in the House and
Senate, although the particulars differed in many respects. The underlying
factional push behind the changes was the ascendancy of the Democratic
party's moderate-to-liberal wing, which tended to dominate the two chambers' procedural workings from the time of the Great Society through the
1980 elections. The immediate policy thrust, to the extent that there was
one, was in the direction of more liberal legislation and spending patterns.
However, the new procedures were available to anyone who could amass the
needed votes; conservatives often modified liberal legislation through
limitation amendments and other provisions, especially legislation relating
to the so-called social issues (abortion, school busing, bilingual education).
Floor amendments were used so effectively that House Democrats in 1980
considered prohibiting them again and two years later partially succeeded in
doing so.

The 1974 Budget Act developed, it is important to remember, from the
same combination of forces and factions that produced the other 1970s
innovations. Public Law 93–344 was passed by overwhelming margins in
both houses, but its final version was the product of many people, all of
whom had their own views about what the new procedures would accomplish. The measure was a delicate compromise, which, rather than curtailing
anyone's powers directly, overlaid the existing power centers with an
"ambiguous and permissive process," complete with an array of committees, timetables, and supporting agencies.[23]

It is therefore proper to speak of the 1974 act as a "treaty" among
suspicious and competing committees and factions.[24] Legislators agreed that
Congress's power of the purse needed defending and that a truly congressional budget process was the only way to achieve this. Beyond that,
however, the consensus dissolved. Fiscal conservatives wanted to limit
congressional spending and close the "back doors;" their reward was the
second budget resolution, with its ceiling and its promise of reconciliation.
Liberals wanted wider discretion and a "debate on national priorities;" the
first budget resolution, with its spending targets, was designed with this in

mind. For the appropriations committees, most backdoor spending was eliminated; they gambled that the budget committees would not encroach on their domain by moving from functional spending totals to line items. The taxing committees preserved their jurisdiction over tax expenditures but accepted provisions that would draw more attention to those items. The authorizing panels preserved existing "back doors" at the cost of eliminating most new ones and accepted deadlines for reporting authorizations, although not for enacting them. As Schick concluded: "Budget power is not directly taken from the authorizing, appropriating, or taxing committees. No direct change is made in their jurisdiction."[25]

With such divergent motivations and differing jurisdictions to protect, it is little wonder that a giant question mark existed with regard to what the new process was supposed to do. Nor is it surprising that this ambiguity and lack of consensus still persist today. The brief flurry of debate about whether the act's founders did or did not envision the 1981-style reconciliation is a case in point.[26]

All parties to the compromise nevertheless sensed that the true meaning of the act would become apparent only as it was implemented. In time-honored legislative fashion, the act had addressed substantive issues with a procedural solution. The procedures themselves remained to be tested, and in the testing the results would emerge—the winners and the losers, the beneficiaries and the victims. This open-endedness is typical of organizational innovations, especially on Capitol Hill.

Some Thoughts on Budgeting as Reform

Assessing the effects of the 1974 Budget Act as a "procedural innovation" is a frustrating task. Experts who have immersed themselves in the details of the process are sharply divided on its impact and its benefits. Moreover, like the budget itself, the process is a "moving target;" each year since 1980, the process has changed. Who can say how it will evolve in the future?

The budgetary process, whatever adjustments may be made to it, has become a permanent feature on Capitol Hill. The process itself seems to have gained acceptance, but the House and Senate budget committees have become cockpits of political conflict. Contrary to predictions (the House even provided for rotating membership, partly to encourage people to serve), seats on the panels are highly coveted. Members campaign to gain appointments to the panel; at least one representative, Phil Gramm of Texas, was disciplined by his Democratic colleagues for his behavior on the committee. It is hard to imagine that Gramm's perceived transgression—consorting and sharing privileged information with the opposing party—would have warranted discipline had his actions pertained, for example, to immigration policy or food stamps.

However controversial, the process has institutional components that have a stake in its survival: the two budget panels, their staffs, and the Congressional Budget Office (CBO). These entities have spawned a subculture of budgetary concepts, terminology, and procedures. It would be absurd to say that the budget process has been followed "to the letter;" but its general provisions have survived, with the two budget committees monitoring compliance and passing upon procedural waivers. If for no other reason, the 1974 act will be remembered for its contribution to the expertise available to Congress.

Perhaps the staying power of the budgetary process against powerful odds is due to the fact that it is just about "the only game in town," from the Capitol Hill perspective. As former House Budget Chairman Robert Giaimo (D, Conn.) declared, "It's ineffective, it doesn't work well, it's sloppy like everything else in our government, but it's the only tool we have at hand, and it's beginning to make an impact."[27] This may be inevitable, at least during an era of economic recession and budgetary retrenchment, but it is significant that the budgetary process provided the framework and the forums through which these issues could be resolved.

The subtler and more critical question concerns the organizational consequences of the process for Congress. Beyond the obvious addition of two panels and three staffs, what can be said about the budgetary process as organizational change, as reform? Has the process served Congress's adaptive requirement, its need to respond to external challenges? Has it affected Congress's consolidative impulse, the requirement to serve the goals and purposes of members and committees? Based on the simplified theory of organizational change set forth earlier, what can be concluded about the 1974 Budget Act?

There is little question that budgetary innovations have helped Congress adapt to its external environment—an environment characterized by macroeconomic considerations and presidential budget initiatives. For perhaps the first time in recent memory, members and committees are coping with the same sorts of assumptions and data bases (although not always the same numbers) that economists and executive-branch budget officers have at their disposal. Not only the preoccupation with numbers and totals but also the sophistication regarding the complexities and interdependencies of fiscal decisions is impressive among current members, compared with members of, say, a decade ago. This flows partly from the consuming nature of the process itself and partly from the availability of more detailed information.

Another adaptive feature of the budget process is its tendency to focus and centralize the legislative work load. Budgetary decisions are centralizing and integrative processes within an institution that is singularly decentralized. At the most obvious level, party leaders are heavily involved in shaping the membership of the budget panels—recruiting members for the panels, assuring that the diverse party viewpoints are represented, and even disciplining errant members.[28]

At another level, the budget process has yielded a level of partisanship that is unusual in today's Congress. Especially in the House, party-line voting on budget resolutions has been the rule rather than the exception. Republican unity has been 90 percent or better in virtually all House floor tests of budget resolutions (see table 7.2). In 1981, there were virtually no Republican defections in voting on the FY 1982 budget. Democratic unity,

Table 7.2.   Party Unity on Budget Resolution Votes, 1976–83

Fiscal Years	Resolution	House		Senate	
		Democrats	Republicans	Democrats	Republicans
1976	First	80%	97%	93%	49%
1976	Second	76	92	86	44
1977	First	83	90	88	48
1977	Second	85	90	89	56
1977	Third	82	89	95	50
1978	First[a]	31	99	75	53
1978	First[b]	78	95	—	—
1978	Second	77	97	85	43
1979	First	76	98	86	54
1979	Second	84	99	88	46
1980	First	81	94	90	43
1980	Second[a]	74	97	76	56
1980	Second[b]	80	100	—	—
1981	First	77	86	89	54
1981	Second	82	99	61	63
1982	First[c]	74	100	61	93
1982	First[d]	65	99	—	—
1983	First	77	83	93	94

Source: Author's calculations; raw figures for 1976–80 appear in Allen Schick, *Congress and Money: Budgeting, Spending, and Taxing* (Washington, D.C.: Urban Institute Press, 1980), 239, 257.

[a]First round.

[b]Second round.

[c]Vote to substitute Gramm-Latta for the House Budget Committee resolution; note that previous party positions were reversed.

[d]Vote on the Gramm-Latta substitute resolution; note that previous party positions were reversed.

while not as high, has nonetheless been substantial. In the Senate, the Budget Committee's bipartisan approach during the 1975–80 period yielded high Democratic unity while splitting the Republican ranks. In 1981, however, Republicans showed virtual unanimity in supporting President Reagan's FY 1982 budget program, whereas nearly two-thirds of the Democrats voted for alternatives. In a Congress with many factions that cross party lines, this situation dramatically showed the capacity of the budgetary process to polarize issues and factions.

The budget process has drawn together and focused Congress's scattered work groups and factions in an even deeper sense. Although Congress is a decentralized institution, it requires a certain degree of centralized decision making, if only to adapt coherently to external challenges, such as presidential initiatives that demand expeditious action. With the decentralizing innovations of the 1970s—burgeoning subcommittees, weaker chairmanships, open meetings, and wider participation through floor amendments and conferences—this integration has become harder than ever to achieve. Fiscal decision making was similarly decentralized, for example, through limitations on leaders of the taxing and spending committees which impaired their balance-wheel functions. The budget process has provided a large measure of the integration that was lost with the weakening of the taxing and spending committees.

Making decisions within the budgetary framework serves consolidative as well as adaptive needs. Budgets pose decisions around clusters of issues, each seen in relation to the others. That is a characteristic of all budgets, executive as well as legislative, and it forces policy makers to deal with the whole of their environment. Yet budget decisions also have consolidative aspects. They allow senators and representatives to make summary judgments that avoid "going on the record" concerning controversial specifics. Despite the openness of today's proceedings, members find it useful to limit the possible risk of voting on numerous controversial issues. When funding committees limited floor amendments or when taxing committees arranged for up-or-down votes on revenue measures, they enabled members to evade tough decisions and blame the respective committees for the unpleasant choices. Today, budget resolutions perform a similar function for individual members. They permit members to make difficult choices without the adverse consequences of having to explain each one of them. Even in an open institution, this type of "heat shield" function is indispensable. In other words, when one balance wheel was broken, another was fashioned to take its place.

The budgetary process imposes organizational costs as well as benefits. In adaptive terms, there is a distinct danger of overloading the process—

attaching to it so many controversial decisions that it fails to delineate them in clear fashion. In consolidative terms, the process challenges the hegemony of the very power centers that thought they had protected their interests with the passage of the 1974 act.

A distinct possibility exists that Congress will be propelled by the budget process, with its timetables and numbers. As Congressmen David R. Obey (D, Wis.) and Richard A. Gephardt (D, Mo.) have declared: "The Budget has become the pied piper of Congress. Its schedule dictates when Congress convenes and when it recesses, what happens on the floor and what is stalled on the calendar."[29] These and other representatives who appeared before the House Rules Committee in 1981 to muse on the state of the House envisioned a "three-bill Congress," preoccupied with budget resolutions, some sort of tax legislation, and continuing resolutions.[30] Not only could this crowd out substantive legislation; it could also impair the already limited time devoted to oversight and deliberation of programmatic changes.

A widespread view, both on and off of Capitol Hill, is that the reconciliation exercise forced committees to take a long-overdue "hard look" at programs under their purview. Long-deferred oversight decisions were imposed through the discipline of the budget process. This impression may prove to be inaccurate. At this point, one cannot determine how thorough or thoughtful the 1981 exercise really was; careful and detailed study will be needed to evaluate the committees' behavior during that frantic period. When that history is finally written, however, it may be found that the committees' programmatic decisions were hasty and scattershot. It may also be found that the process did not yield thorough oversight and program redirection but merely frantic slashing of functions in order to develop acceptable sets of numbers.

The feelings of pressure, haste, and ultimate exhaustion have led at least some legislators to call for a lengthening of the process. Senator Wendell Ford (D, Ky.), Congressman Leon Panetta (D, Calif.), and CBO's former director Alice M. Rivlin are a few of those who have spoken in favor of a two-year budgetary process. As Senator Ford noted, the current timetable mandates

> pro forma reviews of most of the budget. There is not sufficient time. No sooner do we finish the job than we have to begin again, and repeat everything for the next fiscal year. Such repetition is not only wasteful. It is counterproductive. It is frenetic activity solely for the sake of activity.
>
> And to what purpose do we continue this frenzy? Do we think that the spectacle of furious action and the excitement of round-the-clock sessions are satisfactory substitutes for insuring the orderly operation of the Government of this great republic?[31]

Demands for an elongated budget process are understandable yet paradoxical. At the very moment when congressional work groups feel most pressed by time contraints, economic conditions have rendered the budget ever more volatile. Because so many expenditures are linked to economic indicators—unemployment levels, the cost of living, interest rates—budget projections are bound to shift almost daily. If Congress is to adapt itself to this reality, some hard choices will have to be made—either Congress will have to register its preferences to monitor the midstream course of federal spending more frequently, or it will have to limit itself to more intermittent types of interventions, which would necessarily be more gross in their effects.

The immediate threat to the budgetary process flows from internal, or consolidative, forces. The process has become a target for committee leaders in both chambers and has the potential to undermine the committee system further. Budget resolutions can "squeeze" and even by-pass the authorizing committees, and the same can happen to the appropriations panels. The assault on the seniority system in the 1970s succeeded in compromising the committees' autonomy and leverage; budget mechanisms threaten to erode the committees' powers still further. Faced with massive reconciliation decisions, the committees were "pushed into line" in 1981, but many members, especially those with a heavy investment in the standing committees, were frustrated by the process. Several of them grumbled that it was "a heck of a way to run a railroad;" some vowed that "it won't happen again."[32]

A final observation can be made about the budget process: no one fully understands it. Few if any citizens comprehend the maze of terminology and the procedural timetables, and many members of Congress, by their own admission, have similar problems. The budget itself is enormously complicated. As former CBO Director Rivlin conceded: "We . . . need a drastic simplification of the federal budget itself. It is too complicated. There are too many accounts. Nobody understands it as it has accreted over the years."[33]

The process itself is equally complex and puzzling. There seems to be a never-ending series of confrontations on budget figures, the result being constant making, remaking, and unmaking of decisions. This is complicated by the fact that the budget timetable is overlaid with the traditional authorizing and taxing processes. The result, to use the current argot, is that a multitude of "windows of vulnerability" have been built into the system. Many participants have noted the exhausting nature of the current process. As Congressmen Obey and Gephardt commented: "Opponents have multiple opportunities to block legislation or load it with damaging riders. If you lose in the budget process, so what? You can resume the battle when the authorization or appropriation bill is on the floor. No victory assures victory and no defeat ends opposition.''[34] For the general public, this confusion is intensified by episodic media reporting, which tends to heighten the discontinuous, almost stroboscopic character of the decisions.

The Congressional Budget and Impoundment Control Act of 1974 illustrates many of the leading characteristics of organizational innovation on Capitol Hill. The outgrowth of a combination of external and internal forces, it embodies a panoply of diverse views concerning its purposes and objectives. It has reshaped traditional work groups and procedures, not by abolishing them but by adding yet another set of actors and timetables. Its implementation manifests both complexity and unanticipated consequences. And it has drawn mixed reviews. No one can tell what the next step may be; its future is as elusive as the process itself.

8

The Budget Act of 1974:
A Further Loss
of Spending Control

LOUIS FISHER

T he Budget Act of 1974 is generally credited with giving Congress a
new and effective means of controlling expenditures. James Sundquist, reviewing the operation of the act after its first six years,
concluded that Congress "demonstrated the capacity to adopt a considered
fiscal policy responding to the political and economic circumstances of a
particular period, and then to enforce that policy on reluctant and resistant
standing committees."[1] The budget committees, he said, are involved at
each stage of the spending process "as a new source of pressure and
restraint."[2]

Other analysts feel that the Budget Act is neutral with regard to spending.
Allen Schick described the process as "neutral on its face." The process
"can be deployed in favor of higher or lower spending, bigger or smaller
deficits."[3] To Dennis Ippolito, the act promised only "limited and relatively
neutral modifications of the congressional budget process."[4]

These are the two dominant interpretations. Either the Budget Act
constrains spending, or it is neutral on spending. Why is there such
reluctance to explore a third alternative—that the Budget Act favors spending? Is it not possible, or at least worth considering, that the structure and
operation of the act encourage more spending than the system it replaced?

It is difficult to separate the effect of the Budget Act from other influences
on spending. Yet this problem has not stopped other analysts from crediting
the act with a restraining influence. Even the neutrality model assumes that
the impact of the act can be analyzed and isolated from competing forces.

The two models of restraint and neutrality have political appeal because
they provide continuing support for the Budget Act. To suggest that the act
encourages spending might jeopardize the fragile coalition that sustains the
process. Even members of Congress who vote consistently against budget

The views expressed in this chapter are the author's and do not necessarily reflect those of
the Congressional Research Service.

resolutions feel an obligation to make positive comments about the act. They praise the process while condemning the product. Congressman Herman Schneebeli, voting against the first budget resolution for FY 1977, voiced strong support for the Budget Act: "This budget process must work—we cannot allow it to fail. To fail is to admit to our constituents that we cannot control our wild Federal spending."[5] Senator Robert Packwood took a similar position that year, "Although I can commend the process whole-heartedly, it is with reluctance that I cannot support the result."[6]

Many members of Congress, like Schneebeli and Packwood, feel trapped. They say complimentary things about an act that produces aggre-gates and priorities they deplore. After almost a decade there should be no need to treat the Budget Act as sacrosanct. It ought to be possible to evaluate its operation, retain its worthwhile features, and modify or discard the rest. Patience wears thin for a process that has been long on promises and short on performance.

A Neutral Process?

Allen Schick, in the most comprehensive and meticulous study available on the Budget Act, characterizes the process as essentially neutral. Congress could not "subscribe to a biased process, that is, to an arrangement which explicitly favored spending cuts over increases . . . . What has emerged, therefore, is a process that is neutral on its face. It can be deployed in favor of higher or lower spending, bigger or smaller deficits. Its effects on budget outcomes will depend on congressional preferences rather than on pro-cedural limitations."[7] Procedural reforms, however, are rarely neutral. As Schick notes, legislative action in 1974 was "complicated by the sure knowledge that no reform could be truly neutral in its impact on future budgetary outcomes."[8] Nevertheless, after reviewing the expenditures added by Carter in 1977 and the budgetary cutbacks achieved by Reagan in 1981, Schick returned to his basic thesis that "the process itself is neutral, but . . . it will not be neutrally used."[9]

One problem is that *neutral* is not a neutral word. It means different things to different people. There are two separate issues: (1) Did Congress intend the Budget Act to be neutral toward spending? and (2) Has it had a neutral effect?

The answer to the first question clearly seems to be no. Members of Congress disagreed on the objectives of budget reform in 1974. Some wanted reduced spending and a balanced budget; others wanted the budget used to stimulate the economy; and still others thought the act would strengthen congressional control over federal spending priorities.[10] But the overwhelming sentiment behind the act was the creation of a procedure capable of restraining the growth of federal spending.

The ability (or inability) of Congress to control federal spending had ripened into an acrimonious issue by the time of the 1972 election. President Nixon and Congress fought bitterly over a spending ceiling of $250 billion for FY 1973. In a message to Congress on 26 July, 1972, Nixon found fault with the "hoary and traditional procedure of the Congress, which now permits action on the various spending programs as if they were unrelated and independent actions."[11] In a nationwide radio address on 7 October, Nixon warned that "excessive spending by the Congress might cause a Congressional tax increase in 1973."[12] John Ehrlichman, the president's domestic adviser, ridiculed the "credit-card Congress" for adding billions of dollars to the budget. He compared lawmakers to a spendthrift brother-in-law "who has gotten hold of the family credit card and is running up big bills" with no thought of paying them.[13]

Many members were quick to volunteer that Congress had indeed been derelict. The premise of congressional irresponsibility led to the creation of the Joint Study Committee on Budget Control (JSC) and had an effect on the committee's report of 18 April 1973. The JSC linked the increasing size of budget deficits to the procedural inadequacies of Congress, "The constant continuation of deficits plus their increasing size illustrates the need for Congress to obtain better control over the budget." The failure of Congress to arrive at budget decisions "on an overall basis has been a contributory factor in this picture."[14] The JSC said that Congress lacked a mechanism for choosing among competing programs: "The present institutional arrangements in many cases appear to make it impossible to decide between competing priorities with the result that spending is made available for many programs where the preference might have been to make choices among the programs rather than providing for spending in all cases."[15]

Given the political climate from 1972 to 1974, it seems incongruous to call the Budget Act neutral toward spending. While the JSC failed to gain support for some of its most stringent measures to restrain spending (the "rule of consistency," which would have required amendments for budget increases to provide for commensurate decreases elsewhere, and a two-thirds majority needed for some waivers), there was a clear expectation that the act would give Congress more effective ways to control federal expenditures. Congressman Bob Giaimo, testifying as the chairman of the House Budget Committee, offered this perspective in 1978: "We don't need a Budget Act to enable us to spend more. We need a Budget Act in order to impose a discipline on ourselves, which was the very purpose of the Budget

Act, to establish and change priorities, but within an overall discipline, within overall limitations."[16]

Four years later, as a private citizen, Giaimo gave this as the principal motivation: "The Budget Act of 1974 was basically a contract whereby Congress agreed to curb its undisciplined spending habits and the president gave up his impoundment powers."[17]

The history of impoundment legislation reinforces the belief that spending would be constrained. Each house passed legislation in 1973 to limit the president's ability to impound funds. However, members were reluctant to enact an impoundment bill because they feared its "prospending" reputation. Members of the House of Representatives were especially worried that voters would interpret congressional action to release impounded funds as just one more sign of uninhibited spending. Impoundment control would be politically safe only if attached to a measure that promised greater congressional control over spending. That union was achieved by making the Impoundment Control Act the last title of the Budget Act.

A Process of Restraint?

When interviewed, members of Congress typically mention spending reductions as one of the major accomplishments of the Budget Act.[18] The act supposedly protects members from outside spending pressures by allowing them to tell private groups that their spending proposals, while meritorious, would violate the totals already agreed to in a budget resolution. Members can therefore use the budget committees as "whipping boys" to scale down the demands of private interest groups.[19]

There are instances in which the budget process yields restraint, but the budget committees also provide another access point for members rebuffed by authorization and appropriations committees. And if the totals in a budget resolution are set at generous levels—as they were for the first three to four years—they increase pressure for spending. The appropriations committees find it difficult to argue against amendments for more spending when the appropriations bills they report are below the amount allowed by a budget resolution. This creates a new incentive or rationale for additional spending.[20]

Under these conditions, the Congressional Budget Act legitimizes spending that would not have occurred in the past.[21] Schick points out that several of the supplemental appropriations enacted by Congress since 1974 "have been loaded with costly programs that might have been deferred had it not been for the availability of a margin in the budget."[22] After extensive questioning of members of Congress and their staffs, he could not find a single person associated with the appropriations process who thought that "it had really been pinched by the budget ceilings."[23] Ippolito concludes that the "simple and inescapable lesson of the six years of the congressional budget process is that Congress has failed to control spending."[24]

A Spending Bias?

How can the Budget Act be isolated from other influences on the budget? OPEC price increases, lobbying by political action committees, the eruption of Mount Saint Helens, high interest rates, and an inflationary economy are just some of the outside forces that increase spending. However, California's adoption of Proposition 13, the national drive for a balanced-budget amendment, and the introduction of budget-balancing and spending-limit bills in Congress have all acted as curbs on spending. Budget control has also been affected by changes in the House Appropriations Committee; including the movement for recorded floor votes, open committee hearings, selection of subcommittee chairmen by the Democratic caucus, and the assignment of program advocates to the appropriations subcommittees.

Unless these factors can be separated from the Budget Act, it is impossible to characterize the act as neutral, antispending, or prospending. This puts the Budget Act in an "untouchable" condition, incapable of being evaluated. To say that contemporary budget problems are the result of *politics* rather than *process* is superficial for several reasons. First, the argument is fickle. When the results please people, as in 1981, no one hesitates to credit the process. Second, this argument makes the process not only irresponsible but also inconsequential. Why defend a process that is unaccountable? Why argue for its survival?

The existence of outside forces, pushing for and against spending, should not become an excuse to avoid fundamental questions about the Budget Act. Does the process encourage or discourage spending? What are the incentives for committees and members? Has the act changed legislative behavior? How has it functioned? How do results compare with intentions?

When Schick called the Budget Act neutral toward spending, he did not mean neutral in distributing power among congressional committees. He argued that the act "took more from the powerful than the weak, more, that is, from the tax committees than from the Appropriations Committees."[25] The authorization committees "risked the least" and "gained the least," whereas the appropriations committees "put their jurisdiction over federal spending on the line" and "were rewarded with expanded jurisdiction."[26] I would describe the act somewhat differently, but if the Budget Act is not neutral on the internal operations of Congress, is it likely to be neutral on budget outcomes?

Problems of Timing

The Budget Act was intended to speed up the legislative process, permitting passage of appropriations bills before the start of a fiscal year. The act established a series of deadlines to accelerate congressional action: submission of a current services budget by the president in November, estimates from congressional committees by 15 March, reporting of authorization bills by 15 May, passage of all regular appropriations bills by early September, and the adoption of budget resolutions in the spring and early fall.

The current services budget was scheduled for November to force early action. Now it is submitted in January, along with the president's budget, and estimates the dollar levels required to support the same level of services for the coming year, as required by law. Although it appears to be a neutral baseline since it projects spending without a change in policy, adjustments are automatically made to the previous year's totals to account for anticipated inflation. One consequence of this is the sheltering of programs from budget-cutting drives in the White House.[27] It is also tempting for Congress to take these numbers as "givens," beyond the realm of legislative control, and to look elsewhere for discretionary action. The concept of current services soon broadened into "current policy," which adjusts the spending levels of every program for inflation even when not mandated by law. In 1977 Senator James McClure called current policy "little more than a giant hold-harmless provision and, as such ... a budgetary anathema."[28] A technique for forcing early action had become a sanction for higher spending.

Committees are required to submit their views and estimates to the budget committees by 15 March. This puts pressure on the authorization committees to behave even more strongly as program advocates, hoping to enhance their positions in the first budget resolution. The incentive is to inflate committee claims beyond what will be reported. Forced to issue recommendations so early in the year, the prudent tactic is to estimate on the high side (without losing credibility) in order to preserve options.[29] Senator William Proxmire admitted that he once estimated on the low side for the banking committee and lived to regret it: "Ever since then I have been a little gunshy and I have attempted to come in high rather than low, and I think that is a common tendency."[30]

The budget committees have no difficulty putting together a spending total that is less than the sum of the 15 March requests. Members can then claim "savings" through the new budget process. Congressman Jerry Patterson, in a typical floor statement, announced that the first budget resolution for FY 1977 reduced the House committees' 15 March recommendations from $442 billion to $413.6 billion, "a savings of over $28 billion."[31] The reputation of the Budget Act rests in part on these artificial reductions.

The process established by the Budget Act supplies more information and a better understanding of macroeconomic developments, but this does not automatically translate into more responsible or intelligent decisions for particular programs. In order to meet the deadlines, members often act with less comprehension than before the act was established. One staff member, after watching his committee mark up nine bills in two days to meet the 15 May deadline for reporting authorization bills, said: "More of our members knew less about what we were doing than any time in memory."[32] The authorization committees could avoid this problem by acting a year in advance or for multiyear periods, but many of them prefer to authorize in the same year as the president's budget and the appropriations bills.[33]

The Budget Act was designed to accelerate action on appropriations bills. This occurred for the first few years, but the tight schedule left less time for hearings by the House Appropriations Committee. When the House took up the defense appropriations bill in 1976, Rep. Daniel Flood reported that

> the requirement to meet the time schedules imposed by the Budget Control Act had a substantial impact on the consideration of the defense appropriation bill this year. The subcommittee did not have time to hold a detailed hearing which has customarily been held in the past. We covered the entire budget request. Much of our deliberation was more general and less detailed than has been the case in recent years. . . . The printed hearings are less voluminous than they have been and you will note that the report is less lengthy.[34]

Schick described hearings by the House Appropriations Committee as being "shallower and more hurried because of time pressures."[35] The result, according to one aide, was that committee members knew less and were "no longer as effective a check and balance on executive branch spending."[36]

Within a few years, the appropriations bills were reported and enacted more slowly. Although this caused serious problems with deadlines, delays could have allowed more time for study. Budget resolutions, however, began to require increasing amounts of time for floor debate; by 1980

Congress had decided to pass reconciliation bills in the spring rather than in the fall, as contemplated by the Budget Act. The problem of a compressed schedule returned with full force. Senator Lowell Weicker voted against reconciliation instructions in April 1981 "because of the precipitate, injudicious way the President's spending reduction package has been considered in this body. We are supposed to be a deliberative body but, instead, we have been a mirror of the administration's program."[37]

Entitlements

The appropriations committees were helped by the restrictions on new backdoors (contract and borrowing authority) in Title IV. Both categories were to be treated in the future as mere authorizations, requiring budget authority before agencies could obligate funds. Old backdoors, however, were protected. A more costly decision was made to give entitlements a preferred status. Members of Congress now seem more sensitive to the need to control entitlement programs, but this problem was well known to the authors of the Budget Act. In 1973 the JSC reported that, of federal spending estimated for FY 1974, "only 44 percent is associated with the items to be considered in the appropriation bills."[38] The remainder consisted of backdoors and entitlements of one form or another. There was no doubt that the growth of entitlements and "uncontrollables" constituted a very serious problem for federal spending.[39]

The Budget Act consciously and deliberately protected entitlements. Trust funds (Social Security and 90 percent self-financed trust funds) were exempt from the controls on backdoors. In cases in which other entitlements exceed the allocation in a budget resolution, the amounts are referred to the appropriations committees for review and recommendation. In such cases the committees may report amendments to limit entitlements, but they have decided to treat these referrals mechanically, not substantively. They have assumed that a vigorous use of referral authority would lack political support on the floor.

What the appropriations committees needed in 1974, and what they did not get, was greater control over entitlements. Was this a compromise by the framers of the Budget Act to assure passage? Yes, but the decision was not a neutral one. The act established a "fast track" for entitlements and assured their explosive growth after 1974.

In their supplemental views on the first budget resolution for FY 1982, Congressmen David Obey and Richard Gephardt said that the "exception of entitlement programs from the annual budget review process in anything but a cursory sense allows the second fastest rising part of the budget to escape rigorous examination and by default focuses the lion's share of budget cutting attention on the 25 percent of the budget which represents investment decisions."[40] Senator Mark Hatfield, chairman of the Appropriations Committee, criticized Title IV for failing to apply the "slightest brake on the growth of entitlement spending." The discretionary programs (those within the jurisdiction of the appropriations committees) "bear the brunt of budget-cutting efforts, as the uncontrollables are so difficult to reach."[41]

The Budget Committees

The JSC recommended the creation of budget committees in each house: twenty-one members in the House and fifteen in the Senate. In each case, one-third of the members would be drawn from the appropriations committee, one-third from the tax committee, and one-third from the authorization committees.[42]

The Budget Act followed a different course. Instead of the appropriations and tax committees having fourteen of the twenty-one House budget seats, the number dropped to ten of twenty-three. That allotment remained fixed as the Budget Committee grew to twenty-five members in 1975, thirty members in 1981, and thirty-one members in 1983. The two-thirds control has therefore declined, over the years, to one-third. (In the case of the Senate Budget Committee, the Budget Act did not provide specific ratios for the appropriations and tax committees.)

Allen Schick concluded that the "most far-reaching dilution of Budget Committee power came as a by-product of the shift from coordinative to representative committees." If the recommendations of the JSC had prevailed, the budget committees "would have operated as agents of the revenue and Appropriations Committees, not as independent power centers" and their position would have been strengthened "by the status of these powerful committees." The act, by tilting toward representativeness, assured the budget committees of "rivals in the contest for budgetary power."[43] A coordinative approach might have limited the spending jurisdiction of Ways and Means, which was responsible for several hundred billion dollars in entitlement programs, including Social Security.

The greater representation of authorization committees on the House Budget Committee might have been necessary to pass the Budget Act. Nevertheless, the decision to discard the coordinative philosophy was a conscious decision to relax congressional control over spending.

By rotating the membership, the act gave the members of the House Budget Committee little stake in that committee. Their main allegiance lay with their other assignments or with committees they planned to join after a brief stay on the Budget Committee. Schick points out that members "try to use their Budget Committee connection to pursue their more permanent substantive interests. . . . As partisans, most are more interested in getting their way on particular programs than in assuring adherence to the dollar levels in budget resolutions."[44]

Schick predicted that the budget committees "would vigilantly protect the new process because their own interests also would be at stake."[45] Other than "protecting the new process," what are those interests? Prior to 1974, everyone knew what interested the House Appropriations Committee—it wanted to cut the president's budget. That was a major reason for its existence, the measuring rod of its success. Authorization committees are primarily program advocates. But what are the prominent and overriding interests of the budget committees? What is their institutional purpose? "Protecting the process" is inadequate grounds for existence.

Nicholas Masters reflected on his staff work with the House Budget Committee: "We spend a lot of our time simply passing resolutions. The hell with substance—how can we get something together that we can pass?"[46] The answer, at least for the first few years, was to keep adding money to a budget resolution until it satisfied a majority. It was theoretically possible to build a majority among conservatives who wanted budget estimates cut, but Schick notes that House Democratic leaders, "in their attempts to make the resolutions more palatable to party liberals, have written off the possibility of attracting Republicans or conservative Democrats."[47]

Because of partisanship in the House Budget Committee, House Democrats had to "buy off" the votes of committee and subcommittee chairmen in order to achieve narrow victories on budget resolutions. According to Masters, "So we are held, on the House side, in hostage a lot of times in terms of our relationships with other committees because we know that if we lose 20 Democratic votes, we'll go down the tube!"[48] Congressman Giaimo, reflecting on his experience as chairman of the House Budget Committee, said that, with only a handful of Republicans willing to support the budget resolutions, he had to "fashion a budget with the entire Democratic majority, and that means a more liberal budget than we would like to adopt in almost every case."[49]

In Schick's analysis, line-item additions to the resolutions drafted by the House Budget Committee became the price "for garnering sufficient liberal Democratic support to overcome Republican and conservative Democratic opposition.''[50] Attention to line items was one factor in increasing spending. A House Democrat explained the dilemma in these words: "It is hard to vote for reductions because we know which programs would be hurt. It is hard not to vote for the increases because we know which programs would benefit."[51] Ippolito puts the matter bluntly: "The fact is, of course, that the House Budget Committee has no choice but to accommodate the spending plans of most committees."[52]

Budget Resolutions

Budget resolutions are highly regarded as vehicles for centralized, systematic, and coherent legislative action. The Budget Act assumed that members of Congress would behave more responsibly by having to vote explicitly on budget aggregates and facing up to totals, rather than deciding their spending actions in piecemeal fashion through separate appropriations and legislative bills. In 1974, as now, it was difficult to defend fragmentation, splintering, and decentralization when reformers pressed eagerly for "coordination" and a "unified budget process."

The model of the executive budget looked appealing. The Budget and Accounting Act of 1921 had assumed that presidential control and responsibility would be improved if the budget process was centralized in the executive branch.[53] There has been no retreat from that principle, but advantages for the president do not necessarily apply to Congress. The risks are high when Congress, possessing very different institutional qualities, tries to emulate the executive branch.

The Budget Act anticipated a contest between two budgets: presidential and congressional. The analogy is weak because the president is head of the executive branch, which is fortified by a central budget office. There is no head in Congress, and there are no comparable powers for the CBO. Congress is inherently decentralized, and no amount of procedural innovation can hide that reality. Congress is divided between two houses, each with a different set of budget priorities. The House Budget Committee is torn between the conflicting goals of Democrats and Republicans. The bipartisan tradition of the Senate Budget Committee, carefully nurtured by Edmund Muskie and Henry Bellmon, gave way to open partisanship during the Reagan years. Senate Republicans met in party conference to hammer out the details of budget resolutions. Moreover, the budget committees must compete with the established authorizations, appropriations, and tax committees.

Another misconception was the belief that budget committees and budget resolutions could avoid the specifics of federal spending. Richard Bolling, serving as House floor manager for the budget reform bill, said that the budget resolution "does not get into particular programs, agencies, appropriations, or projects. To do so would destroy the utility of the congressional budget process as an instrument for making national economic policy."[54]

Using budget resolutions strictly as a tool for macroeconomic policy would have required an extraordinary discipline on the part of budget committee members and Congress as a whole. Instead, legislators continued to take a strong interest in specific programs and activities that affected their constituents. They learned to use budget resolutions to expand programs that were bottled up in other committees. The House of Representatives, for example, used the budget resolution to augment veterans' benefits and to vote on tuition tax credits. Schick says these votes indicate that "the budget process is not neutral with respect to the expectations of Congress. By enabling claimants to bypass closed legislative channels and forcing recorded votes on popular issues, the budget process can give a boost to previously suppressed aspirations."[55]

With each passing year, budget resolutions became ever more involved in program details. For FY 1976 the House of Representatives considered six amendments to the first resolution. Three years later that number had climbed to twenty-six, and by FY 1980 it had reached forty-nine. The House responded by adopting restrictive rules to limit floor amendments. The 15 March reports also became more detailed. Although budget resolutions omit those details, every staff member can refer to committee markup documents or computerized backup sheets to determine whether a particular program or activity is included within the aggregates for functional categories.

It proved to be impossible to restrict budget resolutions to macroeconomic debate. Members wanted to know which programs were being funded. After conducting almost one hundred interviews with members of Congress and their staffs, Schick could find no one who believed that the allocations in budget resolutions had been knowingly set below legislative expectations. A chief clerk of an appropriations subcommittee complained that the target figures in a budget resolution had been set too high: "We were faced with pressure to spend up to the full budget allocation. It's almost as if the Budget Committee bent over backwards to give Appropriations all that it wanted and then some."[56] This process allows members to justify amendments for increases in appropriations by arguing that the higher figure will still be within the totals allowed by the budget resolution.[57]

Thus, instead of keeping within the president's aggregates, members can vote on generous ceilings in a budget resolution and then announce to their constituents that they have "stayed within the budget." Congressman Tom Steed, managing the Treasury–Postal Service appropriations bill for FY 1977, stated in his floor message: "Although we are over the President's budget, we are under the legislative budget . . . . This particular bill will be well within the limit set by the Committee on the Budget of the Congress."[58]

In 1975, acting under the umbrella of a budget resolution, the House Budget Committee proposed spending authority "for nearly every stimulative program that has been passed by a House committee, passed by the House, or recommended by the House leadership."[59] Members can vote in favor of increased spending for popular programs by rationalizing that votes on budget resolutions do not actually authorize or appropriate funds. Only a public law can do that, and yet successful amendments to a budget resolution become the basis for higher authorizations and appropriations.

Conservatives have expressed dismay about the spending levels in budget resolutions. Clarence Miller (R, Ohio) protested in 1976 that "those of us who hoped that the new budget process in general, and the budget resolutions in particular, would provide us with vehicles of fiscal responsibility have been bitterly disappointed. To the contrary, levels in the budget resolution have been set so high that virtually anything we do will be within those levels, and therefore, by some unique logic, 'responsible.'"[60]

Two years later Delbert Latta (R, Ohio) declared that the Budget Act had become the "big spenders' biggest ally." The budget committee encouraged "more spending by putting its blessing on many social welfare proposals so inflationary that the House, left to its own devices, would probably not approve many of them."[61] Barber Conable (R, N.Y.) objected to the congressional budget process because it sanctioned higher numbers for programs, giving them "an aura of responsibility they would not otherwise have had."[62]

These comments could be discounted as partisan rhetoric, but the lack of budget discipline for the first four years has been conceded by Democratic leaders. In 1979 Congressman Giaimo described the first budget resolution for FY 1980 as putting "an end to the spending pattern of recent years, when program after program year after year was given a sizeable incremental funding increase, almost regardless of its effectiveness."[63] A year later he told his colleagues: "This budget marks a departure from past years. It is not a 'spending as usual' budget. It is not loaded with fiscal sweeteners to please this group or that group or this Member or that Member."[64]

The Costs of Centralizing Congress

Increasing the size of a legislative vehicle—from an appropriations bill to a budget resolution—magnifies the scope of legislative conflict and encourages additional concessions to members. It costs more to build a majority.

Prior to the passage of the Budget Act, the appropriations subcommittees operated with considerable autonomy, specialization, reciprocity, and group norms (including bipartisanship) that required staying within the limits of the president's budget. The subcommittees reported bills with limited conflict and therefore less need for concessions. Some bargaining was necessary, but it was restrained by the size and complexity of each appropriations bill. In contrast, the budget resolutions are general vehicles; each member feels qualified to offer amendments.

Ironically, it appears that members could redistribute budgetary priorities more easily under a fragmented system. They could trim the defense appropriations bill and add to the Labor-HEW appropriations bill, without ever explicitly taking money from one department and giving it to another. The budget process of 1974 may have complicated congressional action by focusing attention on budget priorities.[65] Members do not like to vote on amendments that transfer funds between functional categories. They prefer to do this implicitly and by indirection, following the time-honored rule "Never openly do harm." As a consequence, Schick notes, Congress did more reordering of budgetary priorities "before it had a budget process than it has since."[66]

Congress can tolerate only a certain amount of conflict. Annual appropriations, incremental funding, and avoidance of debate on budgetary priorities are some of the mechanisms used by Congress to limit conflict.[67] Budget reforms such as the Planning-Programming-Budgeting System (PPBS) have exacerbated budgetary conflict "by fixing more attention to program objectives, future-year impacts, and cost-effectiveness."[68] When conflict in Congress exceeds a certain point, the result is escapist budgeting; members become less, not more, responsible.

Conflicts in executive budget making force concessions from agencies that compete for a relatively fixed aggregate. These agencies are subordinate to the central control of the president and the Office of Management and Budget. Conditions in Congress are entirely different. There is no fixed aggregate, no central control, and therefore no reason to expect that conflict would produce budgetary restraint. Spending pressures in Congress can be relieved by voting more money or by adopting fanciful economic projections.

General budget making on the floor of Congress invites the same deficiencies as did general tariff making. Logrolling occurred on such a grand scale and with such public embarrassment to Congress that members decided to forgo that exercise. Why should anyone expect something better with budget resolutions or omnibus budget bills?

The choice between decentralized or centralized control is a familiar one for Congress. For a number of decades Congress has relied on the public works committees for approval of specific contracts for public buildings. The process is easily criticized as parochial and irresponsible, since committee members decide these allocations in private. This may not be very desirable, but will the results be improved if these matters are brought to the floor for general consideration? Will this produce greater control and "unified action" or merely a general free-for-all? Congressman Elliott Levitas has warned that floor action on public buildings authorization bills will create an "enormous pork barrel" and give every member of Congress a chance to add favorite construction projects.[69]

The omnibus reconciliation act of 1981 appears to be a case in which Congress used a centralized process to force budgetary cutbacks. However, the final bill was drafted largely by OMB and the Reagan administration.[70] The president successfully exploited a congressional process. The House Appropriations Committee has described how the reconciliation process can play into the hands of the president: "It is much easier for the Executive Branch to gain support for its program when it is packaged in one bill rather than pursuing each and every authorization and appropriation measure to insure compliance with the Executive's program. This device tends to aid the Executive Branch in gaining additional control over budget matters and to circumvent the will of Congress."[71]

The results of 1981 exposed serious weaknesses within Congress. Instead of following CBO's projections or substituting an economic forecast of its own, Congress accepted the administration's assumptions. Although the Budget Act has been praised because it gives Congress an independent technical capability, in 1981 Congress chose to adopt the administration's false premises. And instead of passing a second budget resolution in September, Congress waited for a list of additional spending cuts from Reagan. Senator Pete Domenici deplored the unwillingness of Congress to move on its own: "I disagreed with those of my colleagues who advocated that we wait for the administration before going forward. We were elected to exercise our own judgment in the establishment of fiscal policy, and ultimately it will fall to us to put in place policies which will restore the nation to economic health."[72]

Congress chose to wait several months after the deadline for the fall resolution and then reaffirmed the thoroughly discredited figures of the spring resolution. Although the aggregates in the spring resolution were demonstrably wrong (some supporters of the administration gently called them "noncurrent economic assumptions"), Congress preferred to pass a *pro forma* resolution and postpone action until the following spring. Even at that point, Congress could avoid responsibility. The deficit for FY 1982, revised upward from $37.65 billion to $105.7 billion, required no separate roll-call vote or debate. The higher number was included in the first budget resolution for FY 1983. Few members realized that they were making such major changes in the aggregates for the previous year's budget.

In 1982 and 1983, Congress took a further step to avoid responsibility for budget aggregates. The first budget resolution in each year contained language that triggered a second resolution if Congress failed to act by 1 October. The figures in the spring resolution, no matter how unrealistic, automatically became those of the fall resolution.

The House of Representatives also uses the first budget resolution to avoid a separate vote on the public debt limit. House Rule XLIX, adopted in 1979, lifts the public debt limit from the spring budget resolution and places it in a joint resolution, which is then "deemed" to have passed the House. In effect, the vote on the budget resolution also counts as a vote on the debt limit. Accountability is lost because the public debt limit rarely commands much attention during debate on the budget resolution, and budget resolutions in recent years have been notoriously unrealistic about deficits.

What Might Be Retained?

The Budget Act of 1974 contains some worthwhile features. Title IV has been effective in restricting new backdoors, and the Congressional Budget Office has established itself as a useful agency for estimating the cost of pending legislation, performing scorekeeping functions, and making macroeconomic projections. Important studies have been conducted on federal credit, tax expenditures, and off-budget agencies.

Despite these gains, the congressional budget process is in worse condition than it was in 1974. Appropriations bills are enacted later than ever, and sometimes not at all. The government operates for longer periods of time on continuing resolutions, and deficits are larger, far larger, than before the passage of the Budget Act. Basic functions of Congress—the authorizing and appropriating of funds—have lost priority to perennial battles over budget resolutions and reconciliation bills.

Major changes are needed to restore congressional powers. First, the Budget Act is inconsistent with House and Senate rules. The act requires that authorization bills be reported by 15 May, whereas the House rules require that authorizations be enacted before the appropriations committees can even report their bills. A possible modification would be to change the House rule to allow appropriations bills to be reported whenever authorizations have passed the House. However, based on the record of authorization bills in recent years, this would not give Congress time to enact appropriations bills by the beginning of the fiscal year. Appropriations bills should be allowed to come to the floor after a certain date, such as 1 June, regardless of progress on authorization bills. Dependence on continuing resolutions for large portions of the year is simply too high a cost in terms of agency disruption, uncertainty among state and local governments, and "high noon" confrontations each time a continuing resolution expires.

Would this change give too much power to the appropriations committees? Probably not. Authorizations are not enacted prior to appropriations now, forcing the appropriations committees to seek waivers from the Rules Committee. If the House were to change its rule, instead of routinely waiving it, the appropriations committees could be expected to do what they have done in the past. They would stay within the dollar amounts recommended by the authorization committees at the latest stage of their deliberations: the committee markup, the reported bill, the bill as passed by one house, or the amount provided in a conference report. The revised rule could be written to prohibit the appropriations committees from providing funds for programs that had not previously been authorized. Unless the House passes appropriations bills in June, there is little chance of enacting the bills by 1 October.

Allowing appropriations bills to be reported on or after 1 June, without fear of points of order, would put pressure on the appropriations committees to act expeditiously. As matters now stand, they can blame the authorization committees for not enacting their bills on time, blame Congress for passing the first budget resolution too late, or blame the budget committees for late submission of section 302 allocations. A 1 June go-ahead date would eliminate these excuses.

Another "modest proposal" would be to dispense with budget resolutions. Congress has effectively eliminated the second resolution; discarding the first would free crucial floor time for authorization and appropriations bills. Members of Congress would no longer vote on concurrent resolutions, which have no force of law. As Congressman Bill Frenzel remarked in 1982 during action on the first resolution, "We have been voting in the last 48 hours for ghosts and shadows, based on moonbeams, smoke, and rainbow dust."[73] Without budget resolutions, there would be no need for committees to spend time on 15 March reports. Members could concentrate on basic legislative tasks—the authorizing of programs and the passing of appropriations. In the confused and rushed world of budget resolutions, these basic responsibilities have been pushed to one side; they need to be returned to center stage.

Without budget resolutions, would Congress lose control of the budget? Not necessarily. Even during the Nixon years, when Congress was criticized repeatedly for loose spending habits, the record does not support the charge of legislative irresponsibility. From FY 1969 through FY 1973, appropriations bills were $30.4 billion below the president's requests. The problem was with backdoors and mandatory entitlements, which, over the same period, exceeded the president's budget by $30.4 billion.[74] Through its own informal and decentralized system, Congress had managed to appropriate less than the president wanted while making significant changes in budget priorities. The appropriations committees have lost some of their reputation as ''guardians of the purse'';[75] yet the record of the past decade suggests that they are still forces for restraint.

The same cannot be said for budget resolutions. In recent years, the second budget resolutions have been at odds with economic reality, especially with regard to the size of deficits and the level of federal spending. The conference report on the second budget resolution for FY 1981 projected a deficit of $27.4 billion, even though budget analysts expected a figure twice that size. The actual deficit was $57.9 billion. The second budget resolution for FY 1982 (which reaffirmed the first) projected a $37.65 billion deficit, a $19.05 billion deficit for FY 1983, and a surplus of $1.05 billion for FY 1984. So much for projections in budget resolutions. The actual deficit for FY 1982 reached $110.6 billion, the deficit for FY 1983 topped $200 billion, and the prospect for FY 1984 does not look much better.

Not only have budget resolutions failed to address economic realities, they have also been ineffective restraints on spending. For the first few years, they were intentionally high, giving committees generous scope for their programs. Budget resolutions then became more restrictive, but they did not produce budgetary discipline. After the limits were reached, Congress adopted revised second budget resolutions (buried in the first resolution for the following spring) in order to permit spending in excess of earlier ceilings.

Without budget resolutions, the president's budget (as in the past) would represent the bench mark for congressional action. The phrases ''below budget'' or ''above budget'' would once again have meaning. Members of Congress and the public would not be confused by comparisons between spring resolutions and fall resolutions and between House budgets and Senate budgets or by periodic reestimates, updates, and revised baselines.

Individual appropriations bills should not be postponed by late authorizations, budget resolutions, delayed enrollment, or omnibus budget bills. When the president's budget has been given to the committees of Congress, the appropriations bills should be free to go forward after 1 June. The CBO could then track legislative action by Congress, comparing the reported and enacted bills with the president's requests. The budget committees should retain the important functions of policing backdoors, issuing "early warning reports" (alerting Congress to budgetary excesses), and proposing improvements in the budget process.

A mechanism is needed to coordinate the spending decisions of the authorizing committees. One place to start would be permanent appropriations. In previous years, Congress directed the appropriations committees to study permanent appropriations in order to bring some of these programs under annual control. Nothing materialized because the committees felt they lacked jurisdiction and a political base. The results might be better if Congress instructed each authorization committee to examine permanent appropriations within their jurisdiction and recommend the retention, modification, or termination of programs currently funded without annual action by Congress. These reports could be funneled through the budget committees, thus giving them authority to report legislation. The objective would be to subject a greater portion of federal programs to the annual appropriations process.

Congress could experiment with the budget committees by allowing the leadership to assign other broad duties to them; the budget committees could be reshaped as explicit agents of the party in power. Majority and minority members could be appointed by the leaders after caucus ratification; they would be subject to removal by the party leaders. Specific quotas from committees (for example, five from Ways and Means) and restrictions on tenure should be eliminated; party leaders should appoint and remove members, as needed. Without budget resolutions to manage, the budget committees could propose changes in areas of the budget that need attention: permanent appropriations, entitlements, tax expenditures, federal credit, and off-budget agencies. Recommendations by the budget committees should take the form of a bill, requiring enactment into law.

The purpose of these changes is to eliminate duplicative and divisive legislative actions (budget resolutions), to put pressure on the appropriations committees to enact their bills before the start of the fiscal year, and to tighten the linkage between budget committees and party leaders as a way of encouraging accountability for the spending bills reported by the legislative committees.

The president's budget would remain as a principal constraint on spending. An unfortunate effect of budget resolutions has been to undermine the importance and integrity of the president's budget. Consider this comment in 1983 by House Majority Leader Jim Wright during debate on the Labor–Health and Human Services appropriations bill:

> This bill is not over the budget; the amounts proposed in this amendment
> are well within the budgeted figures. The amounts that we have agreed to

and discussed are not in excess of the congressional budget resolution. That, of course, is the budget.

Now they may be in excess of certain amounts requested by the President in his budget request of last January. But that, of course, is not the budget. Congress makes the budget; the President does not.[76]

It is essential that the White House and OMB reject the concept of "uncontrollability," which currently places three-fourths of the budget outside annual control. The president should prepare a budget that, in his judgment, is truly what he believes to be in the best interest of the nation. This means proposing estimates that require legislative action on entitlements, providing steady leadership, invoking the veto power whenever necessary, and forging an effective relationship with congressional leaders and committee chairmen. A tall order, but those are the constitutional and political duties of a president. Failure to discharge them will encourage the forces who propose outside constraints on spending, either through statutory limitations or constitutional amendments.

9

The Congressional Budget Process: Diagnosis, Prescription, Prognosis

KENNETH A. SHEPSLE

le-gi-sla'-ture, n. A body consisting of no head and 435 bellies.
—Robert Heinlein

To: Chairman, House Budget Committee

From: Kenneth A. Shepsle

Re: The Budget Process in the House—
Diagnosis, Prescription, Prognosis

M r. Chairman, academicians rarely have the opportunity to write for congressmen. And even on those rare occasions, we tend to clog our exposition with academic jargon and other abstractions. In one painful personal experience, a congressman once wrote me to inquire whether I had ever considered taking up English as a second language. I am, therefore, departing from the more traditional mode of academic expression and, instead, am writing down my ideas in the form of a memorandum to you. The main objective is to provoke discussion and action. "Politics," Aristotle observed long ago, "is a practical science." As one scholar asserted more recently, "People study [politics] not only to discover reality but to manipulate it."[1]

Although it is fashionable these days to debate and discuss the effects of budget politics on the institutional life of Congress, the purpose of this memo is to consider precisely the opposite relationship—the effect of the House on the congressional budget process. I shall argue that two "territorial imperatives"—jurisdictional and geographical—have greatly constrained the effectiveness of the budget process. These imperatives stimulated (at least in part) the Nixon impoundments that preceded the budget reforms of 1974 and, in 1981, prompted the Chief Executive and his energetic director of the Office of Management and Budget to exploit procedural opportunities for restraining spending that had been sanctioned (although perhaps not intended) by the congressional reforms of 1974. These imperatives are deeply ingrained in the legislature, but the congressional budget reforms of 1974 have failed to come to grips with them adequately. This, at any rate, is the diagnosis I offer you in the first section of this memo.

I then turn to prescription, offering some ideas I believe would remedy the deficiencies in the current manner of producing a national fiscal policy. In considering them, Mr. Chairman, I ask that you consider the logic behind the ideas, for the ideas themselves may be quite radical and politically problematic. They are the ideas of an outsider and therefore may suffer from the naïveté that any outsider brings to a situation. However, if the logic behind them is persuasive, I would hope it compels insiders like yourself, your staff, and your colleagues to find the practical means by which to implement them.

Finally, let me note that, while academicians may struggle and prevail in the war against jargon, the writing of a tight, one-page staff memo lies outside their ken.

Diagnosis

The establishment of the budget legislation will have the effect at least of visualizing before the appropriating bodies the total expenditures to be made at any given time.

—Mr. Parrish of Texas

I believe that the American people cannot very long be deluded into the belief that Congress is making any substantial reduction in expenditures by adoption of an executive budget without placing the slightest control over the House and Senate in appropriating money of the people of the United States.

—Mr. Hayden of Arizona
5 May 1921

When I first began thinking about the House and the budget process, I decided it might be enlightening to read the congressional debates on the Budget Act—the one in 1921, not 1974! The same kinds of misgivings about fiscal affairs that were later articulated by you and your colleagues in 1974 were expressed in those early debates. Central to both debates was a concern with the diverse processes of taxing and spending recently described as a "war between the parts and the whole."[2] The roots of this "war" extend back to the very earliest Congresses, when the practice of considering the president's budget message in the Committee of the Whole was abandoned. By the time of the debate on the 1921 act, Congress had experimented over the intervening century and a quarter with a variety of institutional arrangements for dealing with fiscal matters.[3] In the previous year, the House had reunited spending measures within the jurisdiction of a single appropriations committee (the Senate followed suit shortly thereafter). Now Congress sought to impose the same integration on the Chief Executive, charging him with responsibility for submitting a single set of budget estimates. As Mr. Parrish's comment suggests, members believed this act would rationalize spending by unifying the consideration of expenditure alternatives.

In 1921, however, the "war between the parts and the whole" was seen as an executive branch problem. Powerful bureaucracies had grown up in post–World War I Washington and, in the absence of the institutional apparatus that is now associated with the modern presidency, the Chief Executive was in a very weak position when dealing with his subordinates. It was the prevailing practice then for cabinet officers and senior agency personnel to prepare the estimates for their respective operations; there was no mechanism or process by which to consider the overall effect of these individual efforts.

In these historical circumstances one can have nothing short of admiration for the prescience of Mr. Hayden. He sought (unsuccessfully) to impress upon his colleagues that the legacy of the Budget and Accounting Act of 1921 would be another "war between the parts and the whole." And this new war would be conducted on legislative, not executive, battlegrounds. Hayden's lengthy speech urged the creation of something close to the process that you and your committee now coordinate in the House, Mr. Chairman. In brief, Mr. Hayden did not view the situation as much improved if a newly integrated set of executive estimates instantaneously broke into pieces when it reached the other end of Pennsylvania Avenue. And this was indeed the experience of the next fifty-three years. Executive estimates were divided among authorizing committees, appropriations subcommittees, and revenue committees in both the House and the Senate. Deliberations proceeded at each level with little impact on one another, and final decisions were reached in a manner that easily exceeded the already strained centripetal forces in Congress. Even "Czar" Reed or "Boss" Cannon would have thrown up his hands in despair.

Mr. Hayden was blessed with a theory of legislative politics—a coherent set of beliefs about the way things worked on the Hill—but things happened over the next half century that even he had not anticipated. Politicians on the electoral side and senior bureaucrats on the administrative side learned how to work the system in a mutually profitable manner. Interest groups began gravitating toward Washington, and the downtown "K Street Corridor" became home for Washington's major growth industry—the public policy lobby. The prospects for a thought-through (if not a thoughtful) national policy on taxing and spending declined with each new "cozy little triangle," "unholy trinity," or "policy whirlpool." Unless taken by surprise or storm, as in the reconciliation initiatives of the Reagan administration in 1981, legislators, lobbyists, and bureaucrats developed successful strategies of survival and sustenance. As Mancur Olson noted at an American Enterprise Institute conference on the budget, it is quite impossible to "ban the ingenuity of politicians and bureaucrats who advance their own careers by satisfying the demands of pressure groups and the electorate."[4] By 1974 (and, sadly, still true today), claims to policy "turf" had been elevated to the status of property rights.

While I cannot in this memo, Mr. Chairman, give full recognition and attention to the currently prevailing wisdom about the Congress and its central role in policy making,[5] let me begin my argument by briefly examining the two arenas of significance for congressional policy making. At the same time, I shall be able to touch on the deleterious effects on governance of "the new individualism," a theme that has considerable currency today in the literature on Congress and that has been articulated most recently by James Sundquist, of the Brookings Institution.[6]

TWO ARENAS: CONSTITUENCY AND COMMITTEE

Congressmen are middlemen. And, like all middlemen, they operate in two arenas, "buying" in one and "selling" in the other. They seek trust and electoral support from their constituents, in exchange for which they deliver ombudsmanlike services in the form of intervention with the bureaucracy (neutrally called casework); legislative facilitation of projects and expenditures important to the economy and welfare of the constituency; and public pronouncements on the major issues of the day, reflective of constituency concern and opinion.

This is intended as description of the manner in which the legislator with the normal stock of ambition, career aspiration, and professionalism adapts to the circumstances of representation and to the necessities of renegotiating his "contract" every other year. It is neither the cynical portrait of the venal legislator nor the virtuous portrait of civics book hyperbole. Grounds for cynicism and disillusionment, however, grow more compelling as the institutional effects on these individually rational adaptations become evident. These institutional effects provide the rationale for, and the answer to, the interesting question asked by Richard Fenno, "If, as Ralph Nader says, Congress is 'the broken branch,' how come we love our congressmen so much?"[7] We love our congressmen and reelect them with such regularity because they tend to our needs for governmental sustenance. We grow cynical toward the collective Congress as we discover that the net effect of every congressman doing this produces collectively undesirable results. Yet, absent any institutional guarantees that every member of Congress will cease and desist from these practices, we continue to reward the congressman who brings his constituency its "fair share."

The tug of geography induces members of Congress to explore the legislative arena for bases of opportunity that may be transformed into electoral advantage in the constituency arena. When they arrive in Washington, they find a highly differentiated division of labor in the legislative arena. The committee system may well have been intended to serve other purposes; its initial development can be traced back to legislative anxiety caused by a division of labor within the executive branch and an aggressive secretary of the Treasury named Hamilton who exploited its advantages. But these intentions bear only slight resemblance to the geographical-electoral objectives currently being served by the "little legislatures." Complementing this division of labor is a committee assignment process that is anxious to please.[8] Legislators are permitted to gravitate to the committees on which they generally wish to serve. And, if this were not enough, the member finds, thanks to the subcommittee bill of rights (again, intended for different reasons), a subcommittee assignment process that allows him to gravitate to an institutional niche where he can effectively respond to the vigorous tugs of geography.

The first point, then, is that sensible adaptations by reasonable and professional legislators to the necessities of representation produce an arrangement in which members gravitate to settings where they can be of benefit for their constituents. Congress, as a consequence, is regarded as "the broken branch" because the system and its arrangements for collective decision making place individual legislators in circumstances in which representational responsibilities go hand-in-hand with, and indeed lead to, collectively "insane" policies.

One should not, however, be too hasty to grab a violin and play 'Hearts and Flowers" for our poor, unfortunate legislators. They not only yield to the "tugs" and adapt accordingly; they are often back home beating the bushes for business and, in Washington, are making their adaptations more and more easily. They have voted themselves generous resources with which, first, to contact constituents, stimulate attention to district problems and concerns, and advertise legislative problem-solving capabilities (trips home, district staff, franking privileges, high-tech media, and computing facilities); and, second, to service these newly induced demands in Washington (case workers, personal and committee legislative staff).

The second point, then, is that legislators have not adapted passively to the necessities of representation; rather, they have voted themselves the means by which to create "enterprises."[9] These staff operations, on the one hand, provide the member with outreach capability that binds him ever more closely to his district and, on the other hand, insulates him from partisan, ideological, and even interpersonal influences. Like businessmen, politicians are agents in search of clients. And the clients are typically not institutional partisans nor ideological fellow travelers, but instead are geographically defined interests. Congressmen have become brokers and entrepreneurs, indeed caterers, to the tugs of geography.

A third point suggests an even more subtle form of adaptation. The tugs of geography have been *institutionalized;* they are not merely reflected in the (possibly transitory) passive and active adaptations of individual legislators to current circumstances. The committees and subcommittees of the House were initially intended to put the legislature on an equal organizational footing with the executive branch, but they have been transformed into institutionalized mechanisms that respond to geographical influences. Geography is ingrained in public policy not only because legislators are bound to particular constituencies but also because the legislature's "eyes and ears" (to quote "Czar" Reed's approving characterization of congressional committees) see and hear in geographic terms. Public policies are a by-product of geographical impacts. Whatever the nominal goals of a policy, the choice of one legislative solution over another is affected by the anticipated effects that solution will have on particular constituencies.

It is by this route that the tugs of geography beget the tugs of jurisdiction. Jurisdictional jealousies, battles over turf, concern with precedent, and other manifestations of legislative territoriality are reflections of the worth of committees to legislators grappling with geographical influences. Committees and constituencies are, in this view, mirror images; their institutionalization is found in the twin forces of geography and jurisdiction.

GEOGRAPHY AND JURISDICTION: TWO TERRITORIAL IMPERATIVES

The necessities of representation entail a responsiveness to geographical influences which, in turn, induce a loyalty to committee jurisdictions. While agricultural policy may be too important to leave to the farmers and interior policy to the westerners, farm and western representatives will object if anything is done to change the situation. And they will do so not only as midwestern farm representatives or western legislators with reclamation concerns, but as representatives of the agriculture and interior committees, respectively. Any brief description of legislative policy making would surely include the idea that policy develops, is formulated, and its implementation ultimately overseen by "interesteds," who have gravitated to the committees and subcommittees on which geographically stimulated interest and jurisdictionally defined policy dovetail. It is this "stylized fact," and the territorial imperatives that support it, that frustrate any efforts to coordinate policy making in a centralized fashion. Whether by a centralized agent (a party leader) or according to a centralized process (the budget process), the demands of coordination must accommadate policy areas spread among many jurisdictions and the fractionalization accompanying the many tugs of geography. This, in turn, requires coping with a rather large number of potential veto groups, which are sensitive to the potential adverse effects on their constituents, their committees, or both. As David Stockman recently stated, "There is no such thing as a fiscal conservative when it comes to his district or his subcommittee."[10]

These lessons, Mr. Chairman, are undoubtedly familiar to anyone involved in the legislative process. They do, however, provide the context onto which the budget process has been imposed, and, more importantly, they imply two fiscal tendencies with which the budget process must grapple. Let me turn now to the distributive tendency and the growth tendency.

THE DISTRIBUTIVE TENDENCY

In a general condemnation of congressional policy making, a young legislative staffer of John Anderson named David Stockman wrote, in 1975, about the "social pork barrel." Social policies, he claimed, resemble the traditional rivers and harbors omnibus inasmuch as each member focuses not on the general policy characteristics of legislation but rather on the manner in which the legislation will affect his constituency. Fiscal incidence—the geographical distribution of taxing and spending effects—has become the basis on which policies are devised and evaluated.

Stockman's condemnation is sweeping and general (and misdirected), catching Democrats and Republicans, liberals and conservatives, in its net.

The social pork barrel, in his view, is a consequence of "conservative duplicity and liberal ideology." Liberals, he claims, have distorted the imperatives of their ideology so that what was once Benthamite utilitarianism is now "the greatest goodies for the greatest number." Unable to formulate programs targeted to those in need of governmental assistance, "the prevailing liberal faith in meeting unfilled 'human needs'" has been replaced "by only a vague notion of who really needs government assistance. Standard rhetorical terms like the 'little guy,' the 'working class,' and the 'average American' can encompass almost the entire electorate, and in liberal practice they usually do." Conservatives, on the other hand, are not merely misguided; they are duplicitous—engaged in a "great ideological charade":

> At the christening of each new domestic program, conservatives loudly complain about yet another boondoggle, more federal red tape and confusion, and a further drain on the over-taxed budget. Most of them vote for gutting amendments during the initial debate, although considerably fewer vote "nay" on final passage. In subsequent years, the ranks continue to erode so that many who initially opposed the program quietly vote for reauthorization and even more vote for annual appropriations.[11]

In sum, "conservatives may profess to be vigilantly watching at the gates of the federal treasury, and liberals may profess to be striving to insure that America's least advantaged are given their due; but in reality, neither side is doing very much of either task."

Stockman's denuciation is misdirected because it condemns individuals for adapting rationally to their circumstances. It would be more appropriate to direct criticism toward the collective arrangement that requires (wishes? hopes for?) individuals to suppress their own private interests in order to further collective objectives. Legislators are neither less principled nor more corrupt than most people, and a modicum of career aspiration should not be judged unsuitable for professional politicians. I accept such aspirations and seek a decision-making arrangement that exploits them by providing incentives that lead career-oriented politicians to produce, as a by-product, some conception of "good public policy." Institutions should check, constrain, and channel self-interest rather than suppress it altogether, as the authors of *The Federalist Papers* stated two hundred years ago. The failure to do so is an institutional defect, not an individual fault.

His moralizing (and mine) aside, however, Stockman's description of the social pork barrel syndrome is characterized by what has come to be known as the distributive tendency. It includes both an outcome and an attitude.

As an outcome, the distributive tendency manifests itself in the traces of geography detected in legislation. It is most blatant in those geographically targeted authorizations and appropriations for which there is little additional justification beyond the fact that some well-positioned legislator received what he wanted. Not all public works projects qualify but, given the propensity of the Army Corps of Engineers to exaggerate benefits and underestimate costs,[12] many do. Traces of geography, however, need not be so conspicuous. The marginal adjustment of a grant formula, for example, to attract a handful of votes; the use of omnibus procedures around which a "coalition of minorities" may form; reciprocity among committees, each of which has a well-defined geographic or demographic clientele—all of these are instances of the distributive tendency. It is important to note that the distributive tendency is a characteristic of most recent legislative policy, not just the (fiscally small) rivers and harbors pork barrel measures. Were this tendency restricted to "bricks and mortar" policies, we could regard it as an aberration of relative insignificance (about 1 percent of the federal budget). But the distributive tendency is a fiscal problem of far greater significance, affecting a considerably larger portion of federal outlays.

Even if the initial source of the distributive tendency is not legislative, rational bureau chiefs and program administrators in the executive branch have come to realize that their anticipatory responses to the tugs of geography make next year's round of appropriations or program renewals a less difficult affair. Thus, subtle pressures in response to or in anticipation of geographic demands come into play. The National Science Foundation, for example, learns not to concentrate all its research awards in Cambridge or the Bay Area; the National Endowment for the Arts finds some criterion by which to avoid spending all its funds in New York City; the Model Cities Program discovers "pockets of poverty" in even the wealthiest of sunbelt cities and "blight" in the smallest of rural hamlets. Bureaucrats, in short, come to appreciate the importance of geography and the membership of relevant legislative committees for the fate of their programs.

The distributive tendency also characterizes an attitude. Members unashamedly carry calculators to the floor of the House in order to compute district benefits according to alternative formulas under consideration. Staffers monitor the proceedings of various committees for their respective members, the purpose being to apprise that representative of potential district-related harms or opportunities. In general, national policies are appraised in terms of their district-related effects rather than against some national policy criterion. And this is regarded as legitimate, since responsiveness to the tugs of geography is seen as the *sine qua non* of representation.

Most members of Congress are familiar with the distributive tendency. Any formal definition would surely include the following characteristics:

1. Benefits are particularized, divisible, and often geographically targeted; costs are generalized, diffused, and are not directly attached to the enjoyment of benefits.

2. The coalition of members whose districts enjoy benefits is large, if not universal—"something for everyone."

3. Failing (2), a policy, the benefits of which are enjoyed by only a minority of districts, is normally part of a reciprocity agreement; nonbenefitting members tolerate the policy in the expectation that their own minority-preferred policy will obtain similar future treatment.

The evidence on the distributive tendency tends to be anecdotal, as in Stockman's 1975 essay or Morris Fiorina's 1977 monograph. A more systematic treatment is found in Douglas Arnold's 1979 monograph on the responsibility for the distributive tendency shared by Congress and the bureaucracy.[13] An especially rigorous quantitative treatment is found in a recent paper by Roderick Kiewiet and Matthew McCubbins.[14] These scholars provide compelling evidence that "Congress was more generous in election years in its treatment of budget requests for agencies which supply particularistic, constituency-oriented benefits. This greater election year generosity did not appear to extend to agencies supplying more collective goods and services." This is precisely what one would expect if the tugs of geography are a prominent factor in policy making, since those influences are heightened in the minds of members in even-numbered years.

I have dwelled on this subject at some length, Mr. Chairman, so let me conclude it by returning to the twin forces of geography / jurisdiction and constituency / committee, for which the distributive tendency is one manifestation. The fiscal implications for this tendency, implications with which centralized fiscal coordination must struggle, include the following. First, many "distributive" programs are wasteful or inefficient in an allocative sense. Since outlays are broadly distributed, they cannot be targeted appropriately. The concept of model cities, for example, began with a tight target of ten severely distressed cities. However, by the time the Model Cities Program became public law, the amount of money had not changed but the number of benefitting cities had grown from 10 cities in severe economic straits to 150 cities in 218 congressional districts. Second, the distributive tendency contains the seeds of spending growth. The spread effect just mentioned allows bureaucrats to return to the Hill at a future time with a "laundry list" of new needs.

THE GROWTH TENDENCY

> *The growth of the cost of government as expressed in the increase of*
> *Federal taxation has been astounding. . . . Our failure to reduce that*
> *cost has called attention to our need of the adoption of a system which*
> *will prevent waste and extravagance with inevitable inefficiency in the*
> *various departments.*
>
> *Our present system cannot be conducive to economic administration,*
> *as it invites increased expenditures through the perfectly natural rivalry*
> *of numerous committees and the inevitable expansion of depart-*
> *ments. . . . Our present system is designed to increase expenditure rather*
> *than reduce it.*
>
> *Each committee in the House quite naturally is jealous of both its*
> *jurisdiction and success in legislation. It will therefore push to the limit*
> *its jurisdiction over legislation and its demand for appropriation that*
> *enlarges the function falling under its jurisdiction. Appropriations from*
> *the several committees become a race between or among rivals to secure*
> *funds from the Treasury rather than to safeguard them. . . . The pressure*
> *is for outlay.*
>
> —Various participants in the debate on the Budget and Accounting Act of 1921

These voices from the past have a familiar ring, Mr. Chairman; their
sentiments have been echoed in 1974 and again today. After sixty years, the
more things change, the more they stay the same. Aaron Wildavsky
expressed this same sentiment recently when he observed that "governments only know how to add, not subtract."[15] The data on federal spending
growth are both familiar and depressing; they are even more shocking at
other levels of government. Let me briefly document the case (using the
figures of the CBO, 1979, which, although dated, tell an accurate story):

● Between FY 1970 and FY 1980, total budget outlays grew from $196.6
  billion to $531.6 billion.

● Controllable spending grew from $73.3 billion to $132.9 billion; uncontrollables (contract authority, entitlements, permanent appropriations,
  but not including borrowing authority and other credit activities) grew
  from $125.8 billion to $404.1 billion. While both grew in nominal
  dollars, controllables actually shrank as a proportion of the budget (from
  about one-third to one-quarter) while uncontrollables grew from two-
  thirds to three-fourths of the budget.

● Controllables grew at an annual rate of 6 percent while uncontrollables
  grew at about a 12 percent rate. Within the controllable category over the
  1970–80 decade, defense outlays grew 49 percent while civilian outlays
  grew 157 percent; within the uncontrollable category for the same
  period, both defense and civilian programs grew about 280 percent.[16]

Given the predominance of uncontrollables (which increased to 78
percent of the FY 1981 budget), it is fair to say that much if not most of the

budget is on "automatic pilot"; we are currently incapable of controlling spending levels and spending growth. As one CBO employee notes, "The purse that the appropriations committees are holding is today only the 'change purse.' "[17]

Contrast this with the view of an earlier era when it could be said that "the appropriations committees, especially in the House, have . . . cast themselves in key *institutional* roles as guardians of the budget and protectors of Congress against its own (and the executive's) enthusiasm."[18] Our institutions have failed as control mechanisms ("governors" is the apt metaphor). The budget process and a decade or more of democratization in the House have so impaired Congress's ability to control spending growth that even strong-willed personalities, like the curmudgeonly, tight-fisted, former chairman of the House Appropriations Committee, Clarence Cannon of Missouri, would doubtless fail to exert much influence today.

The growth tendency is real and has been liberated in the House by the spurt of reforms of the 1970s. Many of these reforms have freed members from control by party leaders (or even influence and persuasion by colleagues), subcommittees (and hence budget authority) from control by powerful authorizing committee chairmen, and especially the Appropriations Committee (and hence outlays) from the normative constraints that had earlier characterized its operation. These reforms have liberated the tugs of geography and jurisdiction, which now have full play to operate. They have, in the words of one student of budgeting, created an institution consisting only of budgetary "claimants."[19]

Two events illustrate this phenomenon. Early in the 1970s, as the Vietnam War was winding down, there was much talk of a fiscal dividend, according to which monies would become available to sate the appetite of previously (and allegedly) "starved" domestic programs and, at the same time, permit budget relief and tax reductions. What happened to this prospect? As Stockman observed, "Congress abhors prospective budget surpluses, preferring to nickel and dime them into oblivion long before they appear."[20] Between FY 1970 and FY 1974, defense outlays fell modestly (from $78.6 billion to $77.8 billion), whereas domestic civilian expenditures jumped dramatically (from $120.5 billion to $195.2 billion).

The second event is of recent vintage and is all the more compelling in light of the current high salience of budget politics and the flood tide of fiscal conservatism. Reported by Richard E. Cohen, it illustrates how legislators have difficulty saying no:

> The Senate showed its budget colors on Nov. 5 [1981] when Armed Services Committee chairman John Tower, R-Texas, proposed an amendment to the energy and water development appropriations bill (HR 4144) to add $509 million for nuclear weapons research. Hatfield objec-

ted, pointing out that the Appropriations Committee had approved $4.68 billion, more than $1 billion over the 1981 level and $157 million short of Reagan's March budget request. He displayed a letter from Stockman opposing the amendment and calling the committee version "sufficient to meet all identified national security requirements." Tower retaliated with a letter from Defense Secretary Caspar W. Weinberger that did not specifically support his amendment but expressed concern about the "serious impact" of the committee's decision to cut the Energy Department's original request. By 49–43, the Senate approved Tower's modified proposal, adding $335 million to the bill.[21]

Fiscal growth, as evidenced by growth in budget categories, understates matters considerably. It captures only the tip of the iceberg since what are technically regarded as outlays underestimate real government spending. In particular, government credit programs[22] and other off-budget items are not incorporated into the budget figures; and these categories are growing more rapidly than the traditional categories. Second, toleration of fiscal growth and of the prospects for future growth is underscored by the growing portion of the budget devoted to so-called uncontrollables. As Clifford Hardin and Kenneth Chilton note,

> As an ever-increasing portion of the budget is made up of indexed entitlements and other indexed programs, the effort to exercise fiscal restraint and to balance the budget becomes increasingly difficult. The well-meaning provision for inflation protection for the beneficiaries of these programs contributes to inflationary pressures and the economy and, in some instances, undermines the fiscal integrity of the programs themselves.[23]

In sum, Mr. Chairman, it would seem that the Congress is its own worst enemy. Recent changes in structural arrangements have given free rein to the tugs of geography and jurisdiction and have unleashed both the distributive and growth tendencies. It is within this context that the budget process must cope. I am reminded of a description, attributed to the economist George Stigler, of the early Interstate Commerce Commission. Illuminating the magnitude of its task in the late 1880s, he noted that the commission's political battle matched fourteen clerks against an industry, the railroads, which controlled more wealth than did Napoleon! The congressional budget process faces equally unfavorable odds.

EFFECTS ON THE BUDGET PROCESS

I have given attention thus far, Mr. Chairman, to the conditions under which the congressional budget process operates. They may be summed up by the wonderful, brief description given many years ago by the historian of Congress, DeAlva Stanwood Alexander: "What is the House? An aggregation of vigorous elements, having different objectives, antagonistic notions, and selfish interests, centered about indefinite party policies and moved by personal, political, and sometimes patriotic purposes."[24]

Grafted onto this "aggregation of vigorous elements" in 1974, the budget process has been seen by some of its most attentive students as seeking to accomplish at least three distinct objectives. First, "the Budget Act was an attempt to reestablish legislative power of the purse by chartering new committees to exercise it in behalf of Congress."[25] Second, the budget process is conceived of as a vehicle for clarifying congressional views on fiscal matters. "It does for Congress what the Budget Act of 1921 did for the executive, namely help it get its act together."[26] Finally, and perhaps most ambitiously, the budget process is a response to the complexities of budgeting. It is a device by which to bring "a new orderliness" to an otherwise obscure, oblique, and confusing set of issues[27]—a "curtain of numbers," as Schick called it.[28] In short, the objective of the authors of the Budget Act was "to fit isolated revenue and expenditure decisions into a logical, coherent process that would treat the federal budget as a rational whole."[29]

The budget process, in my view, is the victim of some very high, indeed self-contradictory, expectations. In order to "get its act together," to "reestablish legislative power of the purse," and to "treat the federal budget as a rational whole," the budget process must attend to that "aggregation of vigorous elements" that Alexander wrote about sixty-five years ago. There is a gross "mismatch of incentives and capabilities" as the process is continually assaulted by the forces of geography and jurisdiction.[30] Whether the budget process has decreased the growth in federal expenditures or the tendency for pork barrel policies is difficult to determine; the appropriate experiments cannot be run. It certainly has not been implemented enthusiastically; about the best that can be said of the process to date is that it has survived. Let me briefly explore the reasons why I believe the objectives of the budget process have been sabotaged.

Consider first the matter of accommodating existing power centers within the House. The Budget and Impoundment Control Act of 1974 was born not only at a time of conflict between the legislature and the executive but also during a period of fingerpointing within the House. Liberals on authorizing committees accused the Appropriations Committee of scuttling their programs. Conservatives saw undisciplined spending and insufficient acknowledgment of the necessity for restraint. The usually collegial Wilbur Mills of Ways and Means accused the former "guardians of the Treasury" on the Appropriations Committee of abandoning their posts under fire, and held tax reductions hostage to spending reductions. George Mahon, chairman of the Appropriations Committee, was uncharacteristically curt in response, strongly asserting that the real responsibility lay with Mills's own committee in its willingness to tolerate revenue losses through tax expenditures. The House was not a happy home during the period of fiscal soul-searching in the early 1970s. As Schick retrospectively concludes:

> The end product was an accommodation to the most salient interests of the affected parties. Conservatives who sought strong budget committees and a restrictive budget process had to settle for a process that does not prevent Congress from spending as it sees fit. [But] liberals who were apprehensive about the possible effect of any budget process on domestic programs had to accept new budget controls. Authorizing committees were able to shelter existing back doors, but not all new ones. They successfully resisted the imposition of deadlines on the enactment of authorizations but could not avert deadlines for the reporting of such legislation. The appropriation committees avoided the allocation of budget amounts among appropriations categories but had to accept allocations among budget functions. The tax committees blocked proposals to specify tax expenditures in the congressional budget, but they acceded to provisions that substantially increase attention to tax expenditures in the federal budget.[31]

This accommodation of existing power centers produced "a respite and a redirection. While it could not assure budget tranquility, it at least provided new conditions under which future battles would be fought."[32] In a sense, the problems—geography and jurisdiction—were made a part of the solution.

This accommodating solution has dogged the budget process throughout its brief life, frustrating all of the objectives it sought to accomplish. To put it bluntly, Mr. Chairman, there is a direct conflict between the centralized requirement of coordinated budgeting and the decentralized requirement of legislative collegiality, which gives priority to committees and constituencies. Something had to give, and I claim it has been the process. The following is a short list of indicators:

• *Reticence about turf.* The House Budget Committee has been very cautious in its dealings with other committees. It avoids floor confrontations and negotiates informally and behind the scenes. It has encouraged committees to discover "legislative savings" in their programs rather than directly confronting the committees about those programs. It has been extremely hesitant to make use of the reconciliation process (although Chairman Giaimo broke the pattern, and events since then have encouraged its more frequent use). This reflects a fear of confronting redistributive issues, of "fiscalizing" legislative debate, and of overloading the fragile budget process. The House Budget Committee has been anxious not to "break faith" with other standing committees. This tentativeness about turf, although receding recently, has certainly compromised the rationalization of legislative fiscal policies.

• *Adding machine function.* Numerous commentators have observed that the process, which only weakly binds in the first budget resolution, has the appearance of an adding machine.[33] The binding second budget resolution, it is argued, simply adjusts the numbers to take previous substantive decisions into account. As Donald Rotunda observed, "the second resolution does not establish policy. It confirms what already has happened."[34] This argument is especially compelling when accompanied by timidity of the Budget Committee to employ reconciliation (a timidity that has abated in the last few years, but at executive, not legislative, initiative.)

• *Budget priorities.* The extent to which the budget committees alter the fiscal priorities that would otherwise emerge from a decentralized, uncoordinated process is unimpressive. As Schick says, "The House and Senate have rebuffed all proposals to reorder the budget's priorities by taking from one function and giving to another."[35]

• *Supplementals versus rescissions.* The record of Congress, as reported by Ippolito, is one in which supplemental appropriations almost always receive a favorable reception, while executive-initiated rescissions are accorded much less favorable treatment.[36] While this is not unequivocal evidence on budget process shortcomings, it surely does not testify to a process with bite. Instead, it confirms Wildavsky's view that governments know how to add but not how to subtract.[37]

• *Procedural accommodations.* Stanley Bach of the Congressional Research Service reports that, of all special rules waiving points of order, the Congressional Budget Act is victimized most frequently.[38] Many of these waivers are technical; nevertheless, it does not give one great confidence in the procedural integrity of the process. In addition, numerous deadlines specified in the act are missed or extended, and, as the events of 1981 displayed, the act is open to procedural exploitation.

• *Substitution effects.* Former OMB Director James McIntyre reminds us that "there are, as we have learned painfully, almost always regulatory . . . equivalents for budget policies."[39] Policy objectives may, and often are, accomplished by substitute means when expenditures are proscribed or restricted. Regulatory solutions, statutory requirements for expenditures by other levels of government and by the private sector, credit and loan guarantee programs, and other off-budget techniques have been steady companions of the budget process.

This list constitutes a powerful indictment of the budget process. While I do not claim outright failure, I do claim that the process is vulnerable to the provincial impulses described earlier.

BUDGET OBJECTIVES VERSUS BUDGET PROCESS: A MISMATCH

The adoption of such a plan [fixing binding authorization ceilings on each committee in advance] would result in a real legislative budget. Until that is done all of the talk about the beneficial effect that is to come from the enactment of budgetary legislation will amount to nothing more than talk. The executive budget can have nothing but a moral effect upon the House and Senate, for it will have no binding force whatsoever.
—Mr. Hayden of Arizona
5 May 1921

Writing about congressional control of executive bureaucracies, Fiorina argues that "procedural changes alone are insufficient to increase control . . .; to achieve their purpose such changes must also provide incentives to exercise that control."[40] In a similar vein, Rohde and I generally suggest that changes in congressional outcomes are not ensured by exclusively altering procedures or exclusively changing incentives; typically, changes in both are required.[41]

Yet, several years after the Congressional Budget Act of 1974, Schick writes that "nothing in the Budget Act ordained specific changes in the behavior of the older committees; the act itself could not ensure that appropriations or tax decisions would be made differently from the way they were made before Congress had its own budget process. What the Budget Act created was an opportunity for change."[42] Wildavsky concurs: "The Budget Act is not designed as a one-way street to reduce expenditure. Congress is encouraged to consider totals, but it has *no greater incentive* than before to reduce those totals [emphasis added]."[43] Indeed, one of the authors and guiding spirits of Public Law 93-344, Richard Bolling of Missouri, has recently suggested that it was the intention of its authors not to provide specific incentives: "The objective of the 1974 Budget Act was not to implement a particular fiscal policy, e.g., a balanced budget. It was to force Congress to be responsible. . . . A budget process that has become identified as inimical to progressive objectives, and as a part of the conservative credo, will suffer from the political rejection of conservatism."[44]

Fiorina, Wildavsky, Schick, and Rohde and Shepsle have all argued, in various contexts, that the alteration of procedures without a concomitant change in incentives may be ineffectual for changing those policies toward which the procedural reform is aimed. Now Bolling claims that the Budget Act was never intended to alter the incentives necessary to effect change but only to "force Congress to be responsible."[45] Is it any wonder that the reform is ineffective? Changing procedures, but giving the new ones no bite and leaving the powerful forces of geography and jurisdiction free to operate, seems, at best, a situation capable of creating what Mr. Hayden of Arizona saw in the Budget and Accounting Act of 1921—a "moral effect" that "will have no binding force whatsoever."

Until the summer of 1981, the budget process sputtered along in the House, despite the able leadership and the good intentions of its Budget Committee. The process has been the captive of partisanship, has been forced to perform primarily an adding machine function, and has been salvaged and sustained time and again by last minute leadership appeals to support the process. But, as Schick points out, "One cannot expect congressmen to forego their substantive interests endlessly, just to keep the budget process alive. As budgeting becomes more commonplace on Capitol Hill, members might become less willing to vote for resolutions that do not reflect their budget priorities. The long-term health of the congressional budget process cannot be secured by frantic appeals to vote against one's interests or instincts."[46]

As it is currently constituted, the budget process cannot, to use Bolling's words, "force Congress to be responsible."[47] As the earlier portions of this memo have argued, legislators, acting as responsible agents for their constitutents and their committees, produce policies that, to all the world, look like irresponsible products of a grand pork-barrel process. Moral exhortation and procedural changes that accommodate rather than check the influences of geography and jurisdiction are not sufficient. More radical changes are required, so let me propose some.

Prescription

As I see it, Mr. Chairman, the House consists of a collection of veto groups which are positioned to defeat or delay action adverse to their interests. This power to veto is the "coin of the realm." Veto groups trade on it in order to accomplish positive purposes. The result is a policy process that looks like a complex reciprocity system. Sometimes it looks exactly like a "you scratch my back, I'll scratch yours" affair. On other occasions it is more subtle, for instance, when the House defers to one of its committees on the basis of the committee's "expertise." Underpinning this veto system and the reciprocity it supports—indeed, driving it—are the tugs of geography and jurisdiction. As noted, the consequences for fiscal policy are deleterious.

My prescriptions are fashioned with an eye to strengthening central institutions, since only they have the incentive to check the centrifugal forces of geography and jurisdiction and to blunt the distributive and growth tendencies, but currently they lack that capability. My recommendations are divided into four categories:

1. Strengthen the executive
2. Strengthen the House Appropriations Committee
3. Strengthen the House Budget Committee
4. Strengthen party leaders

Like all recommendations for reform, mine, too, obey Morris Udall's Fourth Law: Any change or reform you make is going to have consequences you don't like. The basis for discussion and judgment, therefore, is whether or not an improvement has been effected on balance.

STRENGTHEN THE EXECUTIVE

It may seem odd, in light of President Reagan's impressive victories in 1981 and his willingness to go so far as to veto a continuing resolution, which forced a brief shutdown of government in November of that year, to claim that the president needs help. Yet that is precisely the case being made by commentators today, and it is one with which I agree in principle. One reading of the history that provides the backdrop for the Budget Act of 1974 characterizes the actions of Richard Nixon as those of a Chief Executive driven to unconstitutional means to accomplish reasonable objectives denied him by an undisciplined legislative branch. Fiorina makes a very compelling case for the proposition that executives have the proper incentives to work for coordinated and responsible policies but lack the capabilities, while Congress possesses the capabilities but lacks the will.[48] Even after the Reagan-Stockman budget assault of the spring and summer of 1981, Joseph Kraft could write that "only the president is well-qualified [to take the lead in budgeting]. But all the preliminary signs suggest that even a popular leader, relatively new in office, is too boxed in by conflicting pressures and past commitments to swing wide and take the kind of bold actions to get out front of the problem.''[49]

Partisanship undoubtedly further complicates the ''mismatch of incentives and capabilities.'' It surely did during the impoundment disputes prior to the Budget Act, as an overly zealous president sought to take on a Congress of the opposite party, at least in part for purely political reasons. And more recently, as the cohesion of President Reagan's partisans in the House began to erode in the late summer of 1981, about the best that Speaker O'Neill could offer was that Republicans are fighting Republicans. His strategy is ''don't block the view.'' Not exactly a ''profile in courage''! Partisanship is, of course, not an interbranch problem only in eras of divided government; the House Budget Committee has been the victim of partisanship throughout its existence. But here I want to concentrate on improving the executive's ability to blunt the forces of geography and jurisdiction.

In one of his biweekly *Newsweek* columns, George Will promoted the item veto as a ''dandy device for calling the public's bluff. If Americans are as distressed as they say by government today, the item veto is a means of change.''[50] He reports that forty-three of the state governors have some form of item veto. And, as recently as the fall of 1981, President Reagan complained that he had more authority in fiscal matters as governor of California than he has as president.

Yet, historically, Americans have expressed doubts about enabling a Chief Executive to reject pieces of legislative products. To my knowledge there has never been any very visible effort to amend the Constitution in this respect (although it is a possible outcome of a constitutional convention, a call for which lacks but two states). And I suspect interbranch comity will hardly be promoted if the Chief Executive can item veto initiatives of which less than overwhelming legislative majorities approve. Nevertheless, it is precisely those legislative excesses fostered by the tugs of geography and jurisdiction which need, in my opinion, to be reined in.

I propose the following compromise that, I believe, requires no constitutional revision (although I defer to the experts on that matter). Imagine a period just prior to the start of a new fiscal year—call it the Budget Period—during which all thirteen appropriations bills are sent to the president, en masse. Prior to signing them into law the president is empowered to reconcile them with his own spending objectives by proposing an omnibus reconciliation measure, in effect, an omnibus of item vetos, which is returned to the legislature for up or down approval. If the legislature (either chamber) rejects his reconciliation proposal, the president may prepare another or simply sign or veto individual appropriations bills, as he sees fit.

It seems appropriate to give the president the capacity to reconcile (subject to veto by either chamber, as specified), since it is the executive branch, not the legislative, that seems disposed to take a broader national view of fiscal policy. This is precisely the legislative failure that Stockman, Mayhew, Fiorina, and Arnold describe.[51] Yet it also seems appropriate to circumscribe the capacity to reconcile, something untrue of the pure item veto. My omnibus procedure has three distinct advantages. First, all appropriations bills are put before the president, allowing time to coordinate fiscal policy across what are often arbitrarily determined legislative jurisdictions. Second, it gives the president the opportunity to take budget aggregates explicitly into account—surely one of the more important objectives of the 1974 Budget Act still poorly served by a procedure that produces thirteen distinct products. Third, the omnibus procedure allows the president demonstrably to "spread the pain." If, as is often reported, legislators are caught in the cross fire between their own constituency / committee pressures and the deleterious macroeconomic effects of responding to their own provincial concerns, the omnibus reconciliation measure would allow each legislator to compare explicitly the benefits of "trimming all sails" against the cost of having his own particular sail trimmed.

My reconciliation proposal—in effect, the institutionalization of an omnibus rescission after the legislature has worked its will in each of the thirteen appropriations jurisdictions—might be perfected in a variety of ways. But I shall leave that task, if the idea strikes anyone's fancy, to those expert in the business of legislative procedure. Let me, however, mention one possible reservation. Such a procedure may encourage the legislature to increase appropriations bills in the expectation that the president will propose rescinding action. That way, legislators can have it both ways, advertising their appropriations behavior to local interests while supporting "the public interest" by their approval of an omnibus rescission. Legislators have been known to play both ends against the middle, Mr. Chairman, so we should not expect anything different here. In defense of the proposal, I would argue, first, that this "both ends against the middle" opportunity might be precisely what would make an omnibus executive reconciliation palatable to legislators and, second, that the current degree of spending discipline is already so limited that this added incentive would have few noticeable effects.

STRENGTHEN THE APPROPRIATIONS COMMITTEE

The House once had an institutionalized locus of restraint—its Appropriations Committee. As described by Fenno in his 1966 classic, *The Power of the Purse,*[52] this committee saw its dual mission as that of providing adequate monies to operate authorized programs but of doing so in a manner that protected the federal Treasury from raids by various "claimants." A variety of mechanisms characterized this mission; two of them were especially important.

The first, which Fenno called the Cannon-Taber norm (after committee chairman Clarence Cannon of Missouri and ranking minority member John Taber of New York),[53] allowed the two senior partisans of the committee to assign its members to subcommittees in a manner that counteracted nest-feathering tendencies. Farm representatives were not permitted to dominate the agriculture subcommittee nor big-city legislators the urban-oriented subcommittees. Cannon and Taber operated the appropriations subcommittees in a radically different way from the general committee assignment process in the House; under that process, legislators were permitted to gravitate to committees whose jurisdictions closely dovetailed with constituency concerns.[54]

The second mechanism was attitudinal. Party leaders encouraged each party's committee on committees to assign only fiscally responsible legislators to the Appropriations Committee, and a socialization process on the committee encouraged hard work and attention to detail. Thus, the attitude that every budget was "padded with fat" and therefore could be cut was fostered. Consequently, the Appropriations Committee of the House was seen by its members as the last line of defense against an encroaching executive branch, promoters on legislative committees, and an undisciplined Senate.

The death of Cannon and the retirement of Taber in the mid 1960s marked the beginning of the end of this internal regulation. The sweeping reforms of the next decade reduced the former guardians to yet another set of claimants.[55] Today the thirteen subcommittees of appropriations are protectors not of the Treasury but instead of the legislative programs under their care. "As part of their claimant role, the appropriations [sub]committees monitor the formulation of budget resolutions to ensure that there is enough room for their bills"[56]—a far cry from the days of Cannon and Taber! Indicative of the sorry state to which the Appropriations Committee has sunk was the mock surprise expressed by some observers after the omnibus reconciliation move of 1981. Stuart Eizenstadt, for example, expressed shock: "The Gramm-Latta reconciliation in effect says that the appropriations committees cannot be trusted to control spending and that Congress is incapable thereafter of reconciling appropriations bills to the budget."[57] This assessment appears accurate to me.

I propose three procedural changes in the way the appropriations process is conducted. First, I urge that the Appropriations Committee be exempted from the relevant sections of the subcommittee bill of rights in order to permit the committee chairman and the ranking minority member to reclaim their absolute power over subcommittee assignments. The power formerly exercised by Cannon and Taber provided appropriations subcommittees with fiscally responsible incentives. This power was gutted by the subcommittee bill of rights, which allowed full committee members, in effect, to gravitate to subcommittees where their provincial concern conflicted with (and perhaps overwhelmed) the need for fiscal responsibility. The result was a set of money subcommittees that were extensions of the authorizing committees. A redress in the balance is required; the old equilibrium needs restoration.

Second, I propose that the full House report, debate, and dispose of all appropriations measures at the same time and that this consideration be overseen and coordinated by the chairman of the Appropriations Committee. Here I do not advocate an omnibus procedure; each of the thirteen money bills should get separate consideration. But they should not get independent consideration, as they currently do. The full House should have the opportunity to "tear and compare." The members need the opportunity to be educated about the total effects of their decisions. A seriatim procedure like the one currently in use, in which weeks or months separate the consideration of each bill, flies directly in the face of one of the central objectives of the Budget Act. It encourages piecemeal consideration, in which provincial impulses are given prominence. It also gives prominence to the appropriations subcommittees at the expense of the full committee and to logrolling and reciprocity, for which the territorial imperatives described earlier loom large. In my judgment, the chairmanship of the Appropriations Committee is the natural home for an institutional regulator; reforms to strengthen it—and this is just one—are required.

My last recommendation is the most controversial. A recent check revealed that the Holman Rule is still on the books. The rules of the House and their interpretations devote much attention to legislation in appropriations bills; *Deschler's Procedure* devotes forty pages to the subject. Legislative committees have historically feared the power of the purse granted the Appropriations Committee and have rigidly insisted upon the artificial separation between authorization and appropriation—no appropriation is in order until the program or activity for which monies are sought is duly authorized. The Holman Rule is symbolic of this fear and was ultimately responsible for a forty-year dismembering of the Appropriations Committee in the nineteenth century. Formulated in the 1870s, this rule qualified the prohibition against legislation in appropriations measures. The Holman Rule allowed legislative authorizations to be incorporated in appropriations bills by the Appropriations Committee if such authorizations necessarily reduced federal spending. It was a device that could check the tugs of geography and the claimant impulses of legislative committees. It was also, not coincidentally, the vehicle by which the Appropriations Committee concentrated power in its own bailiwick, which led to its disuse and the Appropriations Committee's demise (until the committee was revived in 1920). It is now time to consider the resurrection of this rule.

The dramatic extent to which the entire appropriations process has been by-passed by entitlement programs, permanent appropriations, and other so-called uncontrollables reveals not an inability of the Appropriations Committee to recapture the fiscal initiative but, once again, a lack of will. A Holman Rule procedure would permit the committee to deal with some of the "runaway" uncontrollables in a procedurally sound and circumscribed fashion, which was clearly not the chief characteristic of Reagan's 1981 reconciliation assault.[58] It would, moreover, serve the dual purpose of strengthening the institution's regulator of unhealthy impulses—the Appropriations Committee—and of relying on legislative self-regulation rather than on executive imposition. It is better, in my opinion, to institutionalize self-regulation than to depend exclusively on the Chief Executive.

STRENGTHEN THE HOUSE BUDGET COMMITTEE

Let us also have a legislative budget. Let there be a committee on the budget, a joint committee of the House and Senate, and let its findings be binding upon both bodies. It is only by the creation of such a committee that there can be any real reduction in governmental expenditures. This House may sincerely attempt to practice economy and reduce expenditures by consolidating the authority to make appropriations into one committee, but when the appropriations bills go over to another body where legislation involving heavy commitments may be added, where items of appropriations may be indefinitely increased, without any regard for the President's budget except its mere moral effect, the actual results are sure to be most disappointing.

—Mr. Hayden of Arizona
5 May 1921

Strengthening the Chief Executive and the Appropriations Committee would constrain and regulate the geographic calculus of legislators and the jurisdictional jealousies of committees. Recognition of the need for these changes, however, only acknowledges the overreaction to backbench pressure of the internal reforms of the early 1970s, which destroyed internal regulators. In no sense does it acknowledge the subsequent Congressional Budget Act of 1974. Yet there is a budget process, and any prescription for change must attend to its shortcomings. Central to the process in the House are the Budget Committee itself and its potential role (perhaps shared with the Appropriations Committee) as "guardian of the purse." Certain changes in the manner in which the Budget Committee is constituted and in the process it governs are, in my opinion, advisable.

First, and most obviously, the Budget Committee must be upgraded to a standing committee of full rank. The various requirements on rotation, for members and chairman, must be abandoned so that legislators are free to invest in the committee in career terms. I would even go so far as to recommend that you drop the facade of task forces and go all the way to a permanent subcommittee structure to underscore the career prospects of membership on this committee. Historically, one of the strengths of the House has been its emphasis on legislative specialists. A Budget Committee with a subcommittee structure and a reward system to encourage and foster individual careers of legislative specialization and expertise would both strengthen the House and enhance the capacity of the committee to influence final outcomes.

At the same time, however, and commensurate with my concern for a strong appropriations chairman, I would not want to see these changes come at the expense of the power of the full committee chairman. I think it might be wise to reconsider the idea (abandoned early in the history of the budget process) of setting macrogoals at the beginning of the annual budget cycle and at the full committee level, under the leadership of the chairman, before going into specific functional categories and programs. While budget subcommittees might take responsibility for the nineteen functional categories, a prior agreement on totals by the full committee—a sort of first budget resolution for the committee—would give some bite to the process and some direct influence of macroeconomic objectives upon the committee and its chairman. In addition, I would like to see subcommittee assignment powers returned to the chairman and ranking minority member, as in my recommendation for the Appropriations Committee, by exempting the Budget Committee from the relevant sections of the subcommittee bill of rights.

None of these changes will be anything more than cosmetic unless the products of Budget Committee efforts—the first and second budget resolutions—play a more constraining role on actual outlay decisions. To accomplish this, I propose a novel treatment of the binding second resolution. This resolution, Mr. Chairman, should be reported under a closed rule, to be voted up or down by the House. If approved, the process would proceed as usual. If it fails, however, I propose the following reversion scheme. Rather than require another second resolution, the process would terminate. In place of the (failed) second resolution, the levels either targeted in the first budget resolution or prescribed in the current services budget, whichever is lower, would become binding. What is required is some mechanism that will make it very painful to reject the proposals of the Budget Committee. I believe that either the first budget resolution or the current services budget provides that pain, Mr. Chairman, although you might have an even more imaginative suggestion. The main point is to set the reversion level (the level to which the binding constraint reverts if the second budget resolution is defeated) sufficiently low so that the Budget Committee's recommendations are strengthened. If the reversion scheme works properly, the second budget resolution proposed by a strengthened Budget Committee should never fail; if it does, there should be hell to pay.

This proposal runs contrary to Bolling and Barriere's belief that the budget process should not be tied to a "conservative credo."[59] My reason for advocating it is simple. As I have tried to make very clear throughout this memo, the deck is heavily stacked against fiscal restraint in Congress. In light of the tugs of geography and jurisdiction, the distributive and growth tendencies, and the general inefficacy of coordinating mechanisms like the budget process, the only budgetary risks are on the upside. Since I do not see Congress, year after year, "irresponsibly" running up massive surpluses, to "force Congress to be responsible" can only mean to curb its upside appetite. A strengthened Budget Committee with special clout at the stage of the binding second budget resolution is an integral part of the solution to this problem.

STRENGTHEN PARTY LEADERS

Perhaps more than any other power center in the House, formal party leaders have been victimized by a trend that has liberated backbenchers, committees, committee and subcommittee chairmen, and other informal leaders. Having its roots in the 1910–11 revolt against Speaker Joe Cannon, the decline in the power of the partisan leadership has only occasionally received compensating correctives. One of the most recent in the Democratic caucus gave the Speaker the power to name the majority party members of the Rules Committee. Recognizing the central agenda role played by that committee, and remembering the "barroom brawls" between Speaker Rayburn and an uncooperative Rules Committee Chairman Smith, the caucus concluded that, unlike other standing committees, the Rules

Committee must be responsive to the majority party leadership and must explicitly recognize that its members serve at the pleasure of the Speaker.

Like the Rules Committee, the Budget Committee plays (or could play) a central coordinating role in the House. And, like the Rules Committee, it should be accorded the status of a "Speaker's Committee," its members serving at the Speaker's pleasure. While I am somewhat uneasy about unleashing partisan warfare on the Budget Committee, the committee is already quite partisan and the Speaker already has considerable input on assignments through the Democratic Committee on Committees. I thus regard this recommendation as relatively minor and its effects as unclear. I offer it in the belief that reforms aimed at countering "the new individualism"[60] are appropriate and that such reforms must ultimately include the main organizing coalitions of the legislature—the parties.

Prognosis

At an American Enterprise Institute conference in 1979 on the Constitution and the budget, Arthur Burns provided his usual cogent analysis of the economic problems facing the nation. Although hesitant to endorse a constitutional amendment requiring a limitation on spending or mandating a balanced budget, he believed that solutions would elude us without "drastic therapy." In this context, he did not even mention Congress, as though it were part of the problem and surely not the source of drastic therapy. During the question-and-answer period, he was queried about the congressional budget process. His remarks are instructive:

> I am not [very] enthusiastic . . . but I do think the Congressional Budget Act has to some degree rationalized fiscal discussions in the Congress. It has even led to some reduction in spending; but that has been marginal, and in that sense I have been disappointed. I had expected much more from this legislation. Nevertheless, the act has been a modest, constructive force toward reducing government spending. Rationalizing the budgetary process, so that revenues and expenditures are considered simultaneously, marks a considerable advance over what we had previously. As to the biases of congressmen and their staffs, I doubt whether the Congressional Budget Act has affected them.[61]

The argument of this memorandum, Mr. Chairman, has been an elaboration of Dr. Burns's remarks. The rationalization of fiscal deliberation in Congress can, at best, secure modest improvements in policy. Until and unless it addresses the "biases of congressmen and their staffs," no reform can hope to compete with the two territorial imperatives—geography and jurisdiction. The current budget process, if not a failure, is surely a disappointment precisely because it accommodated rather than deflected those imperatives.

The aim of the prescriptions I have offered is to strengthen those institutions—the Chief Executive, the Appropriations and Budget committees, and the party leaders—that can possibly check and constrain the influences of geography and jurisdiction. I think it fruitless to chastise legislators for yielding to representational impulses. Exhorting them to "act responsibly" is futile rhetoric. The best hope is to make it costly, and hence not in their interest, to pursue provincial interests exclusively. My recommendations—particularly the executive reconciliation procedure, the resurrection of the Holman Rule, and the reversion scheme for the binding second budget resolution—seek not to modify legislators' objectives, nor to accommodate them, but to alter the incentive to pursue them so enthusiastically and unequivocally.

As to a prognosis, I am not sanguine (no one, to my knowledge, is). There is a good deal of advocacy and activity nowadays for a constitutional amendment, a "self-denying ordinance."[62] I cannot be enthusiastic about that either. Like other forms of command-and-control regulation with which our economy has had unpleasant experience, constitutional amendments mandate ends with little regard for means. They either risk stalemate or encourage clever political strategies to mitigate intended effects, for example, off-budget categories (not to mention a good deal of business for Philadelphia lawyers). Tinkering with institutions (incentive-based solutions) rather than amending the Constitution (command-and-control regulation) holds more promise.

I hope, Mr. Chairman, that I have clearly charted some of the underlying causes of the current institutional difficulty in the House and that I have provided you with some food for thought. Institutional reforms must be geared to a theory of legislator behavior, one that takes legislators as they are, understands how self-interest works, and appreciates the current mismatch between capabilities and incentives. The current budget process is little more than "voodoo politics;" institutional relief is in order. The ball is now in your court.

Notes

1. The Politics of Congressional Budget Reform

1. For an account of these various reform eras, see W. Thomas Wander, "Patterns of Change in the Congressional Budget Process, 1865–1974," *Congress and the Presidency* 9, no. 2 (1982): 23–49.

2. Roger H. Davidson and Walter J. Oleszek, "Adaptation and Consolidation: Structural Innovation in the U.S. House of Representatives," *Legislative Studies Quarterly* 1 (1976): 37–65. In this important article, the authors label the second type of reform *consolidative*. I believe, however, that the term is somewhat misleading. It connotes that changes in response to internal pressures will tend to consolidate something. What I have found with respect to congressional budget reforms, however, is that innovations prompted by such considerations tend to decentralize or fragment power. To call such a decentralizing reform consolidative is, I think, unnecessarily confusing. The term *ameliorative* is a more neutral term, suggesting that changes are made to reduce or ease internal tensions or to ameliorate them, but it does not imply anything about how that might be done.

3. See Wander, "Patterns of Change," for a fuller discussion of these issues.

4. It is true that the figures for the 1972–74 era are not nearly so dramatic and were not nearly so decisive in inducing reform as those found in some earlier periods. As will be seen below, however, the economic consequences of Lyndon Johnson's guns-and-butter prosecution of the Vietnam War did include several politically significant numbers, and they, in turn, provided the context within which expenditure ceilings and presidential impoundments became issues of moment and the flaws of the congressional budget process became palpable.

5. *Hearings before the Joint Committee on the Organization of Congress*, 79th Cong., 1st sess., 1945, 615–16.

6. Norman J. Ornstein, "Subcommittee Reforms in the House of Representatives, 1970–1973," in *Congress in Change: Evolution and Reform*, ed. Norman J. Ornstein (New York: Praeger Publishers, 1975), 89.

7. Joseph Cannon, "The National Budget," *Harper's Magazine* 139 (1919): 621.

8. James B. March and Herbert A. Simon, *Organizations* (New York: John Wiley & Sons, 1958), 185.

9. See Avery Leiserson, "Coordination of Federal Budgeting and Appropri-

ations Procedures under the Legislative Reorganization Act of 1946," *National Tax Journal* 1 (1948): 118–25.

10. Joseph A. Pechman, ed., *Setting National Priorities: The 1980 Budget* (Washington, D.C.: Brookings Institution, 1979), 58.

11. "Federal Spending," the president's address on nationwide radio from Camp David, 7 October 1972, *Weekly Compilation of Presidential Documents* 8, no. 41:1497–99.

12. See generally the excellent account in Louis Fisher, *Presidential Spending Power* (Princeton: Princeton University Press, 1975).

13. James Pfiffner, *The President, the Budget, and Congress: Impoundment and the 1974 Budget Act* (Boulder, Colo.: Westview Press, 1979).

14. Although it is true that Congress could not establish priorities directly with a single vote, program priorities could be and were altered substantially. For instance, the budget share for national defense programs declined from 9.6 percent of GNP in 1956–60 to 5.6 percent in 1976, while government payments to individuals increased from 4.1 percent of GNP to 10.4 percent in the same time period. Rudolph G. Penner with Lawrence J. Korb, *The 1978 Budget in Transition* (Washington, D.C.: American Enterprise Institute, 1976), 11.

15. Allen Schick, "Budget Reform Legislation: Reorganizing Congressional Centers of Fiscal Power," *Harvard Journal on Legislation* 11 (February 1974): 312.

16. Ibid., 312–13.

17. Ibid.

18. Joint Study Committee on Budget Control, *Recommendations for Improving Congressional Control over Budgetary Outlays and Receipt Totals*, 93rd Cong., 1st sess., 1973, H. Rept. 147, 10.

19. All unreferenced quotations are taken from open-ended interviews conducted by the author in 1978–79. All respondents were guaranteed anonymity. The author gratefully acknowledges the support of a Brookings Institution Research Fellowship, which made these interviews possible.

20. *Cong. Rec.*, 92nd Cong., 2nd sess., 1972, 118, pt. 26:34612.

21. Fisher, *Presidential Spending Power*, 176.

22. Staff memorandum to Speaker Carl Albert, 14 February 1973.

23. Allen Schick, *Congress and Money: Budgeting, Spending, and Taxing* (Washington, D.C.: Urban Institute Press, 1980), 63.

24. House Committee on Rules, *Budget and Impoundment Control Act of 1973*, 93rd Cong., 1st sess., 1973, H. Rept. 93–658, 40.

25. For a useful discussion of those changes, see Catherine Rudder, "Committee Reform and the Revenue Process," in *Congress Reconsidered*, ed. Lawrence C. Dodd and Bruce I. Oppenheimer (New York: Praeger Publishers, 1977), 117–39.

26. This requirement has since been changed. Members may now serve for six years out of every ten, and under some circumstances, it is possible for the committee chairman to serve eight years out of ten.

27. Membership on the new budget committee was the exception. Following the recommendations of its subcommittee, the Government Operations Committee proposed a fifteen-person committee selected in the same manner as other standing committees. Thus, the principle of representation for the fiscal committees had little support in the Senate.

28. Quoted in Schick, *Congress and Money*, 68.

29. *Cong. Rec.*, 93rd Cong., 2nd sess., 1974, 120, pt. 6:7138–39.

30. Quoted in Schick, *Congress and Money*, 68.

31. Michael P. Cohen, James G. March, and Johan P. Olsen, "People, Problems, Solutions, and the Ambiguity of Relevance," in *Ambiguity and Choice in Organizations*, ed. James G. March and Johan P. Olsen (Oslo: Universitetsforlaget, 1976), 24.

2. *Congressional Budgeting, 1977–1983: Continuity and Change*

1. For examples, see reports on the conference of the Committee for a Responsible Federal Budget held in January 1982 in "Budget Experts Warn Process Could Fall under 1982 Strain," *Congressional Quarterly Weekly Reports* 40 (16 January 1982): 115–18, and in "Democratic Leadership Seeks Role in Reagan's Forthcoming Budget," *New York Times*, 13 January 1982, A7. See also Senate Committee on Governmental Affairs, *Hearing on S. 2629 to Provide for a Two-Year Budget Process and for Other Purposes*, 97th Cong., 2nd sess., 1982.

2. See the discussion of presidential-congressional relationships during this period in Schick, *Congress and Money*, 30–49.

3. Dennis S. Ippolito, *Congressional Spending* (Ithaca, N.Y.: Cornell University Press, 1981), 202.

4. General Accounting Office, *A Glossary of Terms Used in the Federal Budget Process*, 3rd ed. (Washington, D.C.: General Accounting Office, 1981), 57. See also "Legal Status of Entitlement Programs," *Congressional Quarterly Weekly Reports* 38 (19 January 1980): 122.

5. General Accounting Office, *A Glossary of Terms*, 57.

6. Office of Management and Budget, *Budget of the United States Government, Fiscal Year 1984* (Washington, D.C.: Government Printing Office, 1983), 9–39.

7. Eric Hemel, "The Expensive Myth of 'Uncontrollable' Spending," *Journal of Contemporary Studies* (Winter 1981): 15.

8. Schick, *Congress and Money*, 401.

9. Public Law 93–344, Section 3(a)(3).

10. *Congressional Quarterly Weekly Reports* 37 (24 February 1979): 342, as quoted in Ippolito, *Congressional Spending*, 190.

11. House Committee on Rules, *Hearings on H.R. 4882 to Amend Congressional Budget Act of 1974*, 97th Cong., 1st sess., 1981, 141.

12. *Congressional Quarterly Weekly Reports* 38 (6 December 1980): 3487.

13. Fisher, *Presidential Spending Power*, 172.

14. Joel Havemann, *Congress and the Budget* (Bloomington, Ind.: Indiana University Press, 1978), 180–83.

15. Ippolito, *Congressional Spending*, 148–52.

3. *Changes in the House of Representatives after the Passage of the Budget Act of 1974*

1. Rep. Al Ullman claimed that the act was a "revolutionary development" that would return "to Congress the basic powers of budgeting that were originally

intended by the Founding Fathers in the Constitution.'' See the *Cong. Rec.*, 93rd Cong., 2nd sess., 1974, 120, pt. 15:19730.

2. James L. Sundquist, *The Decline and Resurgence of Congress* (Washington, D.C.: Brookings Institution, 1981), 199.

3. This quotation, as well as all other unreferenced quotes in this chapter, are from interviews with members of the House and their staffs, which were conducted by the author. All were guaranteed confidentiality.

4. Allen Schick, "How the Budget Was Lost and Won," in *President and Congress: Assessing Reagan's First Year,* ed. Norman J. Ornstein (Washington, D.C.: American Enterprise Institute, 1982), 15. The House, he notes, had fewer votes on the topic because of its rules, but the amount of time spent on the budget in the two chambers probably did not differ substantially.

5. An example of media concentration on the budget is the cover stories for the *Congressional Quarterly Weekly Reports*. In 1981, the first year of the Reagan presidency, eighteen of the weekly covers (35 percent) dealt directly with the budget; many more dealt with the tax cut, personalities, or appropriations measures.

6. For figures on waivers see Lance T. LeLoup, *The Fiscal Congress* (Westport, Conn.: Greenwood Press, 1980), 139–41. LeLoup suggests that the propensity to grant waivers reflects both the willingness of the Budget Committee to be accommodating and substantial compliance on the part of the House. The entire body, rather than the Budget Committee, grants waivers. In fact, in the House, the Rules Committee makes the recommendation after consultation with the Budget Committee.

7. Most members of the Appropriations Committee believe that the March 15 deadline comes too early for them to know very much about their plans for the year. As a result, they tend to think of the report as a hollow exercise. Routinely, then, they follow a pattern they learned while on the other side of the purse—they pad their requests.

8. This is not a claim that the process has not had an effect on the budget figures (see Lance T. LeLoup, "The First Half Decade: Evaluating Congressional Budget Reforms," in *The Congressional Budget Process: Some Views from the Inside,* proceedings of a conference cosponsored by the Center for the Study of American Business and the Department of Political Science, Washington University, St. Louis, Mo., 22 and 23 February 1980). Also see Schick, *Congress and Money,* chap. 8. "Most members of the budget committees," according to Schick, "do not go looking for a fight. They would rather produce a budget that the affected committees can live with. Tough talk about excessive demands of the other committees often is countered by conciliatory efforts" (310).

9. The *Congressional Quarterly 1976 Almanac* (Washington, D.C.: Congressional Quarterly Press, 1977), 679, 683, describes the sequence of events.

10. Quoted in the *Congressional Quarterly 1978 Almanac* (1979), 40.

11. For an example of that situation, see ibid., 41, which describes the fight between Reps. Ray Roberts and Robert Giaimo, chairmen of the Veteran Affairs Committee and the Budget Committee, respectively. Roberts recommended a substantial increase in the first resolution for changes in veterans' programs, which were being deliberated in committee. Giaimo unsuccessfully defended the Budget Committee's total.

12. An example of that confrontation is former Budget Committee Chairman Giaimo's unsuccessful battle to prevent the inclusion of funds for states in the 1980

reauthorization of revenue sharing. Giaimo asked, "Where do you think that $4.6 billion [for revenue sharing for states] is going to come from? I will tell you where it is going to come from. It's going to come right out of your hide, right out of key gut programs." He added, "My point is that we are not going to be able to fund everything. There is going to be pressure to get control over federal spending and to hold the growth of federal spending down. That means all programs cannot be funded." (*Cong. Rec.*, 96th Cong., 2nd sess., 1980, 126, H10591–97.)

13. This balance is crucial to the success of the resolution on the floor. Compare the account in the *Congressional Quarterly 1979 Almanac* (1980), 169–73, of the first budget resolution for FY 1980, which carefully balanced competing interests and held off efforts to change that balance, with the account of the first resolution for FY 1978 in the *Congressional Quarterly 1977 Almanac* (1978), 192–93, which was not satisfactorily balanced and was unable to withstand amendments. The former passed the House relatively easily, while the latter was defeated by a vote of 84 to 320 and had to be revised.

14. Richard Fenno described the Appropriations Committee during more stable times in his 1966 classic, *The Power of the Purse: Appropriations Politics in Congress* (Boston: Little, Brown & Co.).

15. Schick, in *Congress and Money*, describes many of the changes since Fenno completed his work. The "guardian" label comes from Fenno and the "claimant" label from Schick. Schick's work is an excellent source for detail on this period of transition, but to understand those changes one only needs to listen to today's members of the Appropriations Committee. One of them told me, "If the people give me a chance, I'll be chairman of the Appropriations Committee and I'll run a Brinks truck to my district every weekend."

16. Quoted in the *Congressional Quarterly Weekly Reports*, 37, (12 May 1979): 878.

17. Quoted in the *Congressional Quarterly 1979 Almanac* (1980), 181.

18. Among the few chairmen who did not sign the letter were Richard Bolling, Chairman of the Rules Committee and a key author of the Congressional Budget Act, and Ways and Means Chairman Al Ullman, who had previously served as a chairman of the Budget Committee.

19. The text of the letter and the signers of it can be found in the *Cong. Rec.*, 96th Cong., 2nd sess., 1980, 126, 73, 3318.

20. The comments of both Peyser and Udall were made during debate on 7 May 1980 (*Cong. Rec.*, 96th Cong., 2nd sess., 1980, 126, 73, 3319).

21. Many of the cuts failed to produce savings in the outyears (i.e., after FY 1981), as had been hoped, because many of the changes were limited to one year only. Other changes were produced almost magically. Many members of the Budget Committee had hoped that the Post Office and Civil Service Committee, for example, would change cost-of-living adjustments for federal and military retirees from a semiannual to an annual basis. Both the Senate and House committees flirted with this provision for 1981 only but relied on temporary subsidy cuts and various other relatively minor adjustments to approach the level of savings required. Savings in this area ultimately fell short, and no significant adjustments in COLAs were made. In other areas, primarily health care, long-term benefits were expanded rather than cut in outyears.

22. Leon Panetta, who largely coordinated the reconciliation process, said, "I commend the committees and their chairmen for the hard work that they did in

responding to the instructions that were provided in the budget resolution" (*Cong. Rec.*, 96th Cong., 2nd sess., 1980, 126, 36:H8241). Chairman Giaimo later added: "I certainly want to pay my gratitude and respect to the committees that have been involved in this reconciliation process. . . . They have recommended it [the reconciliation package] and they bring it forth to you here today" (*Cong. Rec.*, H8268). The Republicans, of course, were less enthusiastic. The comment by Bill Frenzel was fairly typical: "The bill, while far from perfect, is, in its original unamended form, at least a step toward fiscal responsibility at the Federal level" (*Cong. Rec.*, H8242).

23. Under the plan constructed by Chairman James Jones, the Appropriations Committee would have had to cut funding for its programs by almost $24 billion.

24. For a discussion of this practice, see *Congressional Quarterly*'s special report, "Governing by Omnibus," by Dale Tate in *Congressional Quarterly Weekly Reports* 40 (25 September 1982): 2379–83.

25. See, for example, David W. Brady and Charles S. Bullock III, "Coalition Politics in the House of Representatives," in *Congress Reconsidered*, 2nd ed., ed. Lawrence C. Dodd and Bruce I. Oppenheimer (Washington, D.C.: Congressional Quarterly Press, 1981), 186–203, or Julius Turner and Edward V. Schneider, Jr., *Party and Constituency: Pressures on Congress*, 2nd ed. (Baltimore: Johns Hopkins Press, 1970), especially chap. 2.

26. A summary that pulls together a wide range of research and identifies the issues that tend to be partisan is found in Malcom E. Jewell and Samuel C. Patterson, *The Legislative Process in the United States*, 3rd ed. (New York: Random House, 1977), 394–402. In particular, they note that, for state legislatures, "social and economic issues that are associated with the liberal-conservative dichotomy of viewpoints on which major interest groups are likely to have taken conflicting stands" are likely to produce disagreement (394).

27. *Cong. Rec.*, 96th Cong., 2nd sess., 1980, 126, 73:H3324.

28. The vote of everyone, regardless of ideology, is important, but options are more limited for those in the middle than for those at the extremes. The options are also more limited for liberals than for conservatives. Generally, liberal Democrats have offered their own budget and received 75–100 votes for it. At that point they are faced with playing an obstructionist role or supporting the Democratic budget, as preferable to the Republican offering. However, conservative Democrats can not only oppose the Democratic budget but also support the Republican budget, which is what they did in the 97th Congress.

29. For a general discussion of changes in the House, see Lawrence C. Dodd and Bruce I. Oppenheimer, "The House in Transition: Change and Consolidation," in their *Congress Reconsidered*, 2nd ed., 31–61.

30. This listing is from the report of the Rules Committee on the Budget and Impoundment Control Act of 1973, Report No. 93–658. That bill, of course, later became the Congressional Budget and Impoundment Control Act of 1974. That report is included on page 29 of the legislative history of the bill that was printed by the House Committee on the Budget in January 1979. Former Rep. Richard Bolling repeated those points on the House floor during the debates and is generally credited with them. See, for example, the House Committee on Appropriations, *Views and Estimates on the Budget Proposed for Fiscal Year 1983* (Washington, D.C.: Government Printing Office, 1982).

4. The Impact of Budget Reform on the Senate

1. *Cong. Rec.* 97th Cong., 1st sess., 1981, 127, S. 6888.

2. William S. White, *The Citadel* (New York: Harper & Row, 1957).

3. Joseph S. Clark et al., *The Senate Establishment* (New York: Hill & Wang, 1963).

4. Donald Matthews, *U.S. Senators and Their World* (Chapel Hill: University of North Carolina Press, 1960).

5. Randall B. Ripley, *Power in the Senate* (New York: St. Martin's Press, 1969).

6. Norman Ornstein, Robert Peabody, and David Rhode, "The Changing Senate: From the 1950s to the 1970s," in Dodd and Oppenheimer, *Congress Reconsidered,* 3–20.

7. Ibid., 16.

8. *Congressional Quarterly Weekly Reports* 32 (16 March 1974): 679.

9. John W. Ellwood and James A. Thurber, "The New Congressional Budget Process: The Hows and Whys of House-Senate Differences," in Dodd and Oppenheimer, *Congress Reconsidered,* 184.

10. Lance T. LeLoup, "Process versus Policy: The House Committee on the Budget," *Legislative Studies Quarterly* 4 (May 1979): 227–54.

11. ADA ratings provide a rough scale of liberalism. Higher scores are more liberal; lower are more conservative. See *Congressional Quarterly Weekly Reports.* Actual figures for the 94th Congress and comparison with the 97th Congress are included in table 4.2. The same conclusion about ideological splits is reached using Americans for Constitutional Action (ACA) ratings.

12. Richard F. Fenno, *Congressmen in Committees* (Boston: Little, Brown & Co., 1973), 84.

13. John F. Manley, *The Politics of Finance: The House Committee on Ways and Means* (Boston: Little, Brown & Co., 1970), 84.

14. *Cong. Rec.* 95th Cong., 2nd sess., 1978, 124, S6358.

15. Personal interview with author, 1978.

16. *Congressional Quarterly Weekly Reports* 40 (22 May 1982): 1173.

17. Ibid., 1175.

18. *Congressional Quarterly Weekly Reports* 40 (26 June 1982): 1507.

19. See LeLoup, *Fiscal Congress,* 106–18.

20. Ibid., 139–41.

21. Ellwood and Thurber, "New Congressional Budget Process," 177.

22. Quoted in Havemann, *Congress and the Budget,* 159.

23. Ibid., 151.

24. Personal interview with author, 1977.

25. Ibid.

26. Senate Committee on the Budget, *Can Congress Control the Power of the Purse?* Hearings before the Committee on the Budget, 95th Cong., 2nd sess., 6 March 1978.

27. Senate Committee on the Budget, *Tax Expenditures,* 94th Cong., 2nd sess., 17 March 1976.

28. Senate, *Can Congress Control the Power of the Purse?* 45.

29. Havemann, *Congress and the Budget,* 59.

30. Ibid., 68.
31. Ippolito, *Congressional Spending.*
32. Ibid., 104.
33. Schick, *Congress and Money,* 370.
34. Lance T. LeLoup, "After the Blitz: Reagan and the Congressional Budget Process," *Legislative Studies Quarterly* 7, no. 3 (August 1982): 321–39.
35. *Cong. Rec.,* 97th Cong., 1st sess., 1981, 127, S6822.
36. *Cong. Rec.,* 97th Cong., 1st sess., 1981, 127, H3392.

5.   Budget Reforms and Interchamber Relations

1. For example, see Lewis A. Froman, *The Congressional Process: Strategies, Rules and Procedures* (Boston: Little, Brown & Co., 1967); Norman J. Ornstein, "The New House and the New Senate," in *The New Congress,* ed. Thomas E. Mann and Norman J. Ornstein (Washington, D.C.: American Enterprise Institute, 1981); and Nelson Polsby, "Strengthening Congress in National Policy Making," *Yale Review* 59 (Summer 1970): 485–86.

2. See, for example, Fenno, *Congressmen in Committees;* Fenno, *Power of the Purse;* John A. Ferejohn, *Pork Barrel Politics: Rivers and Harbors Legislation, 1947–1968* (Stanford, Calif.: Stanford University Press, 1974); Jeffrey L. Pressman, *House vs. Senate: Conflict in the Appropriations Process* (New Haven: Yale University Press, 1966); David E. Price, *The Commerce Committees* (New York: Grossman Publishers, 1975); and Schick, *Congress and Money.*

3. See John A. Ferejohn, "Who Wins in Conference Committee?" *Journal of Politics* 37 (November 1975): 1033–46; Fenno, *Power of the Purse,* 616–92; Froman, *Congressional Process,* 5–15, 141–48; Manley, *Politics of Finance,* 269–370; Ada G. McCown, *The Congressional Conference Committee* (New York: Columbia University Press, 1927); Walter J. Oleszek, "House-Senate Relationships: Comity and Conflict," in "Changing Congress: The Committee System," ed. Norman J. Ornstein, *Annals of the American Academy of Political and Social Sciences* 411 (January 1974): 75–86; Pressman, *House vs. Senate,* 53–79; Schick, *Congress and Money,* 289–309; Gilbert Steiner, *The Congressional Conference Committee: Seventieth to Eightieth Congresses* (Urbana: University of Illinois Press, 1951); Gerald S. Strom and Barry S. Rundquist, "A Revised Theory of Winning in House-Senate Conferences," *American Political Science Review* 71 (1977): 448–53; David J. Vogler, "Patterns of One House Dominance in Congressional Conference Committees," *Midwest Journal of Political Science* 14 (1970): 303–20; and David J. Vogler, *The Third House: Conference Committees in the U.S. Congress* (Evanston, Ill.: Northwestern University Press, 1971).

4. In analyzing how previous studies had found that the Senate "won" a majority of conference battles, Gerald Strom and Barry Rundquist came to the following conclusion:

> The reason Senate conferees win more often in conference is that the Senate more
> often acts second to the House on legislation. . . .
>   The conferees from the first acting chamber have an incentive to exchange
> marginal amendments in the bill with conferees from the second acting chamber to
> obtain the latter's support for the major aspects of the bill their chamber has
> passed. Thus conferences are best understood as the contexts in which conferees

from the first chamber bargain for the support of the conferees from the second acting chamber, rather than as "the third House" in which the forces that lead to legislative victories are similar to those that lead to legislative victories at earlier stages of the legislative process.

Strom and Rundquist, "Revised Theory of Winning," 452. Ferejohn makes a similar argument in regard to appropriations for the Corps of Engineers projects. See Ferejohn, "Who Wins," 1043–46.

    5. Fenno, *Power of the Purse*, 678.

    6. The notion of congressional budgeting as adjudication among congressional committees acting as claimants (for outside groups) is taken from Schick, *Congress and Money*.

    7. Interview with House Republican staff member; the open-ended interviews for this chapter were granted on condition that those being interviewed not be quoted or specifically identified.

    8. To preserve the constitutional mandates, the Senate bill was "held at the desk" until the House version had been passed. The crucial point for this analysis, however, is that the Senate bill was developed prior to the House bill. See Allen Schick, *Reconciliation and the Congressional Budget Process* (Washington, D.C.: American Enterprise Institute, 1981), 40.

    9. The Constitution, of course, requires the House to act first on revenue bills. In this case, the intention of that provision was circumvented by attaching the tax bill to a minor House-passed bill as an amendment.

    10. It should be noted that sec. 310 of the Congressional Budget Act does not limit reconciliation instructions to increases in revenues and cuts in budget authority. The inverse is allowed. In fact, in the Omnibus Reconciliation Act of 1980, certain entitlements were changed in ways that led to higher levels of spending.

    11. Oleszek, "House-Senate Relationships," 82.

    12. John W. Ellwood and James A. Thurber, "The Politics of the Congressional Budget Process Re-examined," in Dodd and Oppenheimer, *Congress Reconsidered*, 2nd ed., 246–47.

    13. For example, see Ellwood and Thurber, "Politics of the Budget Process Re-examined"; Havemann, *Congress and the Budget;* and Schick, *Congress and Money*.

    14. Amid all the talk of the upward bias of congressional decision making, it is interesting to note that multiyear budgeting—an example of the triumph of PPBS in the Congress—has created a downward bias, because the multiyear current policy baseline is constructed using economic assumptions that incorporate real growth and inflation. As such, the baseline projections always imply a declining federal public sector as a percentage of the GNP. While it is theoretically possible to use such a baseline to plan new government activity, in practice, except for planning the expansion of defense spending, the baseline has supported those who have advocated a smaller public sector.

    15. This undermining of the traditional House power that had resulted from greater tenure and specialization has occurred generally. See Ornstein, "The New House and the New Senate."

    16. Some might posit that personality styles caused this lack of communication. However, the pattern has existed under three House and three Senate Budget Committee chairmen.

17. John F. Manley, "Congressional Staff and Public Policy-Making: The Joint Committee on Internal Revenue Taxation," *Journal of Politics* 30 (1968): 1046–67, and *Politics of Finance,* 307–19; see also Michael J. Malbin, *Unelected Representatives: Congressional Staff and the Future of Representative Government* (New York: Basic Books, 1979); 166–203.

18. Robert A. Keith, "Budget Reconciliation in 1981," *Public Budgeting and Finance* 1 (Winter 1981): 43–44.

19. Gramm-Latta I was the Republican substitute for the first concurrent resolution and reconciliation instructions that were reported out by the Democratic-controlled House Budget Committee. Gramm-Latta II was the Republican substitute for the reconciliation bill that had been drafted in response to the instructions of Gramm-Latta I. Both substitutes were adopted.

20. The Republican leadership of the House also met and formed a legislative timetable. They then met with the Democratic leadership and reached agreement on a House timetable. Based on my interviews, this degree of planning and coordination was unknown in the House prior to the first session of the 97th Congress. To the extent that the act of budgeting is driven by deadlines, the increasing dominance of congressional activity by the budgetary perspective has increased the degree of internal coordination within each chamber.

21. Walter J. Oleszek, *Congressional Procedures and the Policy Process* (Washington, D.C.: Congressional Quarterly Press, 1978), 181.

22. Since Senator Muskie left the chairmanship of the Senate Budget Committee, its decision-making process has become somewhat more collective. Chairman Domenici holds many more Republican caucuses than did Senator Bellmon (or, in the case of Democratic caucuses, Chairman Muskie). It is difficult to evaluate the increase in partisanship on the Senate Budget Committee. Partisanship certainly increased during the first year of the Reagan administration. A similar, although less dramatic, pattern occurred during the first year of the Carter administration.

23. Although available, data for the conference for the first concurrent resolution for FY 1982 were excluded from the data for this paragraph because what appear to be much larger Senate numbers for budget authority and outlays are almost totally due to a rejection by the Senate of the Reagan administration's overly optimistic interest rate assumptions.

24. As a marginal percentage, the absolute difference in budget authority declined from 3.9 percent for the first resolution to 3.3 percent for the second, and the absolute difference in outlays declined from 2.4 percent for the first resolution to 1.9 percent for the second.

25. The degree of aggressiveness reflected in the mark in table 5.1 does not change over time.

26. One exception was the first concurrent resolution of FY 1976, when Senator Muskie persuaded the committee to place its economic stimulus package in the allowances function rather than distribute it across the functions. This strategy, which will be described more fully later in the chapter, was adopted in order to maximize the coalition behind the package by avoiding specificity as to its exact make-up.

27. While some of these programs, food stamps, AFDC, and public housing assistance, go through the appropriations process, the appropriations committees have been unable to "cap" their spending. In practice, these "appropriated entitlements" have been treated as uncontrollables.

28. The acceptance by the Reagan administration of extreme supply-side theory in its initial budget broke this constraint. This, in turn, allowed Congress to pass budget resolutions and taxing and spending legislation that would normally have been inconsistent with the constraints of budgeting. Thus, the politically vital myth of supply-side theory should not be underestimated when analyzing the budget politics of calendar year 1981.

29. In the sequence illustrated in table 5.3, lower estimates for the many entitlement programs that make up the income security function also freed up monies that the Senate conferees could distribute to functions 450 and 500 without increasing the aggregates for budget authority and outlays and the size of the deficit. In the case under study, the income security estimates were lowered when the House agreed to the Senate assumption that entitlement changes would be made in order to achieve savings in food stamps, AFDC, and Social Security. One can see the upward spending bias in distributive bargaining at work: assumptions about savings that never materialize are traded for assumptions that encourage new programs.

30. In fact, in this case, the final deficit estimate was lower than that contained in the Senate resolution. This was achieved by the Senate agreeing to lower outlays for national defense and for the smaller, less conflict-ridden functions.

31. It could be argued that this coding scheme favored the Senate. To test this, the traditional coding of *1* if the result favored the House, *3* if it was at the midpoint, and *5* if it favored the Senate was also calculated. This traditional calculation produced results more favorable to the Senate than the measure described above and set out in table 5.5.

32. Fenno, *Power of the Purse*, 616–92; Manley, *Politics of Finance*, 269–370; and Strom and Rundquist, "Revised Theory of Winning," 448–53.

33. Oleszek, *Congressional Procedure and the Policy Process*, 189.

34. During the conference on the second concurrent resolution for FY 1979, the Senate managers opposed a House resolution assumption of $2 billion in new budget authority for accelerated public works (in function 450). The Senate managers refused to compromise with the House, and Muskie returned to the Senate and obtained a resolution (S. R. 562) instructing the Senate managers to insist on no new funding for public works. The dispute was eventually settled by the conferees, who agreed to a budget figure but remained silent on the programmatic assumptions upon which it was based.

35. Fenno, *Power of the Purse*, 653.

36. Schick, *Congress and Money*, 302. The two sequences set out in tables 5.3 and 5.4 are from the first two years of the budget process. It was after this period that the pattern of conference compromises turned in the Senate's favor. Using Schick's coding system, during the first two years of the process, 55 percent of the settlements in conference favored the House position, while only 38 percent favored that of the Senate. From Fiscal Years 1978 through 1980, however, the Senate won 65 percent of the disputes, while the House won only 25 percent.

37. These categories are used by Fenno, *Power of the Purse*, 650.

38. Even when they are willing to do so, the leaders of a conference are frequently hampered in their bargaining by additional constraints. The major additional constraint is the position of their chamber, committee, or party on an issue. A second constraint is the need to placate powerful members on their side in the conference. Many conferees are interested in protecting funding levels for those programs that are under the jurisdiction of their other committees.

Finally, those who want to reach a quick settlement must combat the tendency for many conferees to seek the little extra concession that will "ice" their side's victory. Although it is true that a major goal of the conferees is to bring back a compromise that can be passed in both chambers, it is also true that, within a range, many members will strive for that little "extra" victory.

6. Reform, Congress, and the President

1. Fenno, *Power of the Purse*, xiii.
2. *Cong. Rec.*, 93rd Cong., 1st sess., 1973, 119, pt. 6:39344.
3. Richard E. Neustadt, *Presidential Power: The Politics of Leadership with Reflections on Johnson and Nixon* (New York: John Wiley & Sons, 1976), 66.
4. Havemann, *Congress and the Budget*, 4.
5. *Cong. Rec.*, 93rd Cong., 2nd sess., 1974, 120, pt. 6:7175.
6. Ibid., 19684.
7. Using FY 1972 prices; see *Budget of the United States Government, Fiscal Year 1978* (Washington, D.C.: Government Printing Office, 1977), 436.
8. This rate is for Fiscal Years 1970–75.
9. This rate is for Fiscal Years 1962–69.
10. Human resources spending includes several budget functions: education, employment, training, and social services; health; income security; and veterans' benefits and services.
11. See Ippolito, *Congressional Spending*, 51.
12. Havemann, *Congress and the Budget*, 154–55.
13. Aaron Wildavsky, *The Politics of the Budgetary Process*, 2nd ed. (Boston: Little, Brown & Co., 1974), 210–11.
14. See Pfiffner, *The President, the Budget, and Congress*, 41.
15. Quoted in House Committee on the Budget, *Congressional Budget and Impoundment Control Act of 1974* (Washington, D.C.: Government Printing Office, 1975), 18.
16. *Budget of the United States Government, Fiscal Year 1980* (Washington, D.C.: Government Printing Office, 1979), 13.
17. Louis Fisher, "Effect of the Budget Act of 1974 on Agency Operations" (Paper presented to the American Enterprise Institute, Washington, D.C., 22 October 1978), 4, 6.
18. Allen Schick, *The First Years of the Congressional Budget Process* (Washington, D.C.: Congressional Research Service, 10 June 1976), 31–38; Ippolito, *Congressional Spending*, 154.
19. See Ippolito, *Congressional Spending*, 157–60.
20. *Congressional Quarterly Weekly Report* 39 (4 July 1981): 1168.

7. The Congressional Budget: How Much Change? How Much Reform?

1. "Federal Spending," the president's address on nationwide radio, 7 October 1972, 1497–99.

2. Quoted by John Herbers, "President Denounces Budget Process," *New York Times*, 29 May 1982, 44.

3. LeLoup, *Fiscal Congress*, 16.

4. Louis Fisher, "In Dubious Battle? Congress and the Budget," *Brookings Bulletin* 17 (1981): 9–10.

5. Davidson and Oleszek, "Adaptation and Consolidation," 37–65; Joseph Cooper, "Organization and Innovation in the House of Representatives," in *The House at Work*, ed. Joseph Cooper and G. Calvin Mackenzie (Austin: University of Texas Press, 1981), 319–55.

6. Edward S. Corwin, *The President: Office and Powers 1787–1957*, 4th ed. (N.Y.: New York University Press, 1957), 171.

7. Davidson and Oleszek, "Adaptation and Consolidation," 40–41.

8. See, for example, Kenneth Shepsle, *The Giant Jigsaw Puzzle: Democratic Committee Assignments in the Modern House* (Chicago: University of Chicago Press, 1978), 227; Fenno, *Congressmen in Committees*, 2–5.

9. Wander, "Patterns of Change in the Congressional Budget Process."

10. Ibid., 45.

11. Fisher, *Presidential Spending Power*, chaps. 7–8.

12. Quoted in House Committee on the Budget, *Congressional Budget and Impoundment Control Act of 1974: Legislative History* (January 1979), 335.

13. Ibid., 327.

14. Ibid., 339.

15. Carol F. Goss, "House Committee Characteristics and Distributive Politics" (Paper delivered at the annual meeting of the American Political Science Association, September 1975); see also Roger H. Davidson, "Representation and Congressional Committees," *Annals of the American Academy of Political and Social Science* 411 (1974): 48–62; and Shepsle, *Giant Jigsaw Puzzle*.

16. House Select Committee on Committees, *Committee Organization in the House*, 93rd Cong., 1st sess., 1973, I, 38.

17. Ibid., 66.

18. Louis Fisher, "Congressional Budget Reform: The First Two Years," *Harvard Journal of Legislation* 14 (1977): 415.

19. Ippolito, *Congressional Spending*, 52.

20. Schick, *Congress and Money*, 424–40.

21. See Fenno, *Power of the Purse;* and Aaron Wildavsky, *The Politics of the Budgetary Process*, 4th ed. (Boston: Little, Brown & Co., 1984).

22. See, for example, Roger H. Davidson, "Subcommittee Government: New Channels for Policy Making," in Mann and Ornstein, *The New Congress*, 99–133.

23. The phrase is Schick's. See Schick, *Congress and Money*, 80.

24. Ibid., chap. 3.

25. Ibid., 78.

26. See, for example, Norman J. Ornstein, "The Breakdown of the Budget Process," *Wall Street Journal*, 24 November 1981, 32; Pete V. Domenici, "Congress' Role in the Budget Process," *Wall Street Journal*, 3 December 1981, 21.

27. Quoted in Fisher, "In Dubious Battle?" 10.

28. Ellwood and Thurber, "Politics of Congressional Budget Process Reexamined," 258.

29. Supplemental views of Congressmen Obey and Gephardt, House Committee on the Budget, *Report on the First Concurrent Resolution in the Budget for Fiscal year 1982*, 97th Cong., 1st sess., 1981, H. Rept. 97–23, 329.

30. House Committee on Rules, Subcommittee on the Legislative Process, *Congressional Oversight of Federal Programs,* 97th Cong., 1st and 2nd sess., 1982.

31. *Cong. Rec.,* 97th Cong., 1st sess., 1981, 127, S14037.

32. House Committee on Rules, *Congressional Oversight.*

33. Fisher, "In Dubious Battle?" 13.

34. House Committee on the Budget, *Report on First Concurrent Resolution.*

8.   The Budget Act of 1974: A Further Loss of Spending Control

1. Sundquist, *Decline and Resurgence of Congress,* 231.

2. Ibid., 234.

3. Schick, *Congress and Money,* 73.

4. Ippolito, *Congressional Spending,* 243.

5. *Cong. Rec.,* 94th Cong., 2nd sess., 122, 13761.

6. Ibid., 10519.

7. Schick, *Congress and Money,* 72–73.

8. Ibid., 52.

9. "Budget Reductions and the Budget Process: An Interview," Urban Institute Policy and Research Report, 11, no. 2 (1981): 1.

10. Fisher, "Congressional Budget Reform," 418–430; Schick, "Budget Reform Legislation," 303.

11. *Public Papers of the Presidents, 1972* (Washington, D.C.: Government Printing Office), 742.

12. Ibid., 964.

13. "Nixon Message Warns Congress against Voting 'Excessive' Money Bills," *Wall Street Journal,* 27 July 1972, 3.

14. Joint Study Committee on Budget Control, *Recommendations for Improving Congressional Control,* 1.

15. Ibid.

16. Senate Committee on the Budget, *Can Congress Control the Power of the Purse?* 13.

17. "Congress Must Get Serious," *Washington Post,* 4 June 1982, A19.

18. LeLoup, *The Fiscal Congress,* 148–50.

19. Timothy E. Wirth, "A Congressman's Perspective on the Budget Process," in *The Congressional Budget Process after Five Years,* ed. Rudolph G. Penner (Washington, D.C.: American Enterprise Institute, 1981), 142; see also Linda L. Smith, "The Congressional Budget Process: Why It Worked This Time," *The Bureaucrat,* 6, no. 1 (1977): 93–94.

20. Schick, *Congress and Money,* 469–70.

21. Ibid., 475–76.

22. Ibid., 479.

23. Ibid., 481.

24. Ippolito, *Congressional Spending,* 256.

25. Schick, *Congress and Money,* 72.

26. Ibid., 79.

27. Ibid., 217.

28. *Cong. Rec.*, 95th Cong., 1st sess., 1977, 123, 13576; see Schick, *Congress and Money,* 217–18, 261–64, 585.

29. Schick, *Congress and Money,* 201–5.

30. Senate Committee on the Budget, *Can Congress Control the Power of the Purse?* 22.

31. *Cong. Rec.*, 94th Cong., 2nd sess., 1976, 122, 15436.

32. Schick, *Congress and Money,* 194.

33. Louis Fisher, "Annual Authorizations: Durable Roadblocks to Biennial Budgeting," *Public Budgeting & Finance* 3 (1983): 23.

34. *Cong. Rec.*, 94th Cong., 2nd sess., 1976, 122, 18953.

35. Schick, *Congress and Money,* 459.

36. Havemann, *Congress and the Budget,* 159.

37. *Cong. Rec.*, 97th Cong., 1st sess., 1981, 127, S3317.

38. Joint Study Committee on Budget Control, *Recommendations for Improving Congressional Control,* 10.

39. Ibid., 12.

40. H. Rept. 97–23, 97th Cong., 1st sess., 1981, 328.

41. Senate Committee on Governmental Affairs, *Review of the Congressional Budget and Impoundment Control Act of 1974,* 97th Cong., 1st sess., 1981, 70.

42. Joint Study Committee on Budget Control, *Recommendations for Improving Congressional Control,* 2.

43. Schick, *Congress and Money,* 84.

44. Ibid., 378–79.

45. Ibid., 83.

46. Nicholas Masters, "The Politics of the Budget Process: A View from the House," in *The Congressional Budget Process: Some Views from the Inside,* proceedings of a conference cosponsored by the Center for the Study of American Business and the Department of Political Science, Washington University, Formal Publication No. 32 (1980): 21.

47. Schick, *Congress and Money,* 246.

48. Masters, "Politics of the Budget Process," 23.

49. Ibid., 64.

50. Schick, *Congress and Money,* 230.

51. Ibid., 231.

52. Ippolito, *Congressional Spending,* 100.

53. For the centralization of executive budgeting from 1789 to 1921, see Fisher, *Presidential Spending Power,* chap. 1.

54. *Cong. Rec.*, 93rd Cong., 2nd sess., 1974, 120, 19673.

55. Schick, *Congress and Money,* 330.

56. Ibid., 313; see also Havemann, *Congress and the Budget,* 152–53.

57. *Cong. Rec.*, 94th Cong., 2nd sess., 1976, 122, 20559–65, McCormack amendment to the Interior appropriations bill for FY 1977, adding $67.5 million for energy conservation programs.

58. *Cong. Rec.*, 94th Cong., 2nd sess., 1976, 122, 17843.

59. *Cong. Rec.*, 94th Cong., 1st sess., 1975, 121, 12399, statement of Congressman Brock Adams.

60. *Cong. Rec.*, 94th Cong., 2nd sess., 1976, 122, 18721.

61. *Cong. Rec.*, 95th Cong., 2nd sess., 1978, 124, 12077.

62. Ibid., 12082.

63. *Cong. Rec.,* 96th Cong., 1st sess., 1979, 125, 9028.

64. *Cong. Rec.,* 96th Cong., 2nd sess., 1980, 126, H2824.

65. Schick, *Congress and Money,* 341.

66. Ibid., 332.

67. Ibid., 19.

68. Ibid., 19, n. 1.

69. *Congressional Quarterly Weekly Report* 39 (30 May 1981): 954.

70. Jean Peters, "Reconciliation 1982: What Happened?" *PS,* 14, no. 4 (1981): 732–36. Schick estimates that more than 75 percent of the reductions approved by the Senate Budget Committee had been initiated by the administration; *Congressional Quarterly Weekly Report* 39 (15 August 1981): 1466.

71. House Committee on Appropriations, *Views and Estimates on the Budget Proposed for Fiscal Year 1983,* 97th Cong., 2nd sess., 1982, 12.

72. *Cong. Rec.,* 97th Cong., 1st sess., 1981, 127, S14725.

73. *Cong. Rec.,* 97th Cong., 2nd sess., 1982, 128, H3015.

74. Joint Study Committee on Budget Control, *Recommendations for Improving Congressional Control,* 39.

75. Schick, *Congress and Money,* 415–40.

76. *Cong. Rec.,* 98th Cong., 1st sess., 1983, 129, H7327.

9.   The Congressional Budget Process: Diagnosis, Prescription, Prognosis

1. William H. Riker, *The Theory of Political Coalitions* (New Haven: Yale University Press, 1962), 243.

2. Ellwood and Thurber, "Politics of the Congressional Budget Process Reexamined," 248.

3. For excellent historical reviews, consult Louis Fisher, "The Authorization-Appropriation Process in Congress: Formal Rules and Informal Practices," *Catholic University Law Review* 29 (1979): 51–105; and Wander, "Pattern of Change in the Congressional Budget Process," 23–49.

4. Mancur Olson, "Is the Balanced Budget Amendment Another Form of Prohibition?" in *The Constitution and the Budget,* ed. W. S. Moore and Rudolph G. Penner (Washington, D.C.: American Enterprise Institute, 1980).

5. See the monographs of David Mayhew, *Congress: The Electoral Connection* (New Haven: Yale University Press, 1974); Morris P. Fiorina, *Congress: Keystone of the Washington Community* (New Haven: Yale University Press, 1977); and R. Douglas Arnold, *Congress and the Bureaucracy: A Theory of Influence* (New Haven: Yale University Press, 1979).

6. Sundquist, *Decline and Resurgence of Congress.*

7. Richard F. Fenno, "If, as Ralph Nader Says, 'Congress Is the Broken Branch,' How Come We Love Our Congressmen So Much?" in Ornstein, *Congress in Change.*

8. Shepsle, *Giant Jigsaw Puzzle.*

9. Robert H. Salisbury and Kenneth A. Shepsle, "U.S. Congressman as Enterprise," *Legislative Studies Quarterly* 6 (1981): 559–76.

10. Martin Tolchin, "Back to the Vineyard for a Second Pressing," *New York Times,* 6 September 1981.

11. All of the quotes by Stockman are from David A. Stockman, "The Social Pork Barrel," *The Public Interest* 39 (Spring 1975): 3–30.

12. Ferejohn, *Pork Barrel Politics.*

13. Stockman, "Social Pork Barrel;" Fiorina, *Congress;* and Arnold, *Congress and the Bureaucracy.*

14. D. Roderick Kiewiet and Matthew D. McCubbins, "In the Mood: The Effect of Election Year Considerations upon the Appropriations Process" (Paper delivered at the annual meeting of the Midwest Political Science Association, Cincinnati, Ohio, 1981).

15. Aaron Wildavsky, "Is Expenditure Limitation Possible without a Constitutional Amendment?" in *The Congressional Budget Process: Some Views from the Inside,* ed. Kenneth A. Shepsle, Formal Publication No. 32 (St. Louis: Center for the Study of American Business, 1980).

16. See Jane Gilbert, "Federal Expenditures: The Impact of the Economy" (Paper delivered at the annual meeting of the American Political Science Association, Washington, D.C., 1979).

17. Ibid.

18. See David Price, "Congressional Committees in the Policy Process," in Dodd and Oppenheimer, *Congress Reconsidered,* 2nd ed.; more generally, see Fenno, *Power of the Purse.*

19. Allen Schick, "The First Five Years of Congressional Budgeting," in *The Congressional Budget Process after Five Years,* ed. Rudolph G. Penner (Washington, D.C.: American Enterprise Institute, 1981).

20. Stockman, "Social Pork Barrel."

21. Richard E. Cohen, "Budget High Jinks," *National Journal* 13 (14 November 1981): 2041.

22. Clifford M. Hardin and Arthur T. Denzau, "The Unrestrained Growth of Federal Credit Programs," Formal Publication No. 45 (St. Louis: Center for the Study of American Business, 1981).

23. Clifford M. Hardin and Kenneth W. Chilton, "Budget Control and Indexed Entitlements: Are They Compatible?" Formal Publication No. 40 (St. Louis: Center for the Study of American Business, 1981).

24. DeAlva Stanwood Alexander, *History and Procedure of the House of Representatives* (Boston: Houghton Mifflin, 1916).

25. Allen Schick, "The Three-Ring Budget Process: The Appropriations, Tax, and Budget Committees in Congress," in Mann and Ornstein, *The New Congress.*

26. Aaron Wildavsky, "Constitutional Expenditure Limitation and Congressional Budget Reform," in *Penner, The Congressional Budget Process after Five Years.*

27. James L. Sundquist, "Congress, the President, and the Crisis of Competence in Government," in Dodd and Oppenheimer, *Congress Reconsidered,* 2nd ed.

28. Schick, "Three-Ring Budget Process."

29. Ellwood and Thurber, "Politics of the Congressional Budget Process Reexamined."

30. Morris P. Fiorina, "Congressional Control of the Bureaucracy: A Mismatch

of Incentives and Capabilities,'' in Dodd and Oppenheimer, *Congress Reconsidered*, 2nd ed.

31. Schick, "First Five Years of Congressional Budgeting."

32. Ibid.

33. See, for examples, Robert Hartman, "Commentary on 'The CBO's Policy Analysis,' " in Penner, *The Congressional Budget Process after Five Years;* and Donald T. Rotunda, "Reconciliation: Not Better the Second Time Around," *Washington Post,* 28 June 1981.

34. Rotunda, "Reconciliation."

35. Schick, "Three-Ring Budget Process."

36. Dennis Ippolito, "Budget Reform, Impoundment, and Supplemental Appropriations," in Shepsle, *The Congressional Budget Process: Some Views from the Inside.*

37. Wildavsky, "Is Expenditure Limitation Possible?"

38. Stanley Bach, "The Structure of Choice in the House of Representatives: The Impact of Complex Special Rules," *Harvard Journal of Legislation* 18 (1981): 553–602.

39. James T. McIntyre, "Discretional Control of the Federal Budget," in Moore and Penner, *The Constitution and the Budget.*

40. Fiorina, "Congressional Control of the Bureaucracy."

41. David W. Rohde and Kenneth A. Shepsle, "Thinking about Legislative Reform," in *Legislative Reform,* ed. Leroy Rieselbach (Lexington: Lexington Books, 1979).

42. Schick, "Three-Ring Circus Process."

43. Wildavsky, "Constitutional Expenditure Limitation."

44. Richard Bolling and John E. Barriere, "Budget-Making Gone Awry," *Washington Post,* 28 June 1981.

45. Ibid.

46. Schick, "First Five Years of Congressional Budgeting."

47. Bolling and Barriere, "Budget-Making Gone Awry."

48. Fiorina, "Congressional Control of the Bureaucracy."

49. Joseph Kraft, "Only the President Can Do It," *Washington Post,* 20 September 1981.

50. George Will, "Power to the President," *Newsweek* 12 October 1981.

51. Stockman, "Social Pork Barrel;" Mayhew, *Congress;* Fiorina, *Congress;* and Arnold, *Congress and the Bureaucracy.*

52. Fenno, *Power of the Purse.*

53. Ibid.

54. Shepsle, *Giant Jigsaw Puzzle.*

55. Schick, "The First Five Years of Congressional Budgeting."

56. Schick, "Three-Ring Circus Process."

57. Stuart E. Eizenstadt, "The Hill's Budget Stampede," *Washington Post,* 21 June 1981.

58. There is some procedural ambiguity about the applicability of a Holman Rule procedure to entitlements. This ambiguity should be clarified by the parliamentarian and / or the Rules Committee.

59. Bolling and Barriere, "Budget-Making Gone Awry."

60. Sundquist, *Decline and Resurgence of Congress.*

61. Arthur F. Burns, ''Prudent Steps toward a Balanced Budget,'' in Moore and Penner, *The Constitution and the Budget*.

62. William H. Riker, ''Constitutional Limitations as Self-denying Ordinances,'' in Moore and Penner, *The Constitution and the Budget*.

Selected Bibliography

Davidson, Roger H., and Walter J. Oleszek. "Adaptation and Consolidation: Structural Innovation in the U.S. House of Representatives." *Legislative Studies Quarterly* 1 (1976): 37–65.

Ellwood, John, and James Thurber. "The New Congressional Budget Process: The Hows and Whys of House-Senate Differences." In *Congress Reconsidered,* edited by Lawrence C. Dodd and Bruce I. Oppenheimer, 163–92. New York: Praeger Publishers, 1977.

———. "The Politics of the Congressional Budget Process Re-examined." In *Congress Reconsidered.* 2nd ed., edited by Lawrence C. Dodd and Bruce I. Oppenheimer, 246–74. Washington, D.C.: Congressional Quarterly Press, 1981.

Fenno, Richard F. *The Power of the Purse: Appropriations Politics in Congress.* Boston: Little, Brown & Co., 1966.

Fisher, Louis. "Congressional Budget Reform: The First Two Years." *Harvard Journal of Legislation* 14 (1977): 413–57.

———. *Presidential Spending Power.* Princeton: Princeton University Press, 1975.

Hardin, Clifford M., and Kenneth W. Chilton. *Budget Control and Indexed Entitlements: Are They Compatible?* St. Louis: Center For the Study of American Business, 1981.

Havemann, Joel. *Congress and the Budget.* Bloomington: Indiana University Press, 1978.

Ippolito, Dennis S. *Congressional Spending.* Ithaca, N.Y.: Cornell University Press and the Twentieth Century Fund, 1981.

Leiserson, Avery. "Coordination of Federal Budgeting and Appropriations Procedures under the Legislative Reorganization Act of 1946." *National Tax Journal* 1 (1948): 118–25.

LeLoup, Lance T. "After the Blitz: Reagan and the Congressional Budget Process." *Legislative Studies Quarterly* 7, no. 3 (1982): 321–39.

———. *The Fiscal Congress: Legislative Control of the Budget.* Westport, Conn.: Greenwood Press, 1980.

———. "Process versus Policy: The House Committee on the Budget." *Legislative Studies Quarterly* 4 (1979): 227–54.

Manley, John F. *The Politics of Finance: The House Committee on Ways and Means.* Boston: Little, Brown & Co., 1970.

Moore, W. S., and Rudolph G. Penner, eds. *The Constitution and the Budget.* Washington, D.C.: American Enterprise Institute, 1980.

Penner, Rudolph G., ed. *The Congressional Budget Process after Five Years.* Washington, D.C.: American Enterprise Institute, 1981.

Peters, Jean. "Reconciliation 1982: What Happened?" *PS* 14, no. 4 (1981): 732–36.

Pfiffner, James. *The President, the Budget, and Congress: Impoundment and the 1974 Budget Act.* Boulder, Colo.: Westview Press, 1979.

Rudder, Catherine. "Committee Reform and the Revenue Process." In *Congress Reconsidered,* edited by Lawrence C. Dodd and Bruce I. Oppenheimer, 117–39. New York: Praeger Publishers, 1977.

Schick, Allen. "Budget Reform Legislation: Reorganizing Congressional Centers of Fiscal Power." *Harvard Journal of Legislation* 11 (1974): 303–50.

———. *Congress and Money: Budgeting, Spending, and Taxing.* Washington, D.C.: Urban Institute Press, 1980.

———. *Reconciliation and the Congressional Budget Process.* Washington, D.C.: American Enterprise Institute, 1981.

———. "The Three-Ring Budget Process: The Appropriations, Tax, and Budget Committees in Congress." In *The New Congress,* edited by Thomas E. Mann and Norman J. Ornstein, 288–328. Washington, D.C.: American Enterprise Institute, 1981.

Shepsle, Kenneth, ed. *The Congressional Budget Process: Some Views from the Inside.* St. Louis: Center for the Study of American Business, 1980.

Smith, Linda L. "The Congressional Budget Process: Why It Worked This Time." *The Bureaucrat* 6, no. 1 (1977): 88–111.

Sundquist, James L. *The Decline and Resurgence of Congress.* Washington, D.C.: Brookings Institution, 1981.

Wander, W. Thomas. "Patterns of Change in the Congressional Budget Process, 1865–1974." *Congress and the Presidency* 9, no. 2 (1982): 23–49.

Wildavsky, Aaron. *The Politics of the Budgetary Process.* 4th ed. Boston: Little, Brown & Co., 1984.

About the Authors

GARY W. COPELAND is an assistant professor in the Carl Albert Congressional Research and Studies Center at the University of Oklahoma. He received his Ph.D. degree from the University of Iowa before serving as an American Political Science Association Congressional Fellow from 1979 to 1980. His research interests include legislative politics and American political processes. His research has appeared in a variety of journals, including the *Journal of Politics, American Politics Quarterly, Social Science Quarterly,* and *Legislative Studies Quarterly.*

ROGER H. DAVIDSON is a senior specialist in American government and public administration at the Congressional Research Service of the Library of Congress—a post that is akin to being a "scholar in residence" for the U.S. Congress. He is also an adjunct professor of government and politics at the University of Maryland. The author or coauthor of nine books and more than seventy articles and reviews, Davidson received his A.B. degree (magna cum laude) from the University of Colorado and his doctorate from Columbia University. He taught at Dartmouth College and at the University of California, Santa Barbara, where he also served as department chair and associate dean. He has worked on Capitol Hill as a professional staff member for House and Senate committees and has been a consultant to several national study commissions. His current research includes studies of the congressional work load and Senate structure and operations.

JOHN W. ELLWOOD is an associate professor of public policy and management at the Amos Tuck School of Business Administration, Dartmouth College. From 1975 through 1980 he was a staff member of the Congressional Budget Office, serving as the special assistant to the director. He has written extensively on budget procedures. Among his latest publications is *Reductions in U.S. Domestic Spending: How They Affect State and Local Governments.*

LOUIS FISHER is a specialist in American national government at the Congressional Research Service of the Library of Congress. He is the author of *President and Congress; Presidential Spending Power; The Constitution between Friends: Congress, the Executive, and the Law;* and *The Politics of Shared Power: Congress and the Executive.* He has taught political science at Queens College, Flushing, N.Y.; Georgetown University; and the American University and is currently a professor of political science at Catholic University. He received his doctorate in political science from the New School for Social Research and has authored approximately sixty-five articles in law reviews, political science journals, magazines, and newspapers on a range of topics related to American politics.

F. TED HEBERT is professor of political science and associate director of the Bureau of Government Research at the University of Oklahoma. His publications include *The Politics of Raising State and Local Revenue* and *Essentials of Public Administration,* as well as numerous journal articles on government budgeting, legislative politics, and state administration.

DENNIS S. IPPOLITO is Eugene McElvaney Professor of Government at Southern Methodist University. His research deals with national political institutions and policy. Included among his works on the federal budget are *The Budget and National Politics; Congressional Spending;* and *Hidden Spending—The Politics of Federal Credit Programs.*

LANCE T. LELOUP is a professor of political science at the University of Missouri—St. Louis. He received his Ph.D. degree from Ohio State University and served on the staff of the Ohio Senate. He is the author of *The Fiscal Congress: Legislative Control of the Budget* and *Budgetary Politics* and has published articles on Congress and the federal budget in a number of journals, including the *American Political Science Review, Public Administration Review, Social Science Quarterly, Polity, Legislative Studies Quarterly,* and *American Politics Quarterly.*

KENNETH A. SHEPSLE is a professor of political science, a research associate of the Center for the Study of American Business, and chairman of the Committee on Political Economy at Washington University in St. Louis. His major research interests are legislative politics, analytical political science, and formal models of political institutions. His publications include *The Giant Jigsaw Puzzle: Democratic Committee Assignments in the Modern House; The Congressional Budget Process: Some Views from the Inside; Political Equilibrium;* and numerous articles in the *American Politi-*

cal Science Review, American Journal of Political Science, Legislative Studies Quarterly, Public Choice, and *Journal of Political Economy.* He is currently a Guggenheim Fellow, in which capacity he is engaged in research on legislative rules and procedures.

W. THOMAS WANDER is an assistant professor of political science and the assistant director of the Carl Albert Congressional Research and Studies Center at the University of Oklahoma. He received his Ph.D. from Stanford University and was a Brookings Institution Research Fellow in 1978–79. He has served as a social science analyst with the Congressional Research Service of the Library of Congress and has taught at the American University. His previous publications have examined structural change in Congress, and he is currently at work on a history of congressional budget reform.

Index

THE JOHNS HOPKINS UNIVERSITY PRESS

Congressional Budgeting

*This book was composed in Times Roman type by Brushwood
Graphics Studio, from a design by Susan P. Fillion. It was
printed on S.D. Warren's 50-lb. Sebago Eggshell Cream paper
and bound in Holliston Roxite A by Bookcrafters.*